What Children Need

What Children Need

JANE WALDFOGEL

HARVARD UNIVERSITY PRESS

Cambridge, Massachusetts
London, England 2006

Library of Congress Cataloging-in-Publication Data

Waldfogel, Jane.
  What children need / Jane Waldfogel.
    p.   cm.
  Includes bibliographical references and index.
  ISBN 0-674-02212-2 (alk. paper)
    1. Child development.   2. Parental influences.   3. Child rearing—United
States.   4. Child care—United States.   5. Children of working parents—
United States.   6. Work and family—United States.   I. Title.
HQ767.9.W35 2006
649′.1—dc22   2005052845

Contents

What Children Need

Introduction

THIS BOOK IS FIRST and foremost about children and what they need. It is also about working mothers and fathers and the decisions they make about who will care for their children while the parents are at work. These decisions are personal and vary from family to family, as well they should. But there is also a larger public interest in these decisions. The care that children receive matters for their development and for the kind of adults they will turn out to be. To grow and thrive, children need not just food and material goods but also care and affection that promotes their health, cognitive development, and social and emotional well-being. When children's needs in these areas are well met, all of us benefit. But when they are not, society suffers. So all of us have an interest in what happens to children when parents work and in how well their needs are met.

Parents are primary in children's lives. Even if they work, parents provide much of the care that children need, particularly when children are young. But many parents can't do it all. One of the most dramatic shifts in the twentieth century was the increase in paid work by mothers, with no corresponding decrease in paid work by fathers. A second dramatic shift was the rise in the share of children being raised by single parents, most of whom work. As a result, parents today are working more hours out of the home than ever before. And this is not likely to change. Most women do not want to go back to the time when mothers stayed home full-time with their children. Others might like to stay home but cannot afford it. As men's wages have stagnated, and as the costs of a middle-class lifestyle have escalated, two-parent families increasingly have come to rely on the earnings of both parents. And single mothers, particularly since welfare reform, have little choice but to work.

The change has been dramatic. Twenty-five years ago, two-thirds of children had a stay-at-home parent. Today, two-thirds do not. So the kind of stay-at-home mom who took care of many of today's adults is no longer the norm. Yet children need as much care as ever. The fact that human infants have a long period of dependency on adults has not changed. Nor has the major system that society provides for the care and supervision of children—the public schools. For the most part, schools operate about six hours a day, eight and a half months a year. Thus, schools cover only about half the hours that a parent working full-time spends at work during the course of a year. Of course, these figures apply only to school-age children. For the most part, schools do not serve children under five (and provide only part-time care for five-year-olds in about half the districts). If you add up all the hours that a parent working full-time is at work between the birth of a child and the day the child turns eighteen, plus an hour and a half each day for commuting to and from work, and contrast that amount with the typical number of hours of care provided by schools, schools cover only one-third of the time that a parent is working.[1]

How can we ensure that children get the best possible care during the other two-thirds of the time—while parents are working and children are not in school? The easy answer—that we can just leave this up to parents—unfortunately won't do. Most parents can't do this on their own; they need help finding and paying for good-quality care for their children or making arrangements to take leave from work to care for their children themselves. Respecting parental choice does not mean leaving parents to do everything on their own.

What can and should policy-makers do to make sure that children are well cared for while their parents work? We each bring our own experience, values, and assumptions to this question. This is only right—experience, values, and assumptions matter, particularly in personal decisions like child care—but we also need to recognize that a lot has changed in the world since we adults were children and that not all families are the same. Parents are of course influenced by how they were raised but may also make different choices when it comes to caring for children than their own parents made. And they will make different choices than their neighbors and co-workers.

Principles for Policy-Making

Fortunately, there are some general principles—which derive from core American values about children and family—that we can bring to bear on policy-making in this area. Three are fundamental.

The first is the importance of respecting choice. Whatever policies we introduce, these policies should, to the extent possible, support families in making their own choices about how their children are cared for. Choice is a strongly held American value, particularly when it comes to the rearing of children, and it is one that policy-makers must respect.

The importance of respecting choice may seem obvious, but it is worth emphasizing, because although many of our current policies are intended to support choice, not all of them do. For instance, parental leave policies in principle give parents the choice as to whether and how long to stay home after the birth of a child, but in reality that choice is limited—about half of private sector workers are not covered by the federal parental leave law (the Family and Medical Leave Act, or FMLA), and those who are covered typically can take only twelve weeks of leave, without pay. Many new parents would like to take more leave but cannot afford to do so. In the area of child care, our system of vouchers and tax credits allows parents to choose their own child care arrangements, but for many parents those choices are constrained by limited availability, poor quality, or high costs. Moreover, if a low-income parent is eligible for a child care subsidy but not paid parental leave, does policy really support parental choice?

A second fundamental principle, and one that sometimes conflicts with choice, is the importance of promoting quality. We now know that the quality of children's care arrangements has a lasting impact on their growth and development. But currently too many children and youth are in care arrangements that are not of good quality. Given the evidence on the benefits of good-quality care and the harm that can be done by poor-quality care, we all have an interest in ensuring that good-quality care is available to all families.

Of course, quality is to some extent in the eye of the beholder. What parents value and see as quality is often highly individual, and there is a potential conflict between choice and quality that we must grapple with. The example of child care regulations is illustrative. Tighter regulations can improve the quality of care along specific dimensions but can also drive some providers that parents might have chosen out of business or out of the formal child-care market. The succeeding chapters will carefully consider tensions such as these and will emphasize policies, such as quality-related rating systems (which recognize and reimburse care at a higher rate if it is of higher quality), that attempt to address the conflict between choice and quality. There are no easy answers here, but by making the key values and principles and the potential tensions between them explicit, we make it easier to identify policies that can potentially resolve these tensions.

The third key principle is the importance of supporting employment. The work ethic is a widely shared American value. And work is a financial necessity for most parents. Single parents have always faced greater pressures to work, which have increased with work-oriented welfare reform. Couples also face increased pressures to work, if they are to manage the costs of raising a family in today's economy, especially with today's housing prices. Changes in the wage structure have led to stagnating or declining earnings for all but the most skilled men and a greater reliance on wives' earnings to keep family incomes rising. The real-estate boom of the 1990s, which continues even now, makes major metropolitan areas prohibitively expensive for couples in the middle class unless they have two middle-class incomes.

Moreover, women's employment is seen by many as key to gender equity and women's well-being. Many Americans feel strongly that as a matter of gender equity, women should not be forced to take a backseat to men in the labor market, just because women have children. In this view, we must be careful not to enact policies that would discourage women from working or that would widen existing gaps between women's and men's employment or earnings.

Another impetus for emphasizing women's employment comes from the recent welfare-to-work reforms, which have required work for low-income mothers as a condition of receiving means-tested welfare benefits. The reforms, along with a strong economy, have resulted in large increases in single mothers' employment and large declines in welfare caseloads. Work-family policies that weaken work incentives and encourage women to return to welfare would be unwelcome from this vantage point as well.

Yet, here again, tensions among values arise. If we truly value choice, we must respect that some parents would prefer to not work outside the home or to work fewer hours, particularly when they have young children. And, if we value quality of care, and if parents can in some instances or in some periods of a child's life provide the best-quality care, our policies should support such parental care, even at the risk of discouraging employment.

Identifying tensions such as these is the first step toward developing creative solutions. In the first year of life, for instance, extended parental leave policies, giving parents the choice to stay home, could be paired with policies to improve the quality, availability, and affordability of infant child care. Policies such as these would better support choice and quality of care in the first year of life than the status quo, without creating huge disincentives in terms of employment.

To recap, then, there are three fundamental value-based principles that we can bring to bear when thinking about how to meet children's needs when parents work: respecting choice, promoting quality, and supporting employment. Sometimes these values collide, and we must be careful to strike the right balance. For instance, mindful of quality, we may decide to put some limits on the kind of care children can be placed in and to develop policies that encourage the use of higher-quality care. Mindful of choice, we should steer clear of policies that assume every parent will work a certain number of hours per week or will use a particular type of care.

Principles for Allocating Public Resources

In thinking about public policies, we also need to recognize that public resources are limited. Governments must spend public money wisely, in a way that advances agreed-upon social goals and that is consistent with the best possible evidence.

Philosophers have long debated what principles should be used to decide how to allocate public resources. Should governments aim to do the most for the worst-off in society or to do at least something for the largest number of people? What outcomes should be valued? Is economic well-being all that matters? To what extent should governments worry about inequality or social cohesion or rights?

Welfare economics, a branch of economics and public policy that specifically tackles such questions, offers useful guidance. Welfare economics articulates two main goals that policy-makers should aim to achieve in allocating public resources. The first is efficiency. Efficiency means that a dollar should be spent on a social program only if the benefit of that program exceeds its cost and if the net benefit from the program exceeds the benefit that could be gained from some alternative use of the dollar. So, efficiency has to do with making sure we get the largest possible return for our investments. For instance, if we are going to spend public funds on a preschool program for four-year-olds, we want to be sure that the benefits of the program outweigh its costs and also that the benefits of this particular program are larger than those of alternative programs that might be funded in its place.

The second goal of welfare economics is equity. Increasing equity means ensuring that members of society have a more equal set of opportunities or outcomes than they would have in the absence of the intervention. Articulating the value of equity is important because sometimes efficiency and equity may be at odds. If equity is valued, an investment that promotes equity can be socially worthwhile even if it is not efficient. So, in the preschool example, we might decide to invest in a preschool program for disadvantaged four-year-olds if it narrowed the gap between their school readiness and that of more advantaged four-year-olds, even if the cost of the program exceeded its dollar benefits.

Equity can encompass a fairly broad set of objectives. In recent years, many European countries have emphasized social inclusion and social cohesion—making sure that no groups in society are excluded or cut off from the mainstream and that all groups feel a sense of belonging and social citizenship. Another theme that is increasingly emphasized both in the United States and Europe is the right of children to a happy and healthy childhood, not just because this will lead to better outcomes for them and their neighbors, but because there are certain experiences children intrinsically ought to have—good health, a happy home, opportunities for play and learning, and so on. These broader conceptions of equity suggest that there are some experiences that all children should have access to and also some minimal levels of care to which all children should be entitled, as a matter of right and as a way of building a better society.

For many Americans, the notion of equity includes concepts of social inclusion, cohesion, and rights. If we think about the ideals that motivated some of the major American social programs—such as the public schools or the War on Poverty—we can see that a fairly broad definition of equity was in place. For this reason, I use equity in the broader sense that encompasses not just equality of economic opportunity but also outcomes such as social inclusion, cohesion, and rights.

Standards of Evidence

Another challenge for public policy-making is to base decisions on the best possible evidence. Issues involving parental employment and the care of children are controversial, and social scientists may disagree as to what research tells us is best for children.

Fortunately, there is little disagreement when it comes to standards of evidence. Social scientists concur that, where available, the strongest evidence comes from controlled experiments. Such experiments randomly assign one group, the treatment group, to receive an intervention and another group, the control group, to not receive it. If the samples are large enough and if the groups have been randomly assigned, it is possible to measure the effect of an intervention by comparing the change in a given outcome for the treatment group to that for the control group.

In the area of nonparental child care, we rarely have such experiments, because we believe so strongly in the importance of parental choice. Parents would object to an experiment that randomly assigned their infant to be enrolled in nonparental versus parental care; parents want to make those decisions themselves, particularly when they involve very young children.

In the absence of a controlled experiment, we can sometimes make use of natural experiments. A natural experiment mimics a laboratory experiment by randomly exposing one group to an intervention. For instance, one state or a few states (the treatment group) might implement a new program for infants, while other states (the control group) do not. If the two groups of states are otherwise comparable, outcomes for the treatment and control groups can be compared, and the effect of the new program can be gauged.

We are fortunate in the United States to have many different types of policies, in both the private and public sector. There is much we can learn from these natural experiments about ways to meet children's needs when their parents work. There is also much we can learn from other countries. Many European countries have long-established and more-advanced programs in areas such as child care, giving us an additional set of natural experiments to draw from. Of course, we need to be careful in drawing lessons from Europe, to take other cross-cultural differences into account. But if we are careful, lessons from European countries can be informative, just as lessons from the U.S. often can be for them.

Often we lack either a laboratory or natural experiment, in which case we have to rely on observational studies. Such studies take advantage of naturally occurring variation in experiences among individuals and then attempt to measure the impact of those experiences, holding all else equal. In the infant care example, we could identify families who used out-of-home child care for their infants and compare them to families who did not. If we could hold all else equal and compare children who were identical except for the difference in their early child care experience, we would be able to estimate the effect of early child care.

In the real world, however, it is often impossible to hold all else equal. There may be many differences between children who did attend infant child care and those who did not, and researchers may not be able to control for all variables. Researchers call this the "selection bias" problem, and it is a serious challenge in observational studies. Families who send their children to infant care may be more interested in learning and may teach their children more at home as well. If so, a naive researcher might overestimate the benefits of infant care for children's learning. Conversely, parents may use out-of-home infant care in a compensatory manner, enrolling children who they feel need extra help because their learning is lagging. If so, a naive researcher might incorrectly conclude that infant child care harmed children's development.

For this reason, we have to be very cautious in drawing conclusions from observational studies and should place the most weight on studies that use rigorous methods to test whether the associations found in observational data are likely to be causal. Studies with a longitudinal design (following children over time) are valuable because they allow researchers to control for how children were doing before they experienced the child care or intervention. Studies using state-of-the-art econometric methods (such as sibling analyses, instrumental variables models, or propensity score matching) are useful because such methods specifically address different types of potential bias. When studies use these types of methods and when several studies all point in the same direction, we can have greater confidence in the evidence from observational studies.

The Way Forward

We now have the tools we need to move forward in thinking about what children need and how to meet those needs when parents work. We have three fundamental principles that are key to thinking about work-family issues: respecting choice, promoting quality of care, and supporting employment. We also have two principles of welfare economics that must be respected in allocating public resources: efficiency, that is, getting the greatest return for our investment of public dollars; and equity, broadly defined to include increasing social inclusion and cohesion, children's rights, and equality of opportunity. And we have standards of evidence, which give first priority to random assignment experiments, second priority to natural experiments that mimic laboratory experiments, third priority to rigorous observational studies (that use longitudinal data or state-of-the-art methods to address bias and test for causality), and lowest priority to other observational studies. Together, these principles and standards of evidence form the analytic framework that we will use throughout the book to think about how to meet children's needs when parents work.

The next chapter provides an overview of what children need to grow and thrive and how parents and others influence child health and development. Chapter 1 also looks at what parents are currently doing; what parents can and cannot provide themselves, given their commitments in the workplace; and what policy supports exist currently.

The succeeding chapters then consider each stage of childhood in turn, because what children need and what parents can and can't do vary greatly by developmental stage. Chapter 2 considers the infant and toddler years (the first three years of life), when children's needs for care are most acute and when the potential for conflict between work and family is the greatest. Chapter 3 looks at the preschool years (children aged three to five), the period in which the influence of child care has been most studied but about which considerable controversy remains. Chapter 4 looks at the middle-childhood years (children aged six to twelve), a period that has been relatively neglected by social scientists but a time when children still need considerable amounts of care while their parents work. Chapter 5 moves on to the adolescent years (children aged thirteen to eighteen), a period when children's needs for care are rapidly changing but when parents and other adults still play an important role. Chapter 6 concludes by returning to the overarching question of what children need, drawing together conclusions and implications for policy.

✒ 1

Children and Parents

THIS CHAPTER PROVIDES an overview of what children need in the key domains of health, cognitive development, and social and emotional well-being and how parents, and others, influence children's development in these domains. The bottom-line message of the research is clear: what parents and others do with children matters a lot. Although we now know much more than we did in the past about genetic determinants of child health and development, the research shows that experiences are important too. Parents have a primary role to play, both in the care they provide directly and in the care arrangements they choose for their children. There is also a role for the rest of us—we all share responsibility for the quality of the care arrangements that are available to families. High-quality arrangements will pay long-term benefits; but all of us will bear the costs of poor-quality care.

This chapter also reviews recent trends in parental work and caregiving and provides an up-to-date picture of what parents can and cannot do in terms of providing care for children themselves. Today, with two-thirds of children living in families with every adult working, out-of-home child care is a reality for an increasing number of American children and for an increasing number of hours. This chapter describes that reality and shows how it varies by who the child is and by what type of family she or he lives in.

What Children Need

Human infants differ from the young of other species in their long period of dependency on adults. Young children cannot fend for themselves—they need years of adult care and supervision to survive. But
parents want more for their children than just to survive. Parents want
children to grow up to be healthy, happy, successful, and decent members of society.[1] To do so, children need what economists call "human
capital"—a good supply of health, skills, and knowledge that they can
apply to the situations they encounter on the playground, in school,
and eventually in the workplace. Children also need "social capital"—
supportive families, extended families, and communities that provide
them with all the things that children need to grow and thrive, including love, attention, discipline, morals, nourishing food, safe drinking
water, clean clothes to wear to school, adequate health care, a good education, and, eventually, opportunities for higher education and meaningful and rewarding employment.

Many people feel that raising children is more challenging than it
used to be. The world we live in is growing increasingly complex, and
the set of skills that a child must have is growing too. At the same time,
as economic inequality in the labor market has grown, parents are
painfully aware that it is more important than ever that their child has
the human and social capital to succeed in that labor market. The days
when a high school dropout or high school graduate could get a well-
paying job that would support a middle-class lifestyle are gone. Parents
fear that their children must be even better educated than they were just
to stand still, let alone to get ahead. And education, as provided by the
schools, is just one component of what parents feel children need to
learn. Middle-class parents schedule their children into a host of other
activities designed to increase their skills and knowledge as well as their
stock of social and cultural capital. From after-school tutoring to soccer
or other team sports to music lessons, children today, particularly if they
live in moderate-income or affluent suburban families, are leading much
busier lives, and lives that require more extensive parental chauffeuring
and planning. Even playtime has become more structured, as "hanging
around" has given way to scheduled (and often supervised) "play dates."[2]

Of course, parents' views of what their children need are motivated
by more than just economics. As family sizes have grown smaller, and

parents, particularly those who are well educated, have waited longer to have children, parents have come to place more emotional value on their children. And they have developed a broader and more demanding view of what a child needs and what they themselves must do to meet those needs. A hundred years ago, there was little discussion of "quality time," and children spent long hours on their own or with their many siblings. Most children, like Abe Lincoln, walked to school, even at young ages. Today's families are smaller and have parents who are older and better educated. These parents set higher standards for their parenting, valuing quality time and providing much more one-on-one care and supervision. And many fewer children walk to school.

There are also objective reasons why the job of parenting has become more demanding. The environments in which we live have become more complex and less safe for children to navigate on their own. In many cities, children live at a distance from their schools or would have to walk through unsafe neighborhoods to get there. Even in the suburbs, walking to school may not be safe, as many new areas have been developed without space set aside for sidewalks. And children face other, less tangible risks. Many parents worry about how much and how early children are exposed to drugs, sex, and violence, through television, other media, and what they see and hear about in their families and communities. The world seems a much riskier place than it was a century ago.

Against this backdrop, families' attitudes toward child rearing have changed. Parenting has come to be seen as a more challenging and complex job, by parents and by the many experts who advise them.[3] A hundred years ago, baby books focused on childhood illnesses, feeding, and sleep schedules. Other issues of infant care and parenting during the rest of childhood received less attention, being seen as relatively straightforward. But, over the course of the twentieth century, parents came to see parenting as a more serious job, and experts reinforced that view, expanding the set of issues on which they offered advice and extending their guidance beyond the first few years into the preschool years, middle childhood, and adolescence. As they did so, the number of books on parenting grew exponentially, increasing fivefold in just the last twenty-five years of the century.[4] At the same time, the Internet became a major source of information. By the end of the century, there were more Web sites on parenting than on any other subject—except for sex.[5]

During the course of the twentieth century, as scientists learned more about the developing child, their understanding of what children need from an early age expanded. Babies, it turned out, needed not just feeding and diapering—they were active learners, and the experiences that parents provided for them would lay the groundwork for their future success. The attention to children as early learners accelerated in the 1980s and 1990s, with a cover story in *Time* titled "What Do Babies Know?" in 1983 and a special issue of *Newsweek*, "Your Child From Birth to Three" in 1997. Also in the 1980s and 1990s, attention to issues of character development and morality accelerated, with a burst of books and publications on "the moral child."[6]

The result, ironically, is that at the same time that fewer children have two parents and more children have working parents, standards for what children need from their parents have ratcheted up. As families changed, experts such as Dr. Spock revised their manuals to recognize that fewer children had a parent home full time.[7] But expert opinion about working parents is still divided. While many experts advise working parents about how to choose child care and how to manage the conflicts between family and work, some also express a clear preference for parental care, particularly when children are young. Penelope Leach, the author of the best-selling *Your Baby and Child*, says parental care for young children is best, and she calls for extended parental leave and part-time work options to make this possible.[8] Two other leading child-rearing experts, Berry Brazelton and Stanley Greenspan, see the need for parental care extending further into childhood, prescribing that "one parent needs to be home in the afternoon and both at home (in a two-parent family) by 6:00 PM" and then going on to specify what parents must do in those hours to assure their children's development in all the important domains.[9]

As Ann Hulbert concludes in her review of a century of child-rearing advice, experts by the end of the century were conveying a "daunting message" to parents:

> It presumed parents and children to be in need of step-by-step guidance in an endeavor that, given the vigilance it demanded, could not help sounding fraught with danger. Relations between a child and her mother and father required constant monitoring and recalibrating . . . At stake was not merely growth, or social adjustment, or emotional health, but anxiously calculated moral worth.[10]

As daunting as this message is, it would be even more so for working parents, who would be hard-pressed to meet these new higher standards. It is little wonder, then, that today's parents are so stressed and that working parents are left feeling "still guilty after all these years."[11] Mothers, who were always seen as playing the primary role in child rearing, are being held to a higher standard than in the past, with the development of new ideals for "intensive mothering."[12] These ideals are reinforced by messages from the media and marketing and find a receptive audience among women who have come to be more achievement oriented in their work lives and who bring that spirit of competition home with them as well.

Fathers are being held to a higher standard too. As women have demanded more equality in the home and as experts have emphasized the importance of parenting, fathers have come to see their role in a new light and have increased their time with children. Fathers still spend less time with children on average than mothers do, but in the last twenty-five years, they have narrowed the gap, raising their time with children by an hour a day. Since women have not substantially increased their time with children over the same period—as their work hours have increased—the gap between mothers and fathers has narrowed.[13] Roles within the home continue to be unequal, with women continuing to bear more responsibility on average for the "second shift" of work at home, but roles are certainly more equal than they were fifty years ago.[14]

The Importance of Parents

At the same time that the job of parenting has come to be seen as more complex, questions persist about how important parents are, given all the other influences in children's lives. Seventeenth-century English philosopher John Locke and his successors (eighteenth-century Scottish philosopher David Hume and nineteenth-century English philosopher John Stuart Mill), who espoused a tabula rasa point of view, argued that children's minds were blank slates at birth and that parents could shape a child to become anything they wanted. American behaviorist John Watson asserted in the 1920s, "Give me a dozen healthy infants, well-formed, and my own specified world to bring them up in and I'll guarantee to take any one at random and train him to become any type of specialist I might select—a doctor, lawyer, artist, merchant-chief and yes, even beggar-man and thief, regardless of his talents, penchants, tendencies, abilities, vocations, and race of his ancestors."[15] Others have argued to the contrary, saying that genes are paramount and that parents have little influence. This point of view was expressed in 1875 by British geographer Francis Galton, who conducted an early study comparing identical and nonidentical twins and who concluded, "There is no escape from the conclusion that nature prevails enormously over nurture."[16]

Although such extreme positions have gone out of fashion, these debates continue to the present day. Three questions are particularly contested and have particular importance for how we think about the well-being of children of working parents. The first concerns the relative importance of nature versus nurture. The second concerns the primacy of early versus later experiences. And the third has to do with the influence of parents as opposed to peers. The sections that follow review the evidence on each of these questions.

Nature versus Nurture

Although the nature-nurture question has been hotly debated for centuries, in many ways this is a false dichotomy. Increasingly, scientists have come to understand the central importance, not of nature or nurture, but the interplay between them, what Matt Ridley calls "nature via nurture."[17] Thus, knowing more about the human genome does not mean that experience does not matter. Experience does matter but in a more complicated way than we had previously imagined.

The field of behavioral genetics has made huge strides in more precisely specifying the role played by heredity, environment, and gene-environment interactions in influencing the course of a child's health and development.[18] In the controversial area of intelligence, for instance, we now know that intelligence is highly heritable but that it is also strongly influenced by environment. This was shown strikingly in recent research on adopted children in France. Researchers followed four-to-six-year-old children with low IQs (ranging from 60 to 86, and averaging just under 80) who were then adopted into families of varying socioeconomic status. All the children gained in IQ subsequent to their adoption, but what was particularly striking was that the gain a child made corresponded strongly to how well-off his or her adoptive family was. Children adopted into the most affluent families—who presumably offered the richest learning environments—saw their IQs rise from just under 80 to nearly 100. But children adopted into the lowest-income families—who presumably offered the least stimulating learning environments—gained much less, as the children's IQ scores rose from about the same starting level to only about 85.[19]

Research on children's social and emotional growth and development has also yielded important insights about nature versus nurture. Recent longitudinal work on antisocial behavior, for instance, has powerfully shown the importance of gene-environment interactions. Researchers have been following a cohort of children in New Zealand for thirty years now, gathering data on their family backgrounds and also on the environments in which they have grown up. The researchers have also gathered genetic data, unusual for a study of this kind. Analyzing all this information together led to a striking discovery: children who had a specific gene associated with antisocial behavior were indeed at higher risk of developing antisocial behavior as they moved into adolescence and young adulthood, but the magnitude of the risk was strongly influenced by the parenting they experienced. Children who had the gene but experienced warm and consistent parenting were no more likely to develop antisocial behaviors than children who did not have the gene and experienced similarly good parenting. But their risk was four times higher than average if they had the gene and also experienced harsh and inconsistent parenting, whereas children who did not have the gene but experienced similarly poor parenting had no elevated risk.[20] Results from Denmark tell a similar story. In this case, children of criminals who were adopted into noncriminal families did have a higher risk of becoming criminals than did children of noncriminals adopted into noncriminal families—20 percent versus 15 percent. But the highest risk was for children who were both born to and raised by criminals—fully 25 percent of these children went on to a life of crime.[21]

The message of these studies is clear: even when there is a gene (or set of genes) that places individuals at risk of poor health or development, the environment can play a decisive role in determining how that gene (or set of genes) is expressed. This message is important, because it means that finding a genetic component to an illness or developmental problem does not mean that environment does not matter. In the case of the antisocial gene studied in New Zealand, environment was key—the gene in fact posed no risk unless combined with a harsh environment. In the case of the criminal gene studied in Denmark, the gene posed some risk on its own, but that risk was compounded if the environment was criminal as well.

Early versus Late Experience

If children's experiences do matter, a second fundamental question has to do with the timing of those experiences. Anyone reading the popular press in the past ten or twenty years could be forgiven for having come away with the impression that early experiences are critical. But the truth is more complicated.

The early years are a period of tremendous growth and development. And we are learning more every day about how important experiences in the early years are for children. Even before a child is born, the prenatal care a mother receives, her nutrition, her use or nonuse of alcohol, tobacco, and drugs, and her exposure to toxins in the home, neighborhood, or workplace, all affect the child's health and development. Fathers' experiences, including their exposure to toxins in the workplace, also influence their children prenatally.[22]

After birth, experiences continue to exert a powerful influence on children's health and development. Children master an extraordinary number of tasks in their first days, weeks, and months of life, and the care and support they receive plays an enormously important role in this process. Pediatricians Barry Zuckerman and Robert Kahn beautifully illustrate this point by contrasting the care of two babies, John and Sean, both two months old.[23] John wakes up hungry and crying, is sensitively fed and soothed by his mother, and goes peacefully back to sleep, having learned that when he cries, a caring and responsive adult will be there to meet his needs. Sean, who also wakes up hungry and crying, is picked up roughly by his troubled mother, does not feed well, and goes unhappily back to sleep, having learned that when he cries, a harsh and insensitive adult will not meet his needs. These kinds of experiences occur many times a day throughout the first few years of life and set the stage for how a young child grows and develops, not just socially and emotionally, but also cognitively and physically.

The fact that experiences in the early years are important, however, does not mean that they are all-important. Recently, the early years have been touted as a "critical period," particularly for brain development. During the 1990s—heralded as "the decade of the brain"—a series of well-publicized events informed parents of new advances in brain science that indicated for the first time just how much growth was occurring in the early years and how critical early experiences were in that process. While much of what was presented in this decade was true, some was exaggerated.[24] Take the term "critical" for instance. To a lay person, critical means very important or fundamental. In this sense, it would be correct to describe the early years as a critical period—a very important or fundamental period. But neuroscientists reserve the term "critical period" for something much more specific—a period that is uniquely important for development, in the sense that an individual must have a certain experience in that time frame if development is not to be permanently altered. So, in the classic example, there is a critical period for the development of vision in cats. If a cat's eye is patched during this period, so that the brain cannot receive visual input from the eye, the cat will be permanently blind in that eye, even if the patch is later removed. Similar experiments with monkeys showed the existence of a critical period for binocular vision (vision that uses both eyes properly): if a monkey's eyes were alternately patched during the critical period, the monkey would develop normal vision in each eye but would never develop binocular vision, since its brain had never received input from both eyes simultaneously during the critical period.[25]

Under this more specific definition, can we say that the early years are a critical period for human brain development? Basically, no. Although there are a few competencies that do specifically require environmental input at a precise time in early childhood, the vast majority do not. In the area of language, for instance, it is true that children must hear certain sounds by the age of about six months if they are to distinguish them later in life. This is why native speakers of Japanese cannot hear the difference between the letter *r* and the letter *l*: this distinction does not exist in their language and so they have not heard it as infants. There also appear to be critical periods for other aspects of language learning, having to do with accent or syntax, but these occur much later in life. However, most language development does not involve critical periods. A child who does not learn the word "umbrella" by age three can learn it at age thirteen or thirty-three. So too for other types of development—critical periods are the exception, rather than the rule.[26]

Another area of confusion about the early years is the importance of above-average experiences versus below-average experiences. In translating findings from neuroscientific studies, sometimes the media extrapolate results concerning deprivation into conclusions about enrichment. For example, studies showing slower brain development among rats who are placed in deprived environments (cages with nothing at all to play with) are used as evidence to support the hypothesis that providing extra enrichment to children will boost their brain development. Beyond the difficulty of extrapolating from rats (in cages) to babies (in their playpens), there is also the difficulty of assuming that providing extra stimulation will have equal and opposite effects to withdrawing normal stimulation. It could as well be the case that a minimal amount of stimulation is necessary for healthy growth and development, but anything beyond that has no effect or diminishing effects. Early intervention programs have been shown to have dramatic effects, particularly when they are intensive and of high quality and when they serve very disadvantaged children. We also know that placing young children in very deprived environments, such as Romanian orphanages, can do lasting damage. However, the jury is still out on how much extra enrichment in the early years really matters for children whose experiences are in the normal range.[27]

Although the early years are important, the current, more balanced view is that both the early and later years matter. Human brains, it turns out, are remarkably plastic (to use another term from neuroscience), maintaining the ability to grow, develop, and even recover from injury into adolescence and adulthood. So, although much development occurs in the early years, the story—and parents' work—does not end there.

Parents versus Peers

As children grow and develop into more autonomous individuals, they spend less time with parents and more with peers. If early experiences are not determining, and later experiences matter, this leads to a third fundamental question—how important parents are as opposed to peers. The phrasing here is not accidental; the assumption behind the question is typically that peer influences will be at odds with what parents are trying to convey. Given how important peers are, particularly in middle childhood and adolescence, do parents stand a chance at having any influence at all?

A controversial 1995 article and subsequent book by Judith Harris said the answer was basically no. Reviewing the extensive literature in psychology on the role of parents in children's socialization, Harris pointed to what she saw as its fatal flaw—the inattention to the role of genetic influences. Yes, she argued, children are very like their parents, but this does not mean that parents influence their children: the similarities might well be the result of genetics, not environment. She went on to argue that to the extent environment does matter, it is peers, not parents, who are most influential. Particularly once children enter middle childhood (starting at the age of six), they care about and imitate their peers, not their parents. Thus, children will pick up the accent of their peers, and not that of their parents. So too for tastes in fashion, music, and so on.

Although there is some truth in Harris' version of events—peers do matter, as do genes, of course—her conclusion that parents play no role is too strong. Parents matter a good deal, even in middle childhood and adolescence. Parents have a direct influence on their children's development and also have an indirect influence, through the environments that they expose their children to. It is parents, after all, who determine where a family will live and what school a child will attend. These decisions are hugely important in determining the kind of peers with whom a child will grow up. And the kind of relationship parents have with their children and adolescents affects how much influence peers exert. Children and youth who have a close relationship with their parents and feel their parents listen to them and understand their worries are better able to resist peer pressure and to engage in less risky behavior as they move into adolescence. Having a close relationship with a father or father figure seems to be particularly important, although studies have not been sufficiently detailed to show whether this factor has to do with the presence of a second adult or a man per se.

∿ As we have seen, parents play an important role in their children's development. Indeed, some would say what parents do matters now more than ever. But families are changing rapidly. Many have only one parent, at least some of the time, and parents, whether single or married, are working more hours. What realistically can parents do given the time they are at work?

Family Structure and Parental Employment

The literature on parental employment and children is very much gendered. Studies have focused on trends in mothers' employment and their possible implications for child well-being. When fathers are considered, the focus is usually on the possible ill effects of paternal unemployment on family functioning (although more recently, some attention has been paid to the role of fathers as carers and the importance of their involvement for child development).[28] Thus, there is a fundamental asymmetry in how mothers' and fathers' roles have been viewed: the norm is for the father to be working and the mother to be home caring for the children, and studies have focused on the potential harm done when parents deviate from those norms.

However, it is important to not take as given that fathers have primary responsibility for work while mothers have primary responsibility for children. Although in some domains, mothers do tend to have primary responsibility for children, this is not the case for all domains. In the health arena, for instance, mothers usually are responsible for making sure children have a doctor and dentist and that they receive necessary medical care, but fathers tend to be a more important source of health insurance coverage.[29] Nor is the allocation of responsibility between parents constant across families or over time. In some families fathers play a more important role, and in others mothers and fathers are working to play more equal roles.[30]

Therefore, in the sections that follow, I consider both parents' availability and employment, rather than focusing on mothers only. The fact that children spend fewer hours today than they did in the past supervised by a parent and more hours in someone else's care (or on their own) is a reflection of many factors: the increasing share of families with only one parent, the increasing frequency with which mothers work, and the long hours that parents, especially fathers, work. All of these factors combined result in less parental time with children and more need for nonparental care and supervision.

Single-Parent Families

The most dramatic change in children's lives over the past one hundred years has been the growth in the number of children spending at least some portion of their childhood in a single-parent family. Current estimates are that half of all children living today will spend at least some portion of their childhood in a single-parent home. Children are also spending a longer part of their childhood with a single parent. Fifty years ago, the major cause of single parenthood was divorce, so most children living with single parents had spent some of their childhood (and certainly their early years) in a two-parent family before their parents split up. Increasingly, however, children are being born into single-parent families. Fully one-third of children born in 2000 had mothers who were not married.[31] Children born to an unmarried mother will spend at least their early years with a single parent, and many will spend their later years with a single parent as well.

Although most single parents are women, a growing number are men. In 2002, 23 percent of all families with children were headed by a single mother, and 5 percent by a single father; thus, single-father families now make up almost one-fifth of single-parent families.[32]

Many single parents are not truly single, or at least not all the time. Often, the other parent (or another adult with whom the single parent is romantically involved) is either living in the home or visiting the home at least some of the time. The role of these nonmarried parents or parent figures spans a large range. At one extreme, some cohabiting parents are indistinguishable from married-couple parents (and indeed may be viewed as married by those who know them). At the other extreme, there are boyfriends or girlfriends who drift in and out of single parents' lives, providing little care or support to the children to whom they may or may not be related.

In addition, a substantial share of single parents live with other relatives—the children's grandparent, aunt or uncle, or other extended family members. These other relatives can be an important source of care and supervision when parents work (and may also be a source of additional income when parents do not work full-time).

Although the effects of growing up with a single parent continue to be debated and are complicated by the fact that not all single-parent families are alike, on average, children growing up with just one parent do lose out relative to other children.[33] Part of the penalty to single parenthood is financial: single-parent families tend to have lower incomes and, as a result, tend to live in poorer neighborhoods with poorer schools. Another portion of the penalty has to do with time:

children in single-parent families have, by definition, only one parent available to them.

So, unless a family is independently wealthy or benefits from a very generous welfare system (one much more generous than we have ever had in the United States), a single parent will inevitably be stretched thin, taking on the role of breadwinner as well as caregiver. David Ellwood, in his influential analysis of work, welfare, and the needs of poor families, argued that the most that could be expected of single mothers (or fathers) would be to work part-time, given the need for a parent to be home caring for the children at least part-time.[34] But part-time employment among single parents is actually very rare in the United States, in part because of the design of our welfare system, which has traditionally provided much more generous benefits to those who do not work at all. With the welfare reforms of the 1990s, supports for low-income working parents have become more generous, and the share of single parents working part-time has risen a bit. But for the most part, even with more generous in-work supports, single parents pretty much have to work full-time if they are to provide their families with an adequate standard of living.

So how do single parents cope when they are working full-time? As we shall see in the succeeding chapters, families use an array of child care resources, relying extensively on their own extended family, informal resources in the community, and more formal forms of child care and out-of-school care. Families also rely on their children to care for themselves and their siblings, particularly as children become older and more responsible.

Two-Parent Families

Two-parent families have also experienced dramatic changes. For those of us who grew up in the 1950s, the contrast between our families and the families of today could not be starker. Back in 1950, only a quarter of married mothers worked. This share rose to 40 percent by 1970 and then crossed the halfway mark in 1980, when 54 percent of married mothers were in the labor force. By 1990, two-thirds of married mothers were in the labor force, and the figure today is approaching three-quarters.[35]

The changes have been most dramatic for families with young children. Table 1.1 shows that labor force participation of married mothers with children under age six has doubled since 1970, from 30 percent to 61 percent, while the participation of married mothers with older children has risen less steeply, from 49 percent to 77 percent. More detailed data, in Table 1.2, show that the sharpest increases have been for the women with the youngest children, although these increases have tapered off in the last few years. In 1975, only 31 percent of women with a child age one or younger were in the labor force, compared to 57 percent in 2002. Nevertheless, participation rates continue to be higher when children are older, with the highest participation rate—81 percent—when children are teens.

Table 1.1. Labor force participation of married mothers (in percent), 1970 to 2002

	1970	1980	1990	2000	2002
All married mothers	40	54	66	71	70
Married mothers, children under 6	30	45	59	63	61
Married mothers, children 6 to 17	49	62	74	77	77

Source: U.S. Census Bureau, 2003, Table 597, p. 391.

Table 1.2. Labor force participation of married mothers (in percent) by age of child, 1975 and 2002

	1975	2002
All married mothers	45	70
With child ≤ age 1	31	57
With child age 2	37	62
With child age 3	41	62
With child age 4	41	67
With child age 5	44	68
With child age 6 to 13	52	75
With child age 14 to 17	54	81

Source: U.S. Census Bureau, 2003, Table 598, p. 391.

Because fathers have not cut back their employment or working time, the increases in mothers' employment mean that fewer children have a stay-at-home parent. Overall, only 40 percent of married-couple families have a parent who is not working (see Table 1.3), most commonly because only the father is working (30.5 percent) or, less commonly, because only the mother is working (5.5 percent) or because neither parent is working (3.3 percent). Families with children under six are more likely to have a parent who is not working, but even here more than half (53 percent) of married-couple families have both parents working, and this share rises to 67 percent in families with children age six or older.

Table 1.3. Employment status of parents in married-couple families (in percent), 2003

	Both work	Only father	Only mother	Neither works
All married-couple families	60.7	30.5	5.5	3.3
With children under age 6	53.2	39.0	4.4	3.4
With children age 6 to 17	67.0	23.4	6.4	3.2

Source: U.S. Bureau of Labor Statistics, 2004, Table 4.

How do families cope when both parents are working? As we will see in the succeeding chapters, families adopt a range of solutions, depending on the age of the child, their own interests and preferences, and the resources and options available to them. Some parents split shifts, arranging their work hours so that one of them is home to provide care for the children. Others use some form of child care, often patching together more than one arrangement to cover all the hours of care needed. And in some families, particularly as children get older, children care for themselves, are cared for by siblings, or spend time just hanging around with friends.

☞ How MUCH HELP do working parents get in meeting the needs of their children? We consider the current policy landscape next.

Current Policies

Policies can support families with working parents in three main ways: by ensuring parents have the right to take time off to care for their children at particular times or when certain events occur; by providing, or supporting, nonparental care for children while parents work; and by providing financial assistance with the costs of raising children.

In each of these three areas, as we shall see, the role of government policy in the United States is fairly minimal, compared with what is typically the case in other developed nations. The United States has what has been called a "residual" welfare state. In the residual model, the primary source of support for families is the individual's and family's own resources, including those that come from employment, the extended family, and the community. Government help is seen as a last resort, filling in when, due to circumstances beyond the individual's control, those other sources of support have failed or are not available. This residual approach is reflected in each of the three major types of policies the United States has to support families with working parents.

Time Off for Parents

In contrast with virtually all other developed countries, the United States does not have a national policy providing paid and job-protected time off for parents with a newborn or a sick child. As we shall see in chapter 2, the United States was late to pass national family and medical leave legislation, and even now the Family and Medical Leave Act, which specifies certain situations when employers must provide job-protected leave to working parents, covers only about half the private sector workforce and provides unpaid leave only. State laws in some instances are more generous or comprehensive (especially notable in this regard is California, which provides paid parental leave through a state social insurance program), but even these laws are minimal in comparison to the provisions in place in most developed countries.

In the absence of state or federal provisions, employers, either on their own or in negotiation with unions, set their own policies specifying when employees can take time off and under what circumstances that leave will be paid. Such benefits, like other employee benefits, are considered part of the total compensation package, and as a result, leave benefits tend to be more generous in more-highly paid jobs. The unfortunate result is that low-income working parents are the least likely to have access to time off and particularly to time off with pay. Over half (54 percent) of workers in families with incomes below the poverty line have no paid time off at all on their job, and fewer than a third (30 per-

cent) have more than a week of paid time off; in contrast, 43 percent of
those with incomes between 100 and 200 percent of the poverty line,
and 76 percent of those with incomes above 200 percent of poverty have
more than a week of paid leave.[36] Access to paid leave that can be used
to care for a sick child is even more limited: even among the highest-
income workers (those with incomes above $72,000 per year), a third do
not have access to such leave, and the share without leave rises to half
among middle-income workers (incomes between $28,000 and $72,000)
and two-thirds among low-income workers (incomes below $28,000).[37]

It is a concern that so few American employees have the right to take
paid time off from work when a child is sick, and it is clearly inequitable
that low-income workers are the least likely to have such rights. The
medical literature suggests that children recover more quickly and are
more likely to follow doctor recommendations for treatment and follow-
up if a parent does stay home.[38] This is one area where the United
States could learn from other countries, most of whom require employers to offer at least a minimal amount of paid leave each year that
parents can use to meet urgent family responsibilities. The cost of the
leave can be paid for by employers or through a social insurance fund.
But the United States should guarantee all workers the right to take at
least two weeks off work each year with pay and should specifically
guarantee the right of parents to take that time to meet important family needs, including the need to care for a sick child. As I discuss in
more detail in chapter 2, the United States should also move to guarantee all new parents the right to a period of paid time off to be home
with their newborn.

The second type of policy related to time that is commonly found in
other countries but again not the United States is the right for parents
to request to work part-time or to have flexible hours. Part-time working has long been a feature of the U.S. labor market and has been particularly popular with mothers, although it carries high costs, both in
terms of reduced earnings and also the risk that the part-time worker
will be consigned to a secondary labor market of not-so-good jobs.[39]

Working flexible hours, or flextime, is an increasingly popular option
in the U.S. labor market. The share of wage and salary workers with access to traditional flextime (which allows a worker to change his or her
schedule on a permanent basis) increased from 29 percent in 1992 to
43 percent in 2002, while the share with access to daily flextime (which

allows a worker to change his or her schedule on a daily basis) increased from 18 percent to 23 percent.[40] However, many workers still do not have access to flextime, and as with other benefits, inequities exist. The share of high-income workers with access to traditional flextime is double that of low-income workers (62 percent among those earning more than $72,000 per year versus 31 percent among those earning less than $28,000), and the disparity is even greater when it comes to daily flextime (47 percent of workers earning more than $72,000 versus 13 percent of workers earning less than $28,000).[41]

As I discuss in more detail in chapter 2, European countries now commonly give parents the right to request to work part-time or to have flexible hours. Employers are not required to grant requests if doing so would prove too much of a hardship, but they are required to give requests fair consideration. Introducing such a policy in the United States would help ensure that the option of working part-time or having flexible hours is extended to more parents, on a more equitable basis.

Of course, having rights to take time off or to request reduced or flexible hours does not mean that parents will necessarily make use of these benefits. Some workplaces actively discourage employees from using benefits, penalizing those who have taken too much time off or who have reduced their work hours, when it comes to promotions or pay increases. Men in particular report that they are reluctant to use the benefits available to them because they feel that their supervisors would disapprove or because it might harm their careers.[42] These aspects of workplace culture are hard to change, but changing benefits policies and making sure that they include antidiscrimination provisions are sound first steps. It is also possible that more drastic steps are needed. For example, reducing the standard workweek from forty hours to thirty-two hours, as some in Europe are trying to do, would give parents and others the shorter workweek that many say they want. Mandating a minimum amount of paid vacation time to which all employees are entitled—say, four weeks a year, as is common in Europe—would be another way to relieve the pressure on parents and other caregivers.[43]

Help with Child Care

A second way for policies to support families with working parents is by helping with child care. In this regard, policy in the United States is somewhat more developed than in the area of time off, although it still lags in comparison to European countries. The United States since 1954 has provided some support through the tax system for working families who have child care expenses. The two major federal tax programs are the Child and Dependent Care Tax Credit (CDCTC) and the Dependent Care Assistance Plan (DCAP).[44]

The CDCTC provides tax relief for working parents with a child under the age of thirteen and with no other parent in the home or with a spouse who is also working or in school full-time. Families can claim a portion of their child care expenses, up to a specified maximum; as of 2003, the maximum credit a family could claim was $1,050 for one child and $2,100 for two or more children. Because the credit is not refundable, it does not benefit families with incomes too low to owe taxes. Thus, it does not benefit low-income families with children.

Another option is the DCAP program (families may use the CDCTC or DCAP but not both). Under the DCAP program, parents can ask employers to set aside a portion of their salary, up to a maximum of $5,000, to pay for child care or other dependent care expenses. This program provides a tax savings to families with participating employers in that it allows parents to pay for child care expenses using pretax dollars, but like the CDCTC it does not benefit families with incomes too low to owe taxes.

There are also child care subsidy policies targeted to low-income working parents, and these have expanded markedly (and changed name and form several times) in the past ten to fifteen years.[45] Since 1996, the major federal child care subsidy program has been known as the Child Care Development Fund (CCDF). The main purpose of child care subsidies is to offset the costs of child care for low-income parents who are working (or engaging in activities to prepare for employment). Parents who are granted a subsidy can choose their own child care provider or program (so long as it meets all relevant reporting and licensing requirements) and then receive help paying a portion of the costs of that care. (The exact amount that parents pay is determined state by state, but typically parents pay for something like 30 percent of the costs, and the subsidy covers the rest, with the share that parents pay rising as their income rises.)

Funding for child care subsidies has been greatly expanded in the 1990s in the wake of federal welfare reform, but subsidies do not reach all eligible families. The most recent estimates suggest that only about 15 percent of families who are eligible actually receive subsidies. Some of the others are on waiting lists; others have declined to participate because their preferred provider would not meet the requirements or would not agree to participate or because parents themselves were unwilling to go through the hassle and paperwork; and others probably do not know about the program or do not realize that they would be eligible.

Families with working parents may also receive help with child care from preschool or school programs. Head Start, for instance, provides publicly funded child care for low-income children and children with disabilities, without regard to whether their parents are working. However, Head Start programs often operate on a part-time and part-year basis, which limits their use as child care for parents who work full-time and year round. Various state-funded preschool and prekindergarten initiatives also provide early education to preschoolers, again without regard to whether parents are working but again often on a part-time and part-year basis. Schools themselves, of course, also provide care during some of the hours that parents are at work, as do after-school programs. Each of these sources of child care is discussed further in the chapters that follow.

Employer assistance with child care has often been suggested as a way to help working families, but it remains limited. Even among the workers most likely to have access to generous employee benefits— full-time employees in medium or large firms—only 10 percent receive any help with child care, and that help usually consists of information and referral services rather than on-site care or financial assistance. Among workers in less-favored positions—part-time workers or workers in small firms—access to such child care assistance is even rarer.[46] Unlike flexible hours, employer involvement in child care assistance has not increased much over time. This relative lack of involvement on the part of employers suggests that there may be limits to what employers are likely to do in the child care arena.

In the succeeding chapters, I consider the issues having to do with help with child care in more detail and make specific recommendations for children in different age groups, because the need for care and the type of support that makes sense vary by age. But two overall conclusions are clear: one, relying on tax credits will not be sufficient to help low-income families, unless those credits are refundable; and two, relying on employers is not a very realistic way to ensure that large numbers of parents receive help with child care costs on an equitable basis.

Financial Assistance

A third major type of policy to support working families with children (as well as nonworking families with children) is a child benefit or credit to offset some of the costs of raising children. These costs go beyond the cost of a parent taking time off when a child is born or is sick or the cost of child care. Children are extra mouths to feed and need clothes, books, toys, and a myriad of other items as they grow and develop. Again, in keeping with the more residual approach to social policy, the United States tends to provide fairly minimal support. Federal and state tax policies allow families to deduct from their taxes an amount to offset the costs of caring for a child—but such amounts are low and have until very recently been available only to those with incomes high enough to owe taxes. It was not until 2001 that the United States made its child tax credit refundable (that is, available to workers even if their incomes are too low to owe taxes). The 2001 legislation also doubled the value of the credit over the next ten years (from $500 to $1,000 per child), but even ten years out, the value of the credit will be relatively low and families whose earnings do not meet the earnings threshold are excluded.[47]

For the lowest-income families, the United States does have some means-tested financial assistance—welfare—programs. Temporary Assistance for Needy Families (TANF) (formerly AFDC) provides time-limited cash assistance to very low-income families with children. As the program rules have become more stringent and work oriented, fewer families have received cash welfare benefits. Caseloads fell dramatically in the 1990s and remain at very low levels today. There are also various in-kind welfare programs. Food stamps provide help with the costs of food for very low-income families. The Women, Infants, and Children (WIC) program provides additional help to low-income families with a pregnant woman or young child.

Medicaid and other child health insurance programs provide help with the costs of medical care. These medical benefits are important because most Americans receive health insurance through their employers and because lower-income workers are less likely to have good employee benefits. Nearly a third (31 percent) of workers earning less than $28,000 per year do not have employer-provided family health insurance, compared to 14 percent of those earning $28,000 to $72,000, and only 7 percent of those earning more than $72,000.[48]

An important part of the welfare reform of the 1990s was an expansion in what was previously a little-known and little-used federal tax credit targeted to low-income working families, the Earned Income Tax Credit (EITC).[49] Although still not as generous as child benefits in other developed countries, the EITC has become a major source of income for low-income families and now represents the largest government transfer program to them. One downside of the EITC is that it is claimed through the tax system on an annual basis. Thus, it may be less helpful to families than income that they could count on week in and week out. Nevertheless, with an average benefit of over $1,500 per family, the EITC represents an important part of low-income families' budgets and does offset some of the costs of raising children for them.

What about employers? Do they pay workers more when they have more mouths to feed? Although the findings vary somewhat by study and method, on the whole the answer is no. Fathers do tend to work longer hours than men without children, but it is not clear that they earn any more per hour (and, with the demise of the male-breadwinner model, we probably do not want them to). For mothers, the opposite is true—women work shorter hours when they have children and are, if anything, paid less per hour than comparable women without children.[50]

Employment does confer benefits that can help offset the costs of raising children. In the absence of a national health insurance program, most children who have health insurance coverage in the United States obtain this coverage through their parents' employment. Thus, all else being equal, when parents are employed, children are more likely to have health insurance coverage. But the link between parental employment and child health insurance is not airtight. As we have seen, some employers do not offer family health insurance to all employees, and even when they do, parents may face waiting periods or unaffordable premiums and co-payments. In two-parent families, children may be covered through one parent, and thus the other parent's employment may not affect their insurance status. At the same time, expansions in health insurance coverage for low-income children mean that more low-income children are now covered through public health insurance, even if their parents are not working. Thus, for children in two-parent families or low-income families, a parent moving into employment may not necessarily change the likelihood that a child has health insurance coverage.

How much should government help families with the cost of raising children, and how much should that help be tied to parents' work effort? The answers to these questions are inevitably linked to value judgments. To the extent that we value supporting employment, we might not want overly generous government support for children. Yet, to the extent that we value respecting parental choice and promoting quality of care for children, and to the extent that we are concerned about equity, we might want government to take on a more active role in providing support for children.

One way to balance these competing values is to identify a package of minimal support for children, guaranteed to children whether or not their parents work or work full-time, so that children are cushioned if their parents lose their jobs or move out of work or reduce their hours for a period of time. In my view, such a package would include at a minimum a child benefit more generous than the current child tax credit, something along the lines of $2,400 per year per child for low- and moderate-income families, as well as a guarantee of health insurance for all children and their parents.[51] The United States is one of the only advanced industrialized countries not to provide such a package, even though it is one of the most able to afford to do so. Providing a more generous basic child benefit and guaranteed health insurance would help ease the pressures on today's working families and provide vital support to them in meeting their children's needs.

Looking Ahead

As we have seen in this chapter, parents continue to play a primary role in their children's care. But the American family has changed dramatically and far fewer children have a stay-at-home parent than in the past, due to the growth in single-parent families and to the growth in mothers' employment in two-parent families. Government and employer policies have been hard-pressed to keep up with these changes. And, in fairness to employers, there is only so much we can expect them to do. Investing in employees makes good business sense up to a point, but there are limits to what employers can afford and also equity concerns if parents are given more benefits than other workers.

What of the children? With fewer living with a stay-at-home parent, more children are in nonparental care, for longer hours. As the likelihood of children being in nonparental care and their time in care increases, so too does the importance of making sure that children's time in care promotes healthy growth and development. Yet, unfortunately, this is all too often not the case. As we shall see in the chapters that follow, what we know about the quality of care that children are spending time in is not encouraging.

2

Infants and Toddlers

IF YOU ASK PARENTS to think back to the time when their child was born, you will get an outpouring of memories and emotions. The first few weeks and months after the birth of a child are exhilarating but also exhausting. Newborns need almost constant care and attention, and even the hardiest of parents find themselves drained by the demands on their time and energy. Most mothers spend at least a few weeks at home after the birth, time that is essential for the mother's own recovery and also for the infant's adjustment to life outside the womb. Most fathers too spend at least some time at home, to help with the infant and mother. This is a period when breast-feeding, or bottle-feeding, is established and when parents get to know what their child's rhythms are and also how to respond to the infant's needs for care and comfort.

The first few weeks and months are a time that is stressful for all parents but especially for working parents, who must decide when to return to work. On the one hand, they can see how much their infant needs them at home, and they may want very badly to be home. They may also worry about who would care for the baby if they went back to work and whether that care would be good enough to meet their child's needs. On the other hand, there is the pull of work. Parents may not be able to afford to take more time off work or may have to return if they are to keep their jobs. And even parents who can take an extended leave may worry about keeping their careers on track. Some parents may wish that they could go back to work part-time but may find that this is not a viable option. The conflict can be very intense. Indeed, for many families, there is no other time when work and family demands collide in such a dramatic and wrenching way.

Part of what makes the first weeks and months so challenging for parents is how helpless and vulnerable newborns are. It can be hard for parents to imagine anyone else taking good enough care of their child at this stage. But, of course, one of the other things that usually strikes new parents is how quickly their child becomes competent at all kinds of things—smiling, sitting up, rolling over, and, usually by the end of the first year, moving around independently and using language. By the time children are older infants or toddlers, they seem a lot less helpless, and many parents feel they can trust someone else to care for them, although parents still worry a lot about whether someone else can provide good enough care for their child and who that someone else should be.

This chapter reviews the evidence from developmental psychology and other disciplines on what infants and toddlers need to promote their health, cognitive development, and social and emotional well-being and the extent to which others can substitute for parents during the first three years of life. Drawing on the research, including analyses of data from two large longitudinal studies of American families, this chapter addresses the following questions. What do infants and toddlers need in these early years? Does parental employment have adverse effects on children's development? Are there times in the first year or years when a parent should be home, at least part-time? If so, how can policies support parents who stay home? What about situations when parents have to work or want to work? What is best for children in these situations, and what can policies do to support this decision? This chapter considers a range of policies, including parental leave, measures to improve the quality of infant and toddler care, and cash benefits for families with young children. Welfare rules that affect mothers of infants are also discussed.

What Infants and Toddlers Need

Human newborns are heavily dependent on their parents to meet their basic needs and protect them from harm. The physical needs are easiest to see. At a minimum, infants need to be kept warm and to be fed.

Although these may sound like simple matters, they are actually complex, as any first-time parent can attest. There is an art to wrapping babies so that they are warm enough without being smothered. And breast-feeding is not always possible, or straightforward, and when it is not, providing an adequate and safe supply of substitute milk can be a challenge. In the Middle Ages, it was common practice for a mother who could not care for her newborn to bring it to a place of refuge—a foundling home—where it could be cared for or placed in the care of another family. But many of these foundlings did not survive. Although older orphans could survive on orphanage food and with institutional care, newborns could not, and gradually new forms of support came into being to keep infants with their mothers if at all possible.[1]

However, the needs of infants and toddlers go beyond the purely physical. The care that young children receive from their parents and other caregivers lays the foundation not just for their physical growth and health but also for their cognitive and emotional growth and development. Parents recognize this and worry about whether they are providing the "right" type of experiences and interactions for their children. There is a huge market for books that advise parents about how to care for their children. Those books cover not just feeding, sleeping, and coping with childhood illnesses and injuries but also how the young child develops and what parents should do to promote that development.[2]

In recent years, there has been a good deal of attention to early brain development and to the types of stimulation that young children might need to grow and develop to their fullest potential.[3] Research findings have been rapidly translated into prescriptions that parents should buy particular toys or learning items or should make sure their children engage in certain activities. But what infants need is something more fundamental than the latest toy or CD. After all, generations of children have developed quite well without ever having seen a black-and-white crib toy or listening to classical music in utero. As the National Academy of Sciences Committee on Integrating the Science of Early Childhood Development concluded, "there is no scientific evidence that any sort of mobile, toy, computer program, or baby class has a long-term impact on reasoning, intelligence, or learning."[4]

The bottom line message from developmental psychology and developmental neuroscience is that the most important feature of the care children receive in early childhood is its sensitivity and responsiveness. Sensitivity refers to how appropriate the care is to the individual child, while responsiveness has to do with how adaptive it is to changes in the child's needs and status. A caregiver may be warm and well intentioned but may nevertheless not provide sensitive and responsive care if she or he is not familiar with the child or is not good at picking up cues from the child about what the child needs right now. Conversely, a caregiver may know an individual child's needs well, but if the caregiver is harsh or neglectful in responding to those needs, the care provided will not be sensitive and responsive. Thus, sensitivity and responsiveness are attributes both of the caregiver and of the relationship between the caregiver and the child. Both must be in place if the care is to meet the child's needs and enable the child to grow and develop.

The example of the two babies, John and Sean, whom we met in chapter 1, provides a good illustration of sensitive versus insensitive care. When John wakes up hungry in the middle of the night, his mother picks him up tenderly, feeds him while softly rocking and comforting him, and then gently places him back in bed. Thus, the care John's mother provides is sensitive and responsive to his needs, and John takes away from the experience the expectation that his needs will be recognized and responded to. Sean has a different experience. His mother, who had just had a fight with his father, comes in angrily when Sean cries out and picks him up abruptly and speaks to him in a harsh tone. Because of this, Sean does not feed well, which further irritates his mother, who puts him back into his crib before he has finished eating. Sean learns from this encounter that when he cries out or has trouble feeding, he will not be treated kindly and will not have his needs met.

As such encounters are repeated many times a day, day after day (and night after night), parents and children get to know each other and develop a relationship. In the best of situations, the parent will provide sensitive and responsive care all or most of the time, and the relationship between the parent and child will be based on an expectation that each will be attuned and sensitive to the other. In other situations, the parent may provide sensitive and responsive care some of the time but may not do so consistently—either because of difficulties in his or her own life or because she or he finds it hard to be sensitive to this particular child. In these situations, the relationship will be more troubled and less attuned. In extreme cases, the care that the parent provides may become insensitive—harsh and punitive, as in the example of Sean, or detached and neglectful, if the parent responds by disengaging and withdrawing.

Primate studies shed some light on the origins of sensitive and responsive parenting. There is a strong genetic component: some monkeys are born predisposed to be sensitive mothers, just as their own mothers were. But sensitive mothering can also be learned. A baby monkey who is born to an insensitive mother but raised by a sensitive foster mother will go on to become a sensitive mother herself. So experience clearly matters.[5]

It is also clear that the child one is caring for and the specific situation in which one is raising the child matter too. Some children have more difficult temperaments than others, right from birth, and caring for these babies sensitively and responsively can challenge even the most sensitive of moms or dads, as anyone who has ever had a "colicky" baby can attest. And stresses from other parts of parents' lives can spill over into their care of the child, much as they might try to prevent this. If money is tight, or a spouse is being abusive, even a very sensitive parent may have trouble responding warmly and consistently to the many demands that caring for a baby entails.

In the course of these encounters, children are growing and developing in many ways, and the sensitivity of the care they receive plays an important role. This growth and development is charted by the achievement of specific competencies, known as developmental milestones. The physical ones are well-known—sitting up, crawling, walking, and so on. But there are also milestones in cognitive and emotional development. The first three years of life are a period of very rapid, and interrelated, growth in both domains.

In the area of cognitive development, one of the most important tasks for children is learning language. The development of language nicely illustrates the interplay between nature and nurture discussed in chapter 1, and the importance of sensitive and responsive care in the early years. Children are born with much of what they will need to learn language—a sense of grammar, the ability to recognize different sounds and meanings, and so on—and much of language learning is universal. Most children begin talking between ten and fifteen months, and their vocabularies and language use rapidly expand from about eighteen months onwards.[6] But children will not learn to speak a language unless they are exposed to it. And most children will never speak a language fluently unless they are exposed to it in childhood. Children who do not hear human language (or see sign language) until adolescence can never speak any language fluently as adults.[7] Children who learn a second language after puberty also, for the most part, cannot ever speak it as well as their native language.[8]

The amount and quality of the language children are exposed to matters as well. When children's parents use more words in their interactions with them in early childhood, children develop bigger vocabularies and score better on reading tests at school entry.[9] Children's language development also benefits when parents sing to them or play word games. Caregivers' language matters too. The key is for the person caring for the child—parent, caregiver, or both—to be responsive to the child and stimulating and sensitive in talking to and listening to the child. Interactions with the parent or other caregiver are key.[10]

Alongside language development are a host of other tasks related to cognitive development. Infants must master skills related to thinking, memory, relationships, and so on. Parents and other adults help with the development of these skills, and here again, the more sensitive the care provided, the greater the child's cognitive growth will be.[11] These developing cognitive skills in turn help children with language. And both the language and thinking skills help infants develop socially and emotionally.

In the social and emotional arena, one of the major developmental tasks for infants is to develop secure attachments to adults who care for them. Secure attachments provide a sense of basic trust and as such provide the foundation for the infant to explore the world and form attachments with others. Again, sensitivity and responsiveness are key—children can only develop secure attachments if their caregivers are knowledgeable about their needs and are responsive to those needs. If parents and other caregivers do not know a child well or cannot read a child's cues or fail to respond warmly and consistently to what a child needs, the child will still be attached to them, but that attachment will not be secure. Some children may have an attachment that is ambivalent (reflecting the uneven care they have received to date), while others may have a relationship that is characterized by avoidance (if the care they have received has been harsh or interrupted).

These different types of attachment are diagnosed with a laboratory test called the strange situation assessment, developed by Mary Ainsworth. In this test, a mother and infant are brought into the lab, and the mother then leaves the infant and returns, twice. The child's reactions to the two separations and reunions with the mother are coded, and the attachment relationship is then characterized as secure, ambivalent/inconstant, or avoidant.[12]

The importance of attachment first came to the fore in the 1940s and 1950s, when researchers began studying children who had been made homeless or had been orphaned during World War II. Reviewing the evidence on these terribly deprived children, British psychologist John Bowlby concluded that "mother-love . . . is as important for mental health as are vitamins and proteins for physical health."[13] Bowlby set high standards for that mother love: in order to develop a secure attachment, an infant had to receive continuous and sensitive care from an individual caregiver round the clock for the first year of life.

Bowlby was careful to point out that the continuous, sensitive care could be provided by a mother or another consistent caregiver, but his work was widely interpreted as saying that only continuous and uninterrupted mother care would do. Even worse, it was soon forgotten that the evidence on which Bowlby based his conclusions came from studies of institutionalized children (children in orphanages or shelters), who were indeed deeply traumatized by their experiences, but not from studies of children with working mothers.

As we shall see below, attachment theory was taken to suggest that working mothers posed a risk to their children's mental health. (Working fathers were not seen as a problem because it was assumed that it was the mother who would, or should, be there to provide the consistent care.) It was many years before researchers empirically tested whether and how infants with working mothers differed in their attachment relationships from infants with nonworking mothers, and as we shall see later in this chapter, this research did not bear out the dire predictions. Children with working mothers (or fathers) can develop secure attachments to them, just like children with nonworking mothers (or fathers). The key lies in how sensitive and consistent the parent is.

Although Bowlby and his successors were wrong about attachment and working mothers, they were right about the fundamental importance of attachment in children's development. Children's early attachment experiences lay the groundwork for how they approach future relationships and learning experiences. Although early attachment experiences are not deterministic, secure attachments in infancy make it easier for a child to form healthy relationships with others, while insecure attachments make it harder.

Although infants and toddlers spend most of their time with their own family, an increasing share spend time with other children, and children's early attachment relationships carry over to this arena as well. Twenty years ago, researchers estimated that only 10 percent of toddlers' interactions were with peers. Today, with the majority of infants and toddlers in care at least part-time with other children, that figure is surely a good deal higher.[14] Infants and toddlers have a more active social life than we sometimes think. Babies under the age of one are interested in each other and will try to get each other's attention. Toddlers engage even more actively with other children, especially by imitating each other.[15] But this social interaction does not come easily to young children, and parents play an important role in setting up play situations that their children are likely to be able to manage and in intervening and helping out when conflicts arise.[16] Parents also help by providing a secure base from which children can explore the world and engage in other relationships. Children who are securely attached to their parents are more socially competent and get along better with peers.[17]

As developmental psychologist Ross Thompson points out, the importance of early experiences for social and emotional development is a double-edged sword.[18] Sensitive caregiving is an opportunity for parents to help their children develop socially and emotionally. At the same time, however, care that is not sensitive can put children at risk for behavior problems and mental health problems.

How are these developmental tasks affected if parents work? The question of how children are affected if mothers work has received a good deal of attention in the child health and development literature. The assumption has been that a young child would not be affected by one parent working so long as another parent was with the child full-time. Given the usual division of labor—with the father, if present, working full-time in the labor market and the mother being the one to stay home or arrange substitute care—the question has typically been framed in terms of the impact of having a working mother. As I discuss later, this is a flawed way of looking at parental employment, but for the moment, let us follow the convention and consider what the theoretical literature has to say about situations where the mother is the primary caregiver and then goes to work, meaning that the child must then be cared for by someone else, at least part of the time.

Pediatricians and other baby experts have until fairly recently taken the position that a child's development would be harmed if a mother worked in the first three years. This view is reflected in popular baby books and is also evident in the media and public opinion.[19] Why might one think that exclusive mother care would be best for a child, at least in the first three years of life?

One reason has to do with biology. Anthropologist Sarah Hrdy argues that mothers are best equipped to care for newborns and that newborns actively prefer mothers' care. However, Hrdy also points out that other adults can fulfill this role perfectly well. She argues that the real challenge is in finding someone willing to do so. For example, we know that breast-feeding is best for newborns, and we think of breast-feeding as something that only a mother can do. But, of course, the breast-feeding does not necessarily have to be done by the biological mother. Any other lactating woman can breast-feed a child—she just has to be willing to do so.

A second reason to think that exclusive maternal care would be best for infants has to do with the importance of sensitive and responsive care. If the mother has been the primary caregiver for the child since birth, it stands to reason that she would be best equipped to provide sensitive care, since she would know her baby best and would have learned how to respond to the baby's cues. In this view, any substitute caregiver—whether the father, another relative, or a day care provider— would know the child less well and would provide less sensitive and responsive care than the mother would. Another concern is that time away from the baby early on might detract from the sensitivity of the mother's own care for the child, by interfering with the mother's learning to know her child's cues and with the child's developing a secure attachment to her. In this view, the mother working early on could potentially set up a lose-lose situation—with the child receiving less sensitive care from the substitute caregiver and from the mother herself.

However, there are some weaknesses to this argument. First, given individual variation in the ability to read infants' cues and respond to them appropriately, some mothers may not be very good caregivers or may not be as good as available substitutes. Second, even the best of mothers might provide even more sensitive and responsive care if they did not have to provide care twenty-four hours a day, seven days a week. Third, if an infant is with another caregiver on a regular basis, that caregiver could become as good as the mother at knowing the child and reading the child's cues. Fourth, we know too little about the impact of a mother's time away from the baby on the sensitivity of her own care for the child. It might be that when a mother shares the care of the baby with another adult or adults, it is a win-win situation—with the child benefiting from more sensitive care both from the substitute care-giver(s) and the mother herself.

This discussion suggests that whether and how a child's development might be affected by the mother or other parent working is not clear on theoretical grounds. It is what social scientists call an empirical question—one that must be answered with evidence, rather than with theory. The following section reviews that evidence.

Effect of Parental Employment

Is early parental employment harmful to children? It is hard to think of a question in developmental psychology that has been more hotly debated than this one. Hundreds of books and articles have been written on working parents, with most focusing on whether children are harmed by having a working mother or being in nonmaternal child care, particu-larly in the first few years of life.[20] Where have all these studies left us?

To briefly preview the results, in my view the research on this point is now quite clear. Children do fare better on average if their mothers do not work full-time in the first year of life, although, as we shall see, the effects vary by context. But this finding is pretty specific to the first year, and to full-time work in that year. Part-time work in the first year does not have adverse effects on most outcomes, and work after the first year has neutral or positive effects.

In the following sections, I review the evidence on the effects of early parental employment on child outcomes. Three points are worth not-ing at the outset. First, the evidence on the effects of parental employment comes mainly from observational studies, although in some instances we can also draw on "natural experiments." Evidence from randomized experiments, which would establish causality with more certainty, is generally not available, because of ethical barriers to assigning families to early employment or child care. Second, with few exceptions, studies have examined the effects of maternal employment, reflecting researchers' and the public's preoccupation with working mothers (and the lack of data on families in which fathers are present but do not work). I will review the evidence on paternal employment where available, but we know much less about working fathers than working mothers. Third, it is always worth pointing out that research cannot tell us what is best for any individual child. Studies tell us what is true for children on average or for particular groups. A finding that children on average do better on an outcome if their parents follow a particular employment pattern does not mean that this will be true for an individual child or for all children. Effects will vary among children, and what is best for one child or the average child may not be best for another child or for all children.

Health

There are several reasons that early parental employment, particularly if undertaken in the first year of life and particularly if undertaken full-time, might have negative repercussions for child health. Parents who work, particularly full-time, may have less time available to monitor their child's health and to take the child to the doctor for well-baby care and immunizations. It is also well established that a mother's working, particularly full-time, interferes with breast-feeding. Although there may be offsetting factors, these considerations would lead us to expect that on average early parental employment would have adverse effects on child health, and this expectation in fact is borne out by the research.

The most compelling evidence on the links between early parental employment and child health comes from cross-national natural experiment studies. These studies take advantage of the fact that the generosity of parental leave policies varies across countries and over time. Because such policies influence how long parents stay home before returning to work in the labor market, comparing health outcomes for children born to parents who had access to more- or less-generous parental leave policies allows us to infer the effects of having parents stay home for longer or shorter periods of time. Of course, many other factors that might affect child health and parental employment also vary across countries and over time, so it is important to control for those factors. But careful studies that do so are unanimous in finding that longer periods of parental leave are associated with better child health.

A 1998 study examined this question by using twenty-five years of data (from 1969 to 1994) from sixteen member countries of the Organization for Economic Cooperation and Development (OECD) and by controlling for an extensive set of characteristics that vary by country and year and that might also be correlated with child health. Because the study also controlled for what country the data came from and what year, it was able to show what the effects were of changing leave policies within a country over time. The results indicated that when a country extended its period of paid job-protected maternity leave, infant mortality rates fell. The strongest effects were on postneonatal mortality—mortality that occurs after the first twenty-eight days but before the first birthday. Extending paid job-protected maternity leave by ten weeks reduced postneonatal mortality by 3.7 to 4.5 percent. Extending leave beyond the first year of life also had protective effects on later child mortality (i.e., deaths between the ages of one and five).[21]

A subsequent study updated this work, extending the data to 2000 and adding data on two additional countries, the United States and Japan. Because the United States offers mainly unpaid leave, the later study analyzed the effects of both paid leave and unpaid leave. The results confirm that longer periods of paid leave are associated with lower rates of infant mortality but also indicate that unpaid leave does not have the same protective effect (presumably because unpaid leave has relatively little impact on parents' employment). This study, like the earlier one, found that paid job-protected leave had its strongest effects on postneonatal mortality but also had significant effects on neonatal mortality (i.e., infant deaths under twenty-eight days) and later child mortality (i.e., child deaths between the ages of one and five). Paid leave also had some beneficial effects on other health outcomes, significantly reducing low birth weight and maternal mortality.[22]

The evidence from the cross-national studies, although compelling, does not tell us how early parental employment affects child health. It may be that there are some dimensions along which parents simply provide better care than parent substitutes. One such dimension would be breast-feeding, which pediatricians recommend through the first year of life.[23] Another may be parental supervision of children's sleeping position, which is known to be an important factor in the risk for sudden infant death syndrome (SIDS).[24] Or it may be that employment in the first year of life interferes with parents' taking the child to the doctor for well-baby care or immunizations, and that this accounts for the links between early employment and child health.

Recent research in the United States provides evidence that early maternal employment affects both parental care and the child's receipt of health care. In a study using data from the National Longitudinal Survey of Youth-Child Supplement (NLSY-CS) on just under two thousand children born between 1988 and 1996, the mother's returning to work in the first twelve weeks after birth reduced the likelihood that a child was breast-fed and reduced the length of time that breast-feeding lasted.[25] The mother's returning to work in the first twelve weeks also had negative effects on the child being taken for well-baby visits in the first year of life and on the child being fully immunized (with the recommended series of shots for DPT and polio) by eighteen months. All of these effects were larger if the mother returned to work full-time. Because this study was observational, it cannot prove that the early employment caused the health outcomes. However, this pattern of findings was robust to several different methods of controlling for bias. One set of models included an extensive set of controls for child and family characteristics known to be correlated with both maternal employment and child health. A second set of models used a variable external to the family—the share of women workers unionized in the state and year—to estimate instrumental variables (IV) models that better control for the fact that particular women choose to work early.[26] A third set of models used propensity score matching methods to compare women who worked early in the first year to those most like them.[27] Although the IV models were inconclusive, the results were consistent across the other two types of models, increasing confidence that the effects are likely to be causal.

Unfortunately, we know much less about the effects of fathers' leave taking and employment on child health outcomes. Paternity leave is still a relatively new and unstudied phenomenon, and its links with child health outcomes have not been studied in the United States. We do have some evidence from Britain, where the Millennium Birth Cohort Study is following a large sample of babies born at the dawn of the twenty-first century. In this cohort, about 75 percent of fathers took some leave after the birth of their children. In the families where fathers took leave, the children were more likely to be breast-fed. Although one might worry that this just indicated that these families were more health conscious to start with, this relationship held up in instrumental variables models that estimated the effect of fathers' having leave rights at work (rather than relying on which fathers chose to take leave). These results suggest that when fathers have the right to take leave, they are more likely to do so, and their wives (or partners) are more likely to breast-feed (perhaps because the fathers are around to provide support).[28]

Another potential link between early parental employment and child health has to do with the health effects of day care. Because children of parents who work are more likely to be placed into group day care, these children may be at higher risk of illness or infection, particularly in the first few years of life, when children's immune systems are less developed, when they are still in diapers, and when they are most likely to place objects into their mouths. However, these health effects tend to be minor and not long lasting, and there may even be benefits to children (in terms of lower rates of later asthma or allergies) of being exposed to illnesses earlier in life.[29]

Taken together, the evidence on early parental employment and child health points to three important conclusions. One, maternal employment early in the first year of life, particularly if full-time, is associated with poorer health outcomes for children. Two, more generous parental leave policies, which extend the length of time that parents remain home in the first year of life (and sometimes thereafter), are associated with better health outcomes for children. Third, although group child care in the first few years does pose some health risks to children, these are relatively minor and not long lasting.

Cognitive Development

As we have seen, one of the important roles that parents play in their child's development has to do with the stimulation of cognitive and language growth in the first few years of life. Infants and toddlers learn primarily from the adults who care for them. In the area of language development, for example, the more parents talk to a child, the more the child's language and cognitive ability develops. The same is true for child care providers: the more they talk to the children they care for, the better the children score when tested for verbal and cognitive ability.[30] If the adult who cares for a child while the parent is working is less stimulating and less supportive of the child's growth than the parent would have been, the child's cognitive development could suffer. The child care provider would not have to be overtly negligent—she or he might just talk or read less to the child or might allow the child to spend more time in front of the TV. The alternative, of course, is also possible. In some situations, a substitute caregiver might be more stimulating and more supportive of the child's development. Particularly as children get older and out-of-home care looks more like school, it is easier to imagine nonparental care being more supportive of children's cognitive growth.

Another way in which parental employment in the first three years of life might affect children's cognitive development would be if that employment affected the parent's own care for the child during the hours they are together. As already discussed, mothers who work are less likely to breast-feed, which may adversely affect children's cognitive development.[31] Moreover, a parent who is working, particularly for long hours, may come home tired and stressed, and this could in turn affect the way she or he interacted with the child. A parent worn out from a long day on the job may not have the energy to play or read with the child. But here, too, the alternative is also possible. A parent who is challenged and happy at work may be more likely to engage with the child and nurture the child's growth than if she or he had been at home full-time.[32] How the parent feels about working and how the rest of the family feels are likely to matter too.[33]

From this discussion, it is evident that there are few clear theoretical predictions as to how early parental employment might affect children's cognitive development. To a large extent, the effects of parental employment are likely to depend on factors such as the quality of the substitute caregiver and also on the quality of the parent's own care for the child. However, whichever direction the effects operate in, it seems likely that earlier work and full-time work would have stronger effects. For instance, if a parent substitute provides less (or more) stimulating care than the parent would, the effects should be larger the earlier the care begins and also the greater the number of hours it is experienced.

Income is also likely to play an important role. If parental employment brings in enough income that families are able to purchase high-quality care for their children and are also able to afford some relief from work-related stresses and fatigue (by buying extra goods and services for themselves and their families), that employment is likely to have more positive impacts than if families cannot afford good-quality care or extra resources at home. The effects of income are also likely to depend on what other resources are available to the family. An extra $300 per week will mean a lot more to a family with few other resources than it will to a family with another parent already earning $3,000 per week.

So what does the research tell us? A large number of observational studies, mostly using data from the NLSY-CS, has found that maternal employment in the first year of life, particularly if full-time work, is associated with lower cognitive test scores for preschool age children assessed at age three, four, or five.[34] The effects vary by the type of child care the child receives and by the family's socioeconomic status.[35] Studies that have followed children in the NLSY-CS beyond the preschool years have generally found that the effects of early maternal employment on child cognitive outcomes persist. For instance, one recent study found effects of early full-time maternal employment persisting to age seven and eight.[36]

A perennial challenge in observational studies of this kind is that women who work early in a child's life may be different from those who do not, and if studies fail to control fully for those differences, estimates of the effects of early maternal employment could be biased.[37] However, in studies that control in different ways for this "selection" problem, these results hold up. Although such studies cannot establish causality, when different approaches all yield the same set of results, they give us more confidence that the effects are likely to be causal.

One approach to the selection problem is to include controls for many characteristics that might be correlated with both outcomes and maternal employment. A recent NLSY-CS study, for example, includes a very rich set of controls for family background and other factors to control for potential selection bias. That the results are robust across these different specifications—and that in fact the study finds more negative effects of early maternal employment as controls are added for more covariates—increase our confidence that these effects really are negative.[38]

Another way to control for differences between working mothers and other mothers is to limit the sample studied to just those women who were working prior to the child's birth. In analyses of children from the NLSY-CS using this approach, children whose mothers worked prior to the birth and returned in the first three months had lower cognitive scores at ages three and four than children whose mothers worked prior to the birth but did not return to work that early.[39]

A third way to control for selection bias is to use sibling or family fixed effects models. These models take advantage of the fact that in some families siblings have different experiences of their parents' working in the first year but share many other factors that are likely to affect child outcomes but that cannot be controlled for using available data. If ordinary regression models are biased by selection, sibling models should give us more accurate estimates of the true effect of parental employment. In analyses of non-Hispanic white children from the NLSY-CS, there were persistent adverse effects of first-year maternal employment on cognitive outcomes both in ordinary regression models and in sibling models, suggesting that ordinary regression models are not overstating the effects.[40]

Finally, a fourth approach to the selection problem is propensity score matching, a method that has also been used with children from the NLSY. Briefly, propensity score matching restricts comparisons to members of the sample who are most closely matched in terms of characteristics that are associated with the behavior of interest (in this case, early maternal employment). A recent study used this method to compare outcomes for children whose mothers worked full-time in the first year of life to those who were most like them, and found that this method did not substantially change the finding that early full-time maternal employment is associated with poorer cognitive outcomes for children. White, African-American, and Hispanic children were analyzed together, and significant effects were found for the pooled sample. This study also examined the potential for bias associated with cases being excluded because they were missing data (a common problem in survey research) and found that as cases that were missing data were added back into the analysis (by imputing values for the missing data), the negative effects of first-year full-time maternal employment on later cognitive outcomes were somewhat diminished, but several remained significant.[41]

A further challenge to the many studies that have been done with the NLSY-CS is omitted variable bias. That is, the results might be due to features of child care (e.g., quality, type), home environment (e.g., provision of learning), or parenting (e.g., sensitivity) that are correlated with both employment and child cognitive development and that could not be controlled for in the NLSY. To frame the problem in another way, the NLSY studies cannot tell us how early parental employment affects child outcomes—that is, whether the effects are operating through features of child care, the home environment, or parenting.

A 2002 study explored this issue by using data on nine hundred non-Hispanic white children from the National Institute of Child Health and Human Development Study of Early Child Care (NICHD-SECC), which provided information on child cognitive scores at fifteen, twenty-four, and thirty-six months, as well as on home environment (as assessed by the Home Observation for Measurement of the Environment [HOME] Inventory), parental sensitivity, and child care quality and type. The results indicated that maternal employment by the ninth month was linked to lower school readiness at age three (as assessed by the Bracken School Readiness Scale, a widely used measure of cognitive development), with the effects more pronounced when mothers worked thirty hours or more per week. Further analyses revealed that children whose mothers worked full-time in the first nine months went on to receive less sensitive care from their mothers by age three; they were also somewhat less likely to be in good-quality child care than those whose mothers worked only part-time in the first nine months. However, although quality of child care, home environment, and maternal sensitivity all mattered for children's school readiness, children whose mothers had worked thirty or more hours per week in the first nine months still scored six points lower on the Bracken even after researchers controlled for these factors.[42]

These results do not mean that parental care or child care do not matter. Although the quality of parental care and child care did not fully account for the effects of early maternal employment in these NICHD-SECC analyses, both mattered a great deal. The results indicated that moving a child from having very poor care at home to having very good care (as measured by the mother being rated in the top

25 percent on maternal sensitivity rather than the bottom 25 percent) would raise a child's score on the Bracken School Readiness scale by an average of five points. Similarly, moving a child from below-average quality child care to above-average care (as assessed on the NICHD-SECC child care quality scale) would raise a child's score on the Bracken by another five points.[43]

Although the type of child care was not a focus of the study just discussed, there is ample evidence from other studies that participation in center-based care is beneficial for cognitive development. This evidence comes from experiments with high-quality center-based programs, as well as from observational studies of children whose parents placed them into local day care centers, nursery schools, or other forms of center-based child care.[44] These studies uniformly find that children who have attended center-based care, particularly if it is of high quality, are more advanced cognitively than children who remained home or attended informal child care. One reason for the advantage of center-based care over more informal child care is that the staff in center-based care tend to be more highly educated and more likely to provide the type of verbal and cognitive stimulation that promotes children's learning.[45]

Thus, if parents who work are more likely to place their children in center-based care, this would be good for cognitive development. The converse is also true. For instance, a study of children from the NICHD-SECC found that children whose mothers worked nonstandard hours (evenings, nights, or weekends) were less likely than children whose mothers worked standard hours to be placed in center-based care and had lower cognitive scores at age three as a result.[46]

As already noted, income is also likely to play an important role. A recent study using the NICHD-SECC data looked specifically at the role of family income, considering three income groups: low-income families, whose family incomes were at or below 200 percent of the federal poverty line (the mean income for this group when the children were age fifteen months was $18,841); middle-income families, with incomes between 200 and 400 percent of poverty (mean income, $43,611); and high-income families, with incomes above 400 percent of poverty (mean income, $97,665). This study found that living in a middle-income rather than low-income family was associated with an eleven point gain on the Bracken for three-year-olds. Living in a high-income family was associated with a further ten-point gain. Although not all working parents will bring home enough income to translate into such large gains, these results and results of other analyses with the NICHD-SECC data nevertheless indicate that income too is strongly related to children's cognitive development.[47]

It is evident from this review that much of the work on maternal employment and child cognitive outcomes has focused on the first year of life. Studies that have looked specifically at maternal employment in the second or third year of life have generally found either positive or neutral effects of mothers' working (in contrast to the generally negative effects of mothers' working in the first year). This evidence suggests that maternal employment in the second or third year of life is unlikely to have detrimental effects.[48]

We have little evidence on the effects of early paternal employment. The only study in the United States to have controlled for paternal employment in as much detail as maternal employment found that it has generally weak effects, which tend to be neutral or even positive.[49] This finding may suggest that fathers' employment matters less than mothers' employment (perhaps because fathers' employment has less impact on infants' care), but it may also indicate that the few fathers who are not employed in the first year of their child's life may be a very select group. In analyses with the NLSY-CS, children's cognitive outcomes were worse when they had a working mother and a father who was home in the first year of life, but most of the few fathers who were in this category were involuntarily unemployed and had not made a deliberate choice to be at-home caregivers.[50]

So what can we take away from this review? Two findings in particular stand out. One, children whose mothers work in the first year of life, particularly if they work full-time, do tend to have lower cognitive test scores at age three and thereafter. These effects are specific to the first year of life and to full-time employment. Two, we have learned something about how these effects come about. Some of the adverse effects of early maternal employment on later cognitive outcomes are due to children receiving poorer-quality child care or less sensitive care at home. But if maternal employment raises family incomes, there are positive effects on children's cognitive development. How all these effects balance out depends very much on each family's circumstances.

The largest gap in our knowledge concerns fathers. Paternal employment has not been a focus of most studies of child cognitive development, and we know little about the effects of fathers' work in the first three years of life. This is a serious shortcoming in the literature and one that should be addressed in the next generation of research.

Social and Emotional Well-Being

Much of the research to date on parental employment and child outcomes has focused on the question of whether early parental employment and nonparental child care (in particular, if begun in the first year of life) have adverse effects on children's social and emotional development. There has been a particularly vigorous debate about attachment. Attachment theory, as we have seen, emphasizes the importance of a secure attachment relationship with a parent (or other caregiver) in providing a secure base from which children can explore the world and engage in other relationships and also in providing children with a sense of efficacy, as these relationships provide a place where children can see their influence on the world around them.[51]

Several studies conducted in the 1980s found differences in attachment between children who had been in child care in the first year of life and those who had not, but experts disagreed about how to interpret these results. If children who had been in child care as infants engaged differently with their mothers (e.g., reacting less strongly when they were separated in laboratory situations using a test known as Ainsworth's strange situation), this might be a symptom of attachment problems, or it might be a mature, adaptive response to the child care experience. Nor was it clear how such attachment differences might affect later outcomes. As we saw earlier, psychological theory places a lot of weight on the importance of secure relationships with parents as the base that children need to function successfully in other social settings. But psychological theory was less clear about the meaning of different attachment relationships for children who had participated in early child care and the implications those relationships might have in terms of later development.[52]

This line of research and the associated debate dominated the parental employment and nonparental child care research agenda in the United States for many years, as study after study found negative effects of maternal employment or nonmaternal child care in the first year of life on social and emotional development for at least some groups.[53] (Effects of paternal employment were not studied.) For instance, several studies examined the effects of early maternal employment or early child care on children's behavior problems in the NLSY-CS, using a standardized measure of behavior problems, the Behavior Problem Index (BPI), which is administered for children in the NLSY-CS beginning at age four. With few exceptions, these studies found that children whose mothers worked in the first year of life and particularly those whose mothers worked full-time in the first year tended to have more behavior problems when they were first assessed at age four.[54] Studies that distinguished between externalizing problems (children acting aggressively or impulsively) and internalizing problems (children seeming worried or sad) found that early maternal employment mainly affected externalizing problems. Studies that analyzed children separately by gender tended to find that the effects were strongest for boys.

This research, however, left many important questions unanswered. Did early maternal employment or early child care really affect children's social and emotional adjustment, or were the estimates biased by factors that the researchers could not control for? If the effects were real, were they lasting? And how did the effects relate to characteristics of the child, family, and child care provider? In the most recent studies, researchers have turned their attention to these more nuanced questions.

In the absence of experimental data, the most common approach to the question of whether the effects of early maternal employment on child behavior problems were really causal has been to include a richer set of controls for other child and family characteristics that if omitted might lead to biased estimates. For instance, analyses of the NLSY-CS have controlled for an extensive set of other child and family characteristics and still found significant effects of maternal employment, particularly full-time, in the first year of life on behavior problems for non-Hispanic white children at age four, with the largest effects on externalizing problems and on boys.[55] More recently, further analyses of the NLSY-CS have found that children whose mothers returned to work full-time in the first twelve weeks have more externalizing problems at age four, in both ordinary regression models and in propensity score matching models.[56] However, these effects may not be lasting. In studies following children from the NLSY-CS over time, the effects that are present for non-Hispanic white children at age four are generally attenuated and no longer significant after that age. Thus, the evidence from the NLSY-CS suggests that although there are adverse effects of first-year maternal employment on behavior problems, these effects are short lived.[57]

As with the study of cognitive outcomes, the NLSY-CS studies have been limited in that they cannot control for characteristics of the home and child care environments that are likely to be correlated with early parental employment or early child care and also children's development. The NICHD-SECC was specifically designed to capture such factors, so that analyses could yield more reliable estimates of the true effects of early employment or early child care. In another improvement on the NLSY-CS, the NICHD-SECC was designed to include multiple measures of children's social and emotional adjustment rather than just an assessment of behavior problems. And the funding body for the study (the National Institute of Child Health and Development, NICHD) established a research network of leading developmental psychologists representing different views on parental employment and early child care.[58] Given the quality of the data and the strength and diversity of the researchers in the network, studies from the NICHD Early Child Care Research Network deserve special attention. So what do these studies tell us about how the links between early maternal employment or early child care and child social and emotional well-being relate to characteristics of the child, family, and child care provider?

In early research, the NICHD network focused on attachment and found no overall effects of early maternal employment or child care on attachment. On average, infants' attachment to their mothers did not differ significantly by how old they were when their mothers went to work or how many hours they were in nonmaternal care. However, there were some effects for subgroups. Infants had less secure attachments if their mothers did not provide sensitive and responsive care at home and if they also experienced poor-quality care, ten or more hours a week of care, or multiple care arrangements. In addition, boys who were in care for longer hours were somewhat less securely attached.[59]

More recently, in a series of studies on early child care and child social and emotional development, the NICHD network has found that early and extensive child care is associated with more behavior problems and lower social competence. Their findings, from analyses of children at age four and a half and in kindergarten were published in the journal *Child Development* in the summer of 2003. This article reported that the more time children had spent in child care up to age four and a half, the more externalizing behavior problems they displayed, as reported by mothers, child care providers, or teachers, for both boys and girls. The connections between early and extensive child care and later behavior problems remained even when the investigators controlled for the quality of the parents' care and the quality of the child care. The investigators also found some adverse effects of early and extensive child care on mothers' and caregivers' reports of social competence at age four and a half and on caregivers' and teachers' reports of conflict with the child at age four and a half and kindergarten (respectively). In general, effects were strongest when reported by caregivers and teachers (who observe the children in group settings) and smaller when reported by mothers (who see how children behave at home, on their own or in small groups of siblings or peers).[60]

Recognizing how important these findings were and how controversial they might be, given the past debates about working mothers and nonmaternal child care, the editors of *Child Development* published a series of related articles and commentaries in the same issue. Taken together, these articles and commentaries raise a red flag as to the potential adverse effects of long hours of nonmaternal child care in the first three years of life. But they also point to the importance of child, family, and child care provider characteristics.

Several contributors to the *Child Development* issue note that not all children may be similarly affected by early child care. For instance, research based on measurements of levels of cortisol (a stress hormone) shows that some children find long days in child care more stressful than other children.[61] This point about individual differences in the way children might be affected by nonparental care was also made forcefully in the report of the National Academy of Sciences Committee on Integrating the Science of Early Childhood Development.[62] We know that children are born with differences in temperament and that children's reactions to care may also be tempered by the experiences they have in the home before entering child care. It stands to reason that some children would be more affected by nonmaternal child care than others. Research conducted since the NICHD network study was published bears this out. In analyses of children from the

NICHD-SECC sample, the largest effects of early maternal employment on child outcomes are for children who were rated as having
more difficult temperaments in infancy (at age six months).[63] Similarly,
in analyses of toddlers from another sample, the Three City Study of
Welfare Reform, the children who were most affected by their mothers'
employment and welfare transitions were those who had more emotionally reactive temperaments.[64]

Family characteristics are important too. The NICHD network investigators point out themselves that family characteristics, in particular the mother's sensitivity and the family's socioeconomic status, are
more powerful predictors of behavior problems than early child care.
In addition to these direct effects, the child's family situation may also
affect the way a child reacts to child care. A child who does not receive
sensitive care at home may be more vulnerable than other children to
the effects of poor-quality child care but might benefit more from good-
quality child care.

Another clear message from the *Child Development* issue is that child
care characteristics matter a lot. For instance, the generally observed
finding that effects of early nonparental child care are larger for boys
than for girls may have to do with the different experiences that boys and
girls have in child care. Some researchers have found that boys tend to
form less-secure attachments to child care providers. Boys also tend to
spend more time playing with other boys and away from adults, resulting in more rough and aggressive play. Thus, the links between early
child care and children's behavior problems may have less to do with
the separation of a child from his or her mother or father and more to
do with the nature of the child's experience in that early child care. This
is an important distinction, as the two types of explanations have different implications for policy. To promote children's social and emotional well-being and avoid later behavior problems, it may not be
essential to keep children home with their mothers or fathers for the
first three years of life. It may, however, be necessary to change the
quality of the experiences they have while their parents are working.[65]
In this regard, it is informative that behavior problems have not been
found for children who were randomly assigned to high-quality child
care interventions, even when those interventions involved full-time
child care starting in the first year of life. For instance, the Infant
Health and Development Program (IHDP), which provided high-

quality full-day care to low birth weight children from birth up to age three, resulted in children having fewer behavior problems at age three and five, although these gains faded out by age eight.[66] Other high-quality interventions also had either neutral or positive effects on children's social adjustment and behavior.[67]

The focus of the NICHD network analyses has been on early child care. But early child care and early parental employment are not synonymous. For this reason, other studies have focused specifically on the effects of first-year and later maternal employment on social and emotional outcomes. Following as closely as possible the procedures of the NICHD network for how variables are defined and coded, these studies have for the most part produced results that are complementary to the NICHD studies. For instance, in analyses of children at age three, children whose mothers worked full-time in the first year (but not part-time) had significantly higher levels of externalizing behavior problems, as reported by their caregivers, with the strongest effects for boys. It is interesting, however, that these effects were generally not found on mothers' reports of behavior problems, suggesting that the more-aggressive behaviors may appear mainly in child care settings (the alternative suggestion, that mothers are poor or biased reporters, does not seem to account for the pattern of results). This study also found that the effects of first-year and full-time employment were largest for children who had been in below-average quality care at six months of age; in this case, the effects were large enough to appear both in mothers' and caregivers' reports.[68]

Thus, the research on early maternal employment in the NICHD-SECC sample is consistent with the research on early child care in the same sample on two main points. Children whose mothers work long hours in the first year of life or children who spend long hours in child care in the first several years of life have more behavior problems. And these problems are related to and aggravated by children's experiences in poor-quality child care.

☞ THE RESEARCH on child health, cognitive development, and social and emotional well-being provides a clear message about parental employment and the first three years of life. Across all three dimensions, with all else being held equal, children do tend to do worse if their mothers work full-time in the first year of life. Negative effects are found on health, cognitive development, and externalizing behavior problems. Part-time work in the first year or work in the second and third years does not have the same effects.

We need to be careful in interpreting these results, given the lack of data on fathers and given that in nearly all cases studied the fathers were either working full-time themselves or were not in the household at all. These results tell us the effect of having two parents working full-time or a lone mother working full-time. And so their clearest message is that children would tend to do better if they had a parent home at least part-time in the first year of life. They do not tell us that the parent has to be the mother.

The other key message is that across all three years the quality of parental care and the type and quality of child care that the child receives are also very important. Indeed, maternal sensitivity is the most important predictor of child social and emotional development—more important than parental employment, child care, or other child and family factors. (Unfortunately we don't know how important paternal sensitivity is.) And there is a clear relationship between the quality of child care children experience in the first three years of life and the effect of that care on children's growth and development. When children are in low-quality care for long hours, their development suffers. When children are in high-quality care, their development is enhanced.

Implications for Policy

With this evidence in mind, we can now turn to consider what should be done to better meet the needs of infants and toddlers when parents work.

More Time at Home in the First Year of Life

Children in the United States enter child care very early. In the NICHD-SECC (a sample of 1,364 children born in 1991), nearly three-quarters (72 percent) were in some form of nonparental child care by the end of the first year of life. These children started care on average at three months of age and were in care for an average of twenty-eight hours per week.[69] In the Early Childhood Longitudinal Study, Birth Cohort (a nationally representative sample of over ten thousand children born in 2001), 20 percent of children had begun nonparental child care by three months, another 24 percent entered care between three and six months, and a total of 50 percent were in care by about nine months, with nearly a third of this group in care for thirty-one to forty hours per week and another quarter in care for more than forty hours per week.[70] Is entering child care so early, for such long hours, good for children?

The research clearly suggests that at least some children would be better off if their parents could spend more time at home in the first year of life, either by delaying their return to work or by returning to work part-time. But would parents really want to spend more time at home in the first year, and if so, is this feasible?

Parents' preferences about staying home with young children vary tremendously and are also subject to change over time. As we saw in chapter 1, there was a strong trend in the latter part of the twentieth century toward more mothers in the United States returning to work in the first year of life. But, more recently, this trend has slowed. In particular, well-educated married women, who can afford to stay home for a year or even more after the birth of a child, are doing so in increasing numbers. But the experience of this group does not mean that all women would want to stay home longer or would be able to afford to do so. For many women, financial need is an important factor in their decision to return to work early in the first year of life. In the NICHD-SECC, families whose mothers returned to work the earliest (prior to three months) were the most dependent on the mother's earnings and at greatest risk of poverty.[71]

It is even more perilous to make projections as to what men want and what they would do if given the opportunity to stay home longer. Most new fathers currently take parental leave of some kind, but usually for only a week or two. We do not know whether fathers would like to take more leave or would take more if offered.[72]

We have some evidence from the United States as to what happens when parents actually have the opportunity to spend more time at home. Studies that have examined the effects of parental leave extensions, whether through state laws or the federal Family and Medical Leave Act (FMLA), generally find that such extensions do lead to more mothers taking leave and taking longer periods of leave before returning to their jobs. But the effects have been fairly small, and no effects for men have been found. This is likely due to the fact that (with the exception of California's recent paid leave program) the leave provided under U.S. laws has been unpaid. We simply do not know from the U.S. evidence how much paid leave laws would affect how long mothers or fathers stay home with a new baby. The only evidence we have on this point is indirect. In surveys of representative samples of women, conducted for the bipartisan Commission on Family and Medical Leave and the U.S. Department of Labor, about half of women who took leave with no pay or at reduced pay say they would have taken more time off if more pay had been available. And among women who report not having taken any leave when they needed to, finances are the most frequently cited reason.[73] These responses suggest that if paid leave were available, more women would take leave and would take longer leaves, but we must be cautious: what people say in a survey may not predict what they would really do if given a different set of choices.

We also have evidence as to how women in the United States react to employer policies. Although few employers provide paid maternity leave per se, many allow women to use accrued sick leave or vacation time during their job-protected maternity leave. The research indicates that employer policies matter: women who work for an employer who provides a job-protected maternity leave are much less likely to return within the first twelve weeks after the birth than women who don't have such coverage. They are also more likely to return after twelve weeks, when their leave period ends—the chance to return to a prebirth job where they have established their position and seniority is a powerful incentive for women to return at the end of a leave period.[74]

If we believe that parents in the United States may behave like parents elsewhere, evidence from other countries is instructive. In the United Kingdom, maternity leave policies have had a very marked effect on women's employment decisions. Over the past twenty-five years, maternity leave policies in the United Kingdom have been progressively extended, to give more women the right to a job-protected maternity leave and to provide longer and more generously paid periods of leave. As these policies have been extended, women have taken advantage of them, staying home for a period of time but then returning to work at the conclusion of the leave. The net result has been a dramatic increase in the share of mothers working by the time their youngest child is age one.[75] But this does not mean that mothers are working as early as they do in the United States.

Analyses of a large group of women in the United Kingdom who gave birth in 1991, when most mothers who had worked prior to the birth were entitled to four months of paid leave followed by an additional three months of unpaid leave, provide compelling evidence that British women stay home for as long as they can in the first year of life. In this study, few women with maternity leave rights returned in the first three months, but one-third were back at work at four months (when their paid leave ended) and over half were back at work at seven months (when their unpaid leave ended). Moreover, women who had the fewest economic resources were more likely to return at four months, when their paid leave ended, while those who had more resources (e.g., a higher-paying occupation or a working husband) were more likely to take advantage of the unpaid leave period and return at seven months instead.[76]

More recent evidence from the United Kingdom confirms these patterns, with lower-income women tending to return at the end of the paid leave period (which was six months at the time of this study) and higher-income women tending to stay out until the end of the unpaid leave period (twelve months).[77] These results suggest that policies and economic resources both matter.

The United Kingdom also provides some evidence on how men are affected by parental leave policies. In 2000–2001, when a large sample of new parents were interviewed for the Millennium Birth Cohort Study, not all fathers had the right to take leave after the birth of a child (this right was not extended nationwide until April 2003). Analyses of this cohort indicate that fathers who had leave rights through their employer were much more likely to stay home after the birth of their children than other comparable new dads. But another determining factor was income: dads were much less likely to stay home if their families had low incomes.[78] Again, the evidence points to the importance of policies and income.

If as a country we want to give parents the option to spend more time at home in the first year, the most direct way is to provide all new parents with the right to take up to a year of job-protected leave. The evidence indicates that to be effective—that is, to actually alter parents' behavior—that leave will have to be paid. Such a policy would necessarily be more costly than the status quo, but without some form of wage replacement during the leave, at least some mothers and most fathers are unlikely to take it. And, the costs of extending the leave period from what is typically six to twelve weeks currently to fifty-two weeks must be weighed against the benefits of having a parent stay home, at least part-time, in the first year.

There are two main ways to provide a year of paid leave to new parents. The first is to mandate that employers provide paid parental leave benefits to their employees or to a subset of employees meeting particular qualifying conditions, in much the same way that the FMLA currently requires firms to offer twelve weeks of unpaid leave to qualifying employees. The other is for states to provide paid parental leave through a social insurance program, similar to the unemployment insurance programs or disability insurance programs that states already operate. Although both options have costs and benefits, the net benefits of a social insurance program outweigh those of a mandated benefit program.

The main shortcoming of a mandated benefit program is that it imposes costs on employers. Common sense suggests—and economic theory confirms—that unless employers are altruistic (in which case they would go out of business in a competitive economy), they will have to pass on these costs to someone else.[79] Usually, the someone else is the affected workers—in this case, women of child-bearing age would be the first group to come to mind. If the costs cannot be shifted to the affected workers, then employers will reduce their hiring instead, in this case cutting back on hiring women of childbearing age.[80] This is an outcome that economists would view as inefficient and that also is undesirable on equity grounds. If employers are able to pass the cost of the mandate on to affected employees by reducing their wages, a mandated benefit yields what economists would view as a more efficient outcome but one that is still problematic in terms of equity (particularly since the affected group in this case is primarily women).

Social insurance programs also have costs. Assuming that a parental leave program would be funded through payroll taxes, both employers and employees would bear some costs. However, the evidence from California's new paid leave program indicates that such costs may be surprisingly low. California's program extends its temporary disability insurance program to provide a paid leave of six weeks to parents with newborns (or to employees with an ill family member), at a projected cost of about $22 per year in additional payroll taxes per employee in the state.[81] If the cost of a program that provided fifty-two weeks of leave to new parents was proportional to the cost of this program, it could cost as much as $191 per year per employee. However, take-up of a program that offers fifty-two weeks of leave is not likely to be as high as take-up of a program that offers six weeks, since many parents will not take the full year (and we should also factor out the cost of the portion of the program that has to do with caring for an ill family member, since I am not proposing to extend that). So the costs of a program that offered a year of paid parental leave are likely to be considerably lower than the $191-per-year figure above, more on the order of $100 to $150 per year, or roughly $2 to $3 per week.[82] If a state followed California's lead, these costs would be paid by employees, not employers.[83]

This discussion of parental leave has assumed that a parent has a child, takes a period of leave, and then returns to work under the same terms and conditions as before. Yet another way for parents of young children to spend more time at home is to work part-time. The research suggests that if a mother is working in the first year of life, it is full-time, not part-time, employment that is associated with poorer outcomes for the child. So, on the basis of the research, giving parents more options to work part-time, particularly in the first year of life, would be beneficial.

But how could this be brought about? Surely, the government cannot tell employers to create part-time positions. Too heavy-handed an approach might prove burdensome for employers and make them shy away from hiring women at all or offer only very poorly paid part-time jobs. For these reasons, a lighter-touch approach probably makes sense. We could, for instance, borrow from the European Union's model. Under the part-time directive adopted by the European Union in 1997, European countries have put in place policies to encourage employers to grant requests from employees with young children who want to work part-time. Under these policies, employers are required to give consideration to such requests and to grant them if it is feasible. But if it would be unduly costly to the firm, an employer can say no.[84]

Of course, we do not know how many new parents in the United States would take advantage of the right to request part-time work, just as we do not know how many would take advantage of a longer period of parental leave. It is very difficult to gauge parents' preferences until the policy options are actually in place. When the United Kingdom implemented the right for parents (with a young child under age six or a disabled child) to request part-time or flexible hours in April 2003, no one could have predicted that a million parents—one-quarter of those eligible—would make such requests in the first year alone.

Would the right to request part-time or flexible work be as popular in the United States? Perhaps not, given that a lower share of U.S. parents report wanting to work part-time than United Kingdom parents do, but the experience of the United Kingdom suggests that at least some parents would utilize the right to request part-time work when their children were young.

At the same time, the costs do not look to be very large. In the short run—in the first year of life—employees should be able to receive prorated parental leave pay if they work part-time. In the longer run, employees choosing to work part-time may not advance as fast in their careers, but this is a trade-off some parents will be willing to make. And as more employees work part-time, perhaps the culture of work will change, so that part-time work is not penalized as much as it is today. There are, after all, both good and bad part-time jobs.[85] Parents who reduce their hours in an existing job in order to accommodate family responsibilities may be better positioned to move into a good part-time position than a new worker coming in off the street.

Innovations in job sharing have already paved the way in many firms for employers to see that part-time employees can be every bit as productive as full-timers.[86] If particular employers found the costs prohibitive, they could make the case that they should not grant such requests. Again, the experience of the United Kingdom may be instructive. In the first year of their part-time and flexible working policy, employers granted 80 percent of requests and were able to compromise with employees on a further 10 percent. Indeed, one of employers' largest complaints was that the policy was too narrow and should on equity grounds be broadened to other employees with family responsibilities, not just those with young or disabled children.[87]

The discussion thus far has neglected mothers who are not working prior to the birth and who would therefore not be eligible for a parental leave program (or for the right to request to return to work part-time). About 40 percent of women who give birth each year are not working prior to the birth. Most of these nonworking women (about 90 percent in recent years) stay home for at least the first year postbirth.[88] Although it is something of a simplification, these mothers can be thought of as being drawn primarily from two groups. One consists of women who have sufficient economic resources that they did not need to work prior to the birth. We can conveniently ignore this group for the moment on the assumption that if a mother from this group did not work prior to the birth, she is not likely to do so afterwards or at least not on grounds of financial necessity.

But we cannot ignore the other group, women who were not working prior to the birth in spite of having few economic resources. These women may have been on welfare or other forms of public assistance or may have been just getting by, relying on other household members' incomes or help from friends and family. Historically, Aid to Families with Dependent Children (AFDC) provided support for low-income women to stay home for at least the first year of life, as women with young children were exempted from work requirements. When the first work-oriented AFDC program, the Work Incentive Program (WIN), came into effect in 1967, only women with children over the age of sixteen were encouraged to work. In 1979, this policy was changed so that only women with children under age six were exempted. In the 1988 Family Support Act, the age of exemption was dropped again, but women with children under the age of three were still exempted. States could petition to lower this age exemption even further but could not require women to work before their child was one. However, with the passage of the Personal Responsibility and Work Opportunity Reconciliation Act (PRWORA) in 1996, this is no longer the case. States now have the option to require work or work-related activity when children are under the age of one, and twenty states as of 2003 had taken advantage of this option, establishing no exemption at all for women with newborns or exemptions that extend for only three or four months. The remaining states provide longer periods of exemption, but altogether at least forty-six now require welfare recipients to work by the time a child is twelve months old.[89]

Given the evidence on the adverse effects of maternal employment in the first year of life, policies that require mothers on welfare to work when their child is under the age of one are ill-advised. One study has already found that the tougher work requirements for low-income mothers with infants have significantly reduced breast-feeding.[90] Yet these policies may be difficult to overturn, as states may be reluctant to be seen as softening their position on tough, work-oriented welfare reform.

Is there a way out of this dilemma? Perhaps it would be easier to provide support for low-income women with newborns if they were served through a program other than welfare. In this regard, the at-home infant child care programs recently introduced in a few states (and proposed in Congress by Senator Max Cleland in 2004) offer an interesting solution. These programs provide cash benefits to low-income parents with a child under the age of one. But they are not welfare programs, and, unlike welfare, they do not involve work or other activity requirements. Rather, they are a special kind of child care program, one that facilitates a parent—whether the mother or father—providing care for the child themselves. In Minnesota, the first state to enact such a program, the funding comes from the state's child care budget. Families participating in the program receive a grant that is 90 percent of what the state would have paid in child care subsidies if the infants were in nonparental child care.[91]

If the United States were to set up a paid parental leave program, the right to request to return to work part-time for all parents who worked prior to the birth, and an at-home infant child care program for low-income parents who were not working prior to the birth, it would go a long way toward making it possible for at least one parent to stay home at least part-time for a longer period of time in the first year of life. There would still be a small number of parents who fall through the cracks—parents who had not worked long enough to qualify for paid parental leave but whose incomes were too high to qualify for the at-home infant child care subsidy. In European countries, where benefits are provided on a universal basis, this problem does not arise. Virtually all European countries provide a basic child benefit or child allowance that is provided to all families with children. Such programs can be tailored to provide extra help to particular families. For instance, extra benefits can be provided to families that have a child under the age of one, in recognition of the extra costs associated with caring for infants (whether a parent stays home or the family uses child care); this is the case in the United Kingdom, where the baby tax credit doubles the value of support for a family with a child under the age of one. These extra benefits may supplement or replace the maternity allowances that

European countries have typically provided to help families with the one-time costs of buying the gear that new babies require, such as cribs, car seats, and so on.

Although the United States does not have a child benefit system, the child benefit model could nevertheless be adapted to address the problem of how to ensure that support is provided for all new parents to spend some time at home with their child, regardless of their work history. One worthwhile option to consider is an early childhood benefit, targeted to families with young children. Two Nordic countries, Finland and Norway, provide early childhood benefits to any family who has a child under the age of three and who is not using a publicly subsidized child care place. Families use the benefits to offset the costs of staying home from work and caring for the child themselves or the costs of purchasing child care in the private market, or a combination of the two. (If families use a part-time publicly subsidized place, they receive a prorated early childhood benefit.)[92]

If an early childhood benefit were implemented in the United States, alongside a paid parental leave program and the right to request to return to work part-time, the resulting structure would provide a great deal more support and a more uniform system of support for new parents than exist today. Any parent who had worked a sufficient amount to qualify for parental leave would receive a paid and job-protected leave for up to twelve months. Parents would also have the right to request to return to work part-time, and could receive prorated parental leave benefits if they did so in the first year of life. In addition, all new parents would receive a modest early childhood benefit, to offset the costs of staying home with (or purchasing child care for) a newborn in the first year of life. Because the total package of support would be more generous for those who had worked prior to the birth, the positive work incentives of parental leave policies would be preserved. But at the same time some support would be provided for all families with a newborn, in recognition of the extra costs associated with meeting children's needs in that first year of life. Most importantly, the package would give parents the choice as to how to care for their child in the first year of life.

If the United States is not ready to embrace a universal early childhood benefit, the program could be limited to low- or moderate-income families. Or if even a targeted benefit program is not feasible, then alternatively a paid parental leave program and right to request part-time work for qualifying workers could be implemented alongside a means-tested at-home infant child care program for low-income parents who lacked sufficient work history to qualify for paid parental leave. Such a package would cost less than a universal or targeted early childhood benefit but would also leave out families whose incomes are too high to qualify for means-tested at-home infant care but who nevertheless might need financial assistance if a parent is to stay home for longer in the first year of life. So there are trade-offs here, and policy makers will have to think carefully about them in deciding which way to go. But either policy package would go a long way toward allowing parents to spend more time at home in the first year of life.

Better-Quality Care

One of the clearest messages from the research is that quality of care matters. Yet as we shall see, the research also tells us that the quality of care that infants and toddlers receive when their parents are at work is currently not very good. If the measures that we have discussed were implemented, it is likely that more parents would spend more time at home in the first year of life and possibly the first three years of life. But at some point, parents will be working, at least part-time, and children will be in some form of nonparental care. What can we do to make sure that care is good enough to promote infants' and toddlers' health, cognitive development, and social and emotional well-being?

Parents, of course, have primary responsibility for deciding whether to place their child into some form of child care and also what type of child care to use. This is as it should be. The child's parents are best positioned to know their child's needs and to decide which of the options available within their own extended family and community might best meet those needs. Particularly when children are young, parents understandably want to have their child at home or close to home, with someone they know and trust. Many parents choose to care for the child themselves, by having one parent stay home from work altogether or by having parents schedule their work hours such that one parent is always home with the child. About 40 percent of mothers do not work in the first year after the birth. It is important to note that if a parent does stay home, she or he is foregoing wages and benefits that would come from working and is also paying a price in terms of future career options and earning potential. Reentering the labor market after being home for a number of years is tough, and it can take years for parents to catch up to where they would have been had they not stepped out of the labor market.[93] For this reason, the costs of staying home for an extended period of time are much greater than the costs of taking leave and then returning to a prebirth job.[94]

Among families whose mothers do work in the first year, the most common form of child care is parental care, used by 29 percent of families, as shown in Table 2.1. When a mother is working, the category parental care mainly refers to care by the father but can also include care by the mother while she is working. Although parental care becomes a little less common after the first year, it is still the primary arrangement for 22 to 23 percent of toddlers with working mothers. If we look separately at married couples and single-parent families, as shown in Table 2.2, we can see that, as expected, parental care is more common in married-couple families, who take advantage of the presence of both parents to split shifts.

Splitting shifts has its costs. To make split-shift parenting work, at least one of the parents has to work odd hours—evenings, nights, or

Table 2.1. Child care arrangements of infants and toddlers with working mothers: Percentage of each age group in various forms of care

	Age 0	Age 1	Age 2
Parent	29	22	23
Grandparent	26	25	23
Other relative	8	7	7
Center	17	19	24
Family day care	11	14	13
Other nonrelative	9	14	11
Total	100%	101%	101%

Source: Data from the Survey of Income and Program Participation 1996 Panel, wave 10 (spring 1999), as shown in Smolensky and Gootman (eds.) (2003), Table 3-1. Data refer to primary child care arrangements for children whose mothers are employed. Percentages do not always sum to 100 due to rounding.

Table 2.2. Child care arrangements of infants and toddlers with working mothers, by family type: Percentage of each age group in various forms of care

A. Children with married parents	Age 0	Age 1	Age 2
Parent	31	27	27
Grandparent	23	19	20
Other relative	6	5	6
Center	21	20	23
Family day care	11	15	13
Other nonrelative	8	14	11
Total	100%	100%	100%
B. Children with single parents	Age 0	Age 1	Age 2
Parent	25	8	12
Grandparent	31	41	29
Other relative	11	11	11
Center	8	18	26
Family day care	12	10	12
Other nonrelative	13	12	10
Total	100%	100%	100%

Source: Author's calculations of data from the Survey of Income and Program Participation 1996 Panel, wave 10 (spring 1999). Data refer to primary child care arrangements for children whose mothers are employed.

weekends. Particularly when parents work nights, they may then have to care for a child when they would otherwise be sleeping. Split-shift parenting also cuts into the time that parents have together, thus eroding the quality of family life. It is little wonder that research has found that nonstandard work (work during the evenings, nights, or weekends) is associated with poorer health outcomes for the individual working those hours and a higher risk of conflict and instability for the family.[95] It is also a concern that children whose mothers work nonstandard hours in the first three years of life have poorer cognitive outcomes at age three than children whose mothers work standard hours.[96]

Families who do care for their infants and toddlers themselves, either by having one parent stay home full-time or by having two parents adjust their work hours so that one is always home, do not currently receive any support for the costs of this care. Yet if these same families use nonparental child care, they would be eligible for a child care subsidy, if their family income were sufficiently low. Or they would be eligible for support through the Child and Dependent Care Tax Credit or a Dependent Care Assistance Plan, if their income were higher. If we value parental choice and improving the quality of care that children receive in the first three years of life, providing some financial support to families who care for children themselves would make sense. If we want to do this on a targeted basis, for low-income families only, then a program along the lines of the at-home infant child care program, extended to cover toddlers, would make sense. However, targeting is difficult when many families who use parental care are above the cutoff for means-tested benefits but are nevertheless struggling financially. So it would be preferable to adopt an early childhood benefit model, providing financial support on a universal basis to all families with children under the age of three or on a targeted basis to low-income families (but with a more generous income cutoff than traditional means-tested programs so that more low-income families can participate) and allowing families to choose how to use the support. Those who prefer parental care could use the benefit to finance a parent staying home full-time or to cover the costs of a parent working part-time while using some form of child care part-time (or splitting care with the other parent). To introduce an element of progressivity, so that lower-income families would receive more in benefits, larger benefits could be provided to lower-income families, or benefits for higher-income families could be taxed.

The second most common form of care in the first three years of life for children with working mothers is care by a grandparent or other relative. Grandparents care for about 25 percent of infants and toddlers whose mothers work (see Table 2.1). Other relatives care for another 7 to 8 percent. If we look separately at single-parent families, we can see that they rely even more heavily on grandparents and other relatives for care (making up the shortfall in care provided by fathers).

Care by a grandparent or other relative offers many advantages to families, particularly when children are very young and particularly when the father is not available to share care with the mother. However, there are costs of this care as well. Parents often pay for care provided by a grandparent or relative, and, of course, the grandparent or relative pays too, by forgoing work or the other things that he or she could have done with that time. Care by grandparents or other relatives, unlike parental care, is currently eligible for public subsidy. So long as the grandparent or relative is willing to declare the earnings and to meet any applicable licensing or health and safety requirements, the care is eligible for subsidy through either the child care subsidy program or through parents' tax credit programs.

How does grandparent or relative care compare in quality to other forms of child care? The most recent in-depth study of relative and family child care providers, conducted by the Families and Work Institute in 1991 and 1992, found that relatives were significantly less likely to provide good- or adequate-quality care.[97] What seems to matter, with relatives as with other care providers, is whether they are committed to caring for children. In the Families and Work Institute study, 65 percent of the relative caregivers were living in poverty themselves, and 60 percent were taking care of children because they wanted to help out the parents, not because they wanted to care for children. These results suggest that policy should not push parents to use relatives but rather should leave the choice to families. But providing financial support for relative care, similar to that provided for other forms of care, makes sense.

Children who are not with a parent or a relative in the first three years of life are cared for in a variety of other child care settings. The most common of these is center-based care, which is the primary arrangement of 17 percent of infants with a working mother, rising to 19 percent of one-year-olds, and 24 percent of two-year-olds (Table 2.1). These figures represent a dramatic increase in the use of center-based care for children under three with working mothers, only 8 percent of whom were in this form of care in 1977.[98] Infants of single parents are less likely to be enrolled in center-based care than children of married parents, but by the time children are age one or two, enrollment rates are similar across married-couple and single-parent families (see Table 2.2).

Center-based care for infants and toddlers varies widely in quality in the United States. Although experts emphasize different aspects of what constitutes quality in infant and toddler care, two features that are generally agreed upon as indicators of quality are low child-to-staff ratios and well-educated staff. Child-to-staff ratios are particularly important for infants, while the education level of the staff takes on increasing importance for toddlers and older preschoolers.[99] In the last nationally representative survey of child care centers, in 1990, the average child-to-staff child ratios were 4:1 for infants, 6:1 for one-year-olds, and 7:1 for two-year-olds. These ratios are not far from what the National Association for the Education of Young Children (NAEYC) recommended at the time, but these are averages, and centers varied a good deal on this dimension. Centers in the 1990 survey also varied in terms of staff qualifications, although here the picture was considerably brighter. On average, nearly half of teachers had at least a bachelor's degree, and another 40 percent had some college. Only 14 percent had just a high school education or less.[100]

However, knowing the child-to-staff ratio and the qualifications of the teachers can tell us only so much about the quality of children's experiences at a child care center or in another child care setting. Developmental psychologists and others who study child care make a compelling case that the best way to judge the quality of a child's experience is to visit the center and observe the children and staff directly. In this way, the features of care that really matter—its sensitivity and responsiveness to the individual child—can be assessed. Two large-scale studies have done this and rated the quality of care children received on a scale that ranged from one ("inadequate") to seven ("excellent"). The Cost, Quality, and Outcomes (CQO) Study visited centers in four states (California, Colorado, Connecticut, and North Carolina) in 1993 and found that on average infant and toddler classrooms received a rating of 3.33 (just above "minimal") in for-profit centers and 3.57 (between "minimal" and "mediocre") in nonprofit centers. The National Child Care Staffing Study visited five different locations (Boston, Atlanta, Detroit, Phoenix, and Seattle) in 1988 and found that on average infant and toddler classrooms were rated 3.43 in for-profit centers and 4.09 in nonprofit centers.[101]

A third study, the NICHD-SECC, has also observed infants and toddlers in child care settings, in twenty cities across the United States in the early 1990s, using a scale especially developed for the study to rate quality across different types of settings in terms of dimensions of care important for children's cognitive and social and emotional development. Scores ranged from one to four, where one (what I will call "poor") indicates that a particular dimension of positive caregiving was not at all characteristic of the child's experience, two ("fair") indicates that it was somewhat uncharacteristic, three ("good") indicates that it was somewhat characteristic, and four ("very good") indicates that it was highly characteristic. The NICHD-SECC results paint a sobering picture of the quality of center-based care in which infants and toddlers are placed. When the children were fifteen months old, 10 percent of their centers received a rating of one (poor), and 62 percent were rated two (fair). These low ratings rose to 11 percent and 66 percent respectively when the children were age two. Thus, roughly 75 percent of center-based care settings for infants and toddlers in the NICHD-SECC study were rated as poor or fair.[102]

Again, these are averages. Clearly, some center-based care for infants and toddlers is of very poor quality, whether measured by child-to-staff ratio, teacher qualifications, or direct observation. But at the other end of the continuum, some infant and toddler care is of very high quality. The best-quality center care has been shown to yield important benefits for children, with particularly large benefits for the most disadvantaged children. When center-based care is of high quality, it enhances infants' and toddlers' cognitive development, without causing behavior or other problems.[103] As already noted, one of the main reasons for the good performance of high-quality center-based care is its highly educated and motivated providers. It is these providers, not center-based care per se, that make the difference.

Center-based care for low-income children is subsidized, on the same basis as other forms of care. Higher-income taxpayers can claim credit for some of the costs of this care (through the Child and Dependent Care Tax, or CDCT) or can pay for care with pretax dollars (through Dependent Care Assistance Plan, or DCAP programs). But center-based care is expensive, and low- and moderate-income families are less likely to use it, unless they are eligible for a subsidized slot. And even families receiving child care subsidies may be discouraged from using center-based care, if they face high co-payments or if there are no center-based openings in their area. So there may be some problems with limitations on parental choice with regard to using center-based care, and there are certainly some problems with uneven quality.

The next most common form of care used for infants and toddlers whose mothers work is family day care or other nonrelative care (care by babysitters, neighbors, nannies, etc.). Roughly 20 to 30 percent of infants and toddlers with working mothers are in these two types of care (see Table 2.1). Rates of use of these types of care do not differ greatly for married versus single-parent families (see Table 2.2).

Family day care and nonrelative care are particularly popular among women who work full-time, because these forms provide the long hours of care that such mothers need to cover their time at work plus commuting time. Family day care also offers care in a more family-like setting than center care and is generally less expensive. Nonrelative care ranges in cost but is generally less expensive than center care and also offers more individualized attention (although some nonrelative babysitters care for more than one child at a time).

We know less about the quality of family day care and nonrelative care than we do about other forms of care, but the evidence we do have suggests that, like other forms of care, the quality of family day care and nonrelative care is on average not very good and that it is also highly variable. The Profile of Child Care Settings Study, which studied licensed family day care homes in 1990, found that on average these homes had six infants or toddlers per adult. Only 11 percent of providers had a college degree, while 44 percent had only a high school degree or less. The Families and Work Institute Study of Children in Family Child Care and Relative Care, in the early 1990s, found that only 12 percent of regulated providers and 3 percent of unregulated providers were delivering good care, while at the other extreme, 13 percent of regulated providers and 50 percent of unregulated providers were delivering inadequate care.[104] Consistent with this picture of low quality, the NICHD-SECC, also in the early 1990s, found that when children were age fifteen months, 7 percent of family day care homes were rated one (poor) and 44 percent were rated two (fair); the share with these low ratings rose to 9 percent and 50 percent respectively at age two. In-home providers (such as babysitters and nannies) were rated more highly in the NICHD-SECC. Only 3 percent were rated one (poor) and 36 percent rated two (fair) at fifteen months, with 8 percent rated one (poor) and 34 percent two (fair) at twenty-four months, and at both ages 24 percent of in-home providers received the highest possible rating of four (very good).[105]

Families using day care homes or nonrelative providers are currently eligible for subsidies through the same mechanisms as families using other forms of care (so long as the provider is willing to report his or her earnings and to comply with all relevant licensing and safety standards). Thus, parental choice seems not to be a problem in this sector. However, quality is.

What can and should we do to improve the quality of care that infants and toddlers receive? As we have seen, low quality is a problem that cuts across most of the types of care that children receive—with unacceptably high numbers of low-quality settings in center-based care, family day care, and nonrelative care. There is now widespread consensus in the research community that the quality of care for infants and toddlers is not what it should be and that children's outcomes would be better if the quality of that care could be improved.[106] But there is no magic bullet to boost child care quality for infants and toddlers, and experts disagree about how to do it.

My view is that three policy options are worth pursuing. One is to provide more opportunities for parents to use high-quality care. Star-rating systems—that give providers a different number of stars depending on their quality—are already in use in several states to give parents information as to what constitutes high-quality care and to give providers an incentive to deliver it. And subsidy programs can be reconfigured accordingly. For instance, economist David Blau has proposed a program of quality-related vouchers, where the amount that a low-income parent can be reimbursed for child care would vary with the quality of that care.[107]

A second promising policy, advocated by many child care experts, is to tighten existing state regulations for infant and toddler care. Although states cannot dictate what actually happens day-to-day in a center or day care home, they can and do regulate features of care that we know are associated with quality—features such as child-to-staff ratios and teacher qualifications. In 2003, a center in Mississippi could legally operate with just one adult looking after as many as five infants under the age of one (or nine children age one, or twelve children age two), and that adult did not even need to have a high school degree.[108] Raising states' regulations to the level recommended by NAEYC would help to improve the lowest-quality settings and would send a useful message to parents as to what they should expect in child care. Alternatively, states could require programs to meet the standards of accrediting bodies such as the American Public Health Association and the American Academy of Pediatrics. Child care programs that meet the standards of these bodies have been found to provide better care and to have children who score higher in school readiness than programs that do not meet the standards.[109]

A third option worth pursuing is to expand the Early Head Start program. Founded in 1995 as an offshoot of the Head Start program, Early Head Start provides support to parents and child care to low-income or disabled children under the age of three. A national randomized evaluation of Early Head Start has found that it is effective in boosting young children's cognitive development and social and emotional development. Additionally, families receiving Early Head Start scored higher than control group families at the end of the intervention (when children were age three) on the quality of their home environment, parenting behavior, and knowledge of infant and toddler development. But Early Head Start serves only a small portion of eligible infants and toddlers—less than 5 percent.[110] Moving other low-income children, who are currently receiving child care subsidies but attending poorer-quality care, into Early Head Start is worth pursuing.

Raising child care quality is complex and will require additional steps beyond the three highlighted here. And child care quality affects not just infants and toddlers but preschool-age children as well. For this reason, I return to the subject of how to improve child care quality in the next chapter.

Looking Ahead

There is perhaps no other time when our values about children, families, and work collide in such a dramatic way as they do in the first three years of life. Parents feel strongly that they know what is best for their children and do not want choices ruled out or made by others. At the same time, government has an obligation to protect children from unsafe or harmful settings and to use the funds it spends on child care in a way that promotes children's health and development.

In spite of these competing priorities and tensions between deeply held values, there is nevertheless a set of sensible policy options that satisfy the competing priorities and uphold our most cherished values. One set of options has to do with giving parents the opportunity to spend more time at home in the first year of a child's life. There are three key policies here:

instituting a parental leave program that offers all new parents who worked prior to the birth a year of paid leave through the social insurance system, giving new parents the right to request to return to work part-time or to work flexible hours, and providing an at-home infant child care subsidy for low-income parents who do not qualify for parental leave. Together, these supports would give all parents the option to stay home for up to a year after the birth of a child, as well as the option to return to work part-time or to work flexible hours, but would not require anyone to do so; nor would they place an undue cost burden on employers or society. A fourth policy to consider is an early childhood benefit that low- and moderate-income families with a child under age one could use to offset the cost of a parent staying home or the cost of purchasing high-quality child care; this option too would respect parental choice and support quality care, without unduly discouraging employment.

The second set of options has to do with improving the quality of care for infants and toddlers whose parents work, by giving parents more opportunities to use high-quality care, tightening child care regulations, and shifting subsidy dollars to support higher-quality programs such as Early Head Start. These options too respect parental choice, while supporting quality care and parental employment. Providing more opportunities for parents to use high-quality care will help improve outcomes for children without taking choice away from parents. Tightening child care regulations may impose some restrictions on choice, but such restrictions are justified on health and safety grounds. And shifting government subsidy dollars for low-income or disabled children away from poor-quality settings to higher-quality Early Head Start settings makes good sense too.

Many of these same issues will surface again when we turn to older preschoolers in the next chapter. Nonparental care for three- to five-year-olds is less controversial, but, as we shall see, in some ways the stakes involved are even higher for that age group. The experiences they have while their parents are working will have direct effects on how prepared they are when they start primary school. Yet as we shall see, our current system of support for three- to five-year-old children is little better than what we provide for their younger brothers and sisters. In leaving them to the whims of the child care marketplace, we are missing out on a tremendous opportunity to start them toward school on the right footing.

$\sim$ 3

Preschool-Age Children

ONE OF THE MOST dramatic social changes over the past several decades has been the rise in preschool enrollment. Today, nearly half of three-year-olds and about two-thirds of four-year-olds attend some form of preschool—whether or not their parents are working—and virtually all five-year-olds attend kindergarten. Increasingly, care and education for preschool-age children are coming to be seen as pre–primary education rather than day care. Yet questions and controversy persist as to what type of preschool is best for children, what age they should start, and how many hours they should attend. In Washington, D.C., and in the states, policy for preschool-age children is a hot topic, with initiatives to improve quality, reform Head Start, and expand prekindergarten, to name just a few.

Against this backdrop, this chapter looks at children aged three to five—what they need to grow and develop and the role of parents, preschool providers, and others in meeting those needs when parents work. Drawing on extensive evidence, including analyses of data on large samples of American children followed over time, from the National Longitudinal Survey of Youth Child Supplement (NLSY-CS), the National Institute of Child Health and Human Development Study of Early Child Care (NICHD-SECC) data set, and the Early Childhood Longitudinal Study, Kindergarten Cohort (ECLS-K), this chapter considers what we know about the following questions: What is best for children's health, cognitive development, and social and emotional well-being in the pre-school years, and what are the effects of parental employment and of nonparental child care and education in these years? How can policy that respects parental choice and supports employment also support high-quality care and education for preschool-age children? Policies considered in this chapter include child care vouchers and regulations, Head Start, and universal prekindergarten and kindergarten.

What Preschool-Age Children Need

In the preschool years, children build on the gains they made in infancy and toddlerhood but also face new challenges and have new developmental tasks to master.[1] In the health arena, preschool-age children continue to need immunizations and regular health screenings. As they play in more active ways and in more varied settings, they need monitoring and supervision, as well as safe play spaces both inside and outside the home, to protect them from accidents and injuries. The preschool years are also important for establishing good nutritional habits as children begin to eat a wider variety of foods.

In the cognitive domain, children's thinking and language skills are developing rapidly. As Swiss psychologist Jean Piaget documented, preschool-age children develop a progressively stronger sense of numbers and sizes, concepts that will be helpful in preparing them for math at school. Their vocabulary expands greatly, as they absorb the new words they hear spoken by their parents and others with whom they interact. Parents' language has a large impact on children's language development: the richer and more varied a parent's vocabulary is, the more developed the preschooler's language becomes. Child care providers' language also has an influence: the more stimulating a provider's language is, the more developed the child's language and thinking skills are.[2] Preschool-age children are also mastering a variety of tasks related to reading readiness—associating letters with their sounds, understanding what books are, becoming familiar with the structure of stories, and so on. Parents and other adults support this development by reading books with children but also by telling stories, singing songs, playing word games, and so on. By the end of the preschool years, most children will have the skills they need to read and will be ready to begin reading when they start school or shortly thereafter.

In the social and emotional arena, one of the central challenges for preschool-age children is forming friendships and playing cooperatively with peers. Children's interactions are characterized by elaborate rules regarding such things as taking turns, and these rules must be learned in these years. For some children, the preschool years mark the first time they are separated from their parents on a regular basis, and they must learn to manage that separation. For others, the preschool years are a time to consolidate their ability to separate from parents or other caregivers and more generally to make transitions between activities. Preschool-age children are learning to control their attention, emotions, and behaviors, tasks referred to as "self-regulation."[3] As the name indicates, self-regulation is something children must increasingly do for themselves, but parents and other caregivers play an important role in helping children develop this set of skills. Parents provide a secure base for children and also help make sure that their children are in situations that they are likely to be able to manage. When challenges do arise, parents help children learn how to cope with difficult situations and feelings. Self-regulation is essential if children are to get along with other children and adults. All preschool-age children have some trouble controlling their feelings and behaviors, but most increasingly gain mastery over them during these years.

How well children develop in each of these domains will influence their school readiness when they make the transition to school at age five. Thus, school readiness is not just about children's cognitive development—it also depends on their health, and social and emotional development. School readiness has recently become a high priority at both the federal and state level. Educators have increasingly come to recognize that children's school readiness at age five is a major influence on their success as they move through school and into adult life. Teachers, fellow students, and children themselves tend to have lower expectations of children who lag behind their peers when they enter school, and these expectations can have long-run consequences.[4] Although schools can go a long way to help children catch up, educators and policy makers have increasingly come to emphasize the importance of ensuring that children enter school ready to learn. Meeting children's developmental needs during the preschool years is central to meeting this goal.

The Effects of Parental Employment

As we have seen, the developmental needs of preschool-age children are many and varied. For a parent who does not work in the labor market, it can be a full-time job to supervise the child's play activities, provide nutritious and healthy meals, keep up with health care appointments, support the child's language and cognitive development, and help the child learn to manage separations, friendships, and his or her own feelings and behaviors.[5]

What happens when a parent works? We can usefully distinguish between two types of effects. First, when a parent works, the way he or she manages these child-rearing tasks may be affected, whether for better or worse. Second, when a parent works, at least some of these tasks must be taken on by the other parent or by a child care or education provider. Again, the effects could be positive or negative, depending on the quality of the substitute care as compared to the quality of the care the parent would otherwise have provided.

In this section, I review what we know from research about how parental employment affects children's health and development in the preschool years. Then, in the following section I review the research on the effects of care and education for preschool-age children. I consider parental employment separately from child care and education, because these are two different phenomena. Not all parents who work use nonparental care and education for their preschool-age children; and many parents who do not work send their children to preschool, as a way of providing them with opportunities to play with other children and to learn the skills they need to get ready for school.[6]

Before proceeding, it is important to note that here again most studies have focused on mothers, and we know relatively little about the effects of fathers' employment on children's health and development.[7] I will review the evidence on fathers where it exists. Ironically, much of this literature focuses on fathers as a form of child care provider.

Health

There are several pathways by which parental employment in the preschool years might affect children's health. Parents who work may have less time (or energy) to attend to children's health care needs or to keep up with medical appointments. They may also supervise or monitor their children less closely. And working parents may have less time and energy to shop for and prepare healthy and nutritious meals. At the same time, parents who work generally bring in more income, which could allow them to purchase more items to promote their children's health and nutrition. In the United States, employment is also an important source of health insurance coverage, which could in turn lead to higher rates of health care use and closer attention to children's health care needs. Parents who work may also be in better mental health and may lead more organized lives, which could have positive health effects for their children.[8]

Thus, theory suggests the effects of parental employment on preschool-age children's health could be both negative and positive. It is perhaps not surprising, then, that the research tends to find that the overall effects of parental employment on child health in the preschool years are roughly neutral—suggesting that any negative effects are small or are offset by positive ones. In a series of welfare-to-work experiments evaluated by researchers at the Manpower Demonstration Research Corporation (MDRC), there were few significant effects on children's health outcomes when mothers of preschool-age children were subject to work-oriented welfare reforms. However, whether reforms were accompanied by income gains mattered. For instance, a Canadian program that gave parents a cash supplement if they worked full-time had statistically significant positive effects on the health of children who were aged three to five at the time of the experiment (although a similar program in Minnesota had no significant effects on health for children in this age group). In contrast, in two of the six programs that mandated employment without supplementing earnings, the evaluators found negative effects on children's health (in the remaining four programs, the effects on health were not statistically significant).[9]

Observational studies, too, have tended to find few effects of maternal employment on child health in the preschool years.[10] However, one area where some effects have been found is obesity. Several recent observational studies have found that children whose mothers work in the preschool years are more likely to be obese or to be at risk of being overweight, with these effects tending to be strongest in families with the highest incomes.[11] This link between maternal employment and obesity is not found in the infant and toddler years—the risk seems to arise in the preschool (and possibly later) years. These findings, while not conclusive, suggest that there is something about maternal employment in the preschool years that may be detrimental to children's nutrition or exercise habits. The fact that the effects are strongest in more affluent families, where obesity rates would ordinarily be lowest, may indicate that these parents, if not working, would have provided exceptionally good nutrition or supervision or that the changes in these preschool-age children's diets or exercise levels associated with parents' working may be especially harmful. Perhaps higher-income working families are more able to afford, and more likely to turn to, high-calorie take-out food. Or perhaps their children are more likely than children in other families to increase the time they spend watching television—and eating unhealthy snacks—when their parents work.[12]

Cognitive Development

As we saw in chapter 2, there is a good deal of evidence that children's cognitive development tends to be negatively affected when mothers work in the first year of life, particularly if that employment is full-time, but not in the toddler years. What about the preschool years—does maternal employment when children are age three, four, or five harm their cognitive development? For the most part, the answer is no.

In experimental studies of welfare-to-work initiatives, researchers at MDRC found seven of ten programs had no significant effects on the cognitive development of preschool-age children whose mothers were exposed to work-oriented welfare reforms. In the remaining three programs, where significant effects were found, these were positive, with the largest effects in the two programs that provided earnings supplements (the Canadian Self-Sufficiency Program, (SSP) and the Wisconsin New Hope program).[13]

Evidence from observational studies tends to confirm this picture. For instance, a study using data from the NICHD-SECC examines the effects of maternal employment when children are aged three and four and a half on their cognitive scores at those ages and finds no significant effects. Thus, although maternal employment in the first year of life is associated with poorer cognitive outcomes at age three and four and a half for these children, later maternal employment is not.[14] Similarly, in analyses of the NLSY-CS examining the effects of maternal employment when children were age three to eight on their cognitive scores as late as age eleven, the effects are generally not significantly different from zero (this study did not analyze children age three to five separately). The only children for whom there were significant negative effects of maternal employment in these years on child cognitive outcomes are those from families in the top 25 percent of family incomes.[15] This is the same group of children for whom the effects on obesity tended to be the largest, suggesting that there may be something exceptional about the effects of maternal employment in these families. Perhaps high-income mothers provide exceptionally high-quality care if they are not working, and the substitute care they use is not able to match that quality.

This last study also examined the effects of paternal employment during the years when children were age three to eight on their cognitive development as late as age eleven and found no significant effects of fathers' employment or working hours during those years (again, children age three to five were not examined separately). This pattern of noneffects held up even for the highest-income families (where some effects of maternal employment had been found).[16] But with few resident fathers not working, or working part-time, it may be that the study simply did not have the power to detect employment effects. Further evidence on the effects of fathers' employment would be welcome.

Social and Emotional Development

As with cognitive development, most of the evidence on social and emotional development points to negative effects of maternal employment in the first year of life, rather than thereafter. Experimental studies of welfare-to-work reforms, conducted by MDRC, found few significant effects of maternal employment in the preschool years on children's behavioral outcomes. Of the ten programs examined, only three (all of which mandated employment without offering earnings supplements) had significant effects on behavior problems for children aged three to five at the time of the experiment. In one program, located in Grand Rapids, parents reported their children had more behavior problems, while in two others, both located in Atlanta, parents reported fewer problems. The MDRC researchers also examined one program that imposed time limits on welfare receipt for families with children aged one to eight (children aged three to five were not considered separately) and found that the program reduced positive behavior (as reported by the children's parents) four years later.[17] These results suggest that the effects on social and emotional development of maternal employment in the preschool years, at least for the welfare population, are likely to be varied, depending on the context.

Observational studies of a wider range of families have also for the most part not found any negative effects of maternal employment in the preschool years on children's social or emotional development, in contrast to the findings for the first year of life. Analyses of the NLSY-CS did not find any significant effects of maternal employment after the first year of life on behavior problems assessed when children were ages four through eight.[18] Similarly, in the NICHD-SECC, although children whose mothers worked in the first year of life had significantly more behavior problems as reported by the children's caregivers at age three, this was not the case for children whose mothers worked subsequent to the first year.[19] Indeed, in further analyses of the NLSY-CS, children whose mothers worked when they were aged three to eight had significantly fewer behavior problems at age eleven (although it is possible that this result reflects reverse causality, that is, that parents were more likely to work if their children had fewer behavior problems).[20]

☞ AS WE HAVE SEEN, maternal employment in the preschool years is generally not associated with risks for children, although the results do raise a few red flags. In the area of social and emotional development, maternal employment in the preschool years is if anything linked with fewer behavior problems. The only concerns that do emerge about maternal employment in the preschool years are an elevated risk of obesity and poorer cognitive development, but only for children from the highest-income families. On the plus side, low-income children may gain in health and cognitive development if their mothers work and their family incomes increase.

Some of these effects are likely to be mediated or tempered by the type and quality of care and education in which children are placed while their mothers are at work. And many preschool-age children are in some form of care or education, regardless of whether their parents work. Parents of preschool-age children face difficult choices about whether to use care and education and what type of care and education to use. We turn to the effects of that care and education next.

Effects of Child Care and Education

A majority of preschool age children are in some form of child care or education, whether or not their parents work. What do we know about what types of activities or programs best meet children's needs in these years? What is helpful or harmful?

Health

There are four main ways in which nonparental care or education might affect children's health in the preschool years. First, as in the infant and toddler years, group care in the preschool years could pose health risks to preschool-age children by exposing them to communicable illnesses. Such risks have been documented for children this age and are higher as the size of the group in which children are placed gets larger. However, these risks appear to be less pronounced for preschool-age children than for infants and toddlers (because children this age are less likely to put things in their mouths and also are out of diapers).[21]

Second, preschool care can play a preventive role by screening for and treating health problems or disabilities, such as vision or hearing problems, motor problems, or asthma, and by providing good nutrition. However, not all child care or education providers see this as part of their role, and the extent to which providers take on these responsibilities varies tremendously. Head Start programs, for instance, are mandated to serve children with disabilities and to provide comprehensive health services for all the children they serve. On average, Head Start programs spend about 12 percent of their budgets on health and nutrition, and Head Start health expenditures have been found to have beneficial effects on children's school readiness in the areas of reading and behavior, which suggests that these expenditures are improving some aspects of children's health.[22] A random evaluation study completed in 2005 provides further evidence that Head Start programs may improve child health, finding that three- and four-year-olds who attended

Head Start were more likely to have received dental care than non-Head Start children. In addition, three-year-olds who attended Head Start were reported to be in better health than non-Head Start children.[23] We also know little about the role that child care or education programs play in improving child nutrition. Child care providers located in low-income communities are eligible for government funding to offset the costs of nutritious meals for the children they serve, through the Child and Adult Care Food Program, but this program has not been evaluated.[24] Anecdotally, parents often report that preschools expose their children to a wider variety of foods than they eat at home, but there has not been any systematic research on this point.

Third, preschool programs can affect child health by protecting or failing to protect children from accidents and injuries. During the preschool years, children spend a larger portion of their waking hours playing with other children, both indoors and outdoors, and begin to use a wider range of play equipment and large toys than they did as infants and toddlers. Unintentional injuries are the leading cause of death for children in this age range and the cause of millions of emergency room visits each year.[25] Safety is therefore an important concern in these years. How safe are child care settings? The evidence suggests that although children are safer on average in child care settings than they are at home or in other settings, child care settings still are not as safe as they could be.[26] A study of over 200 licensed child care settings in 1998 by the U.S. Consumer Product Safety Commission found numerous safety hazards, as did a 1994 study of roughly 170 settings by the Office of the Inspector General.[27] Research examining the impact of child care regulations has found that when states have tougher child care regulations—in particular, requiring day care center directors to have more education—fewer children are injured in child care settings. However, this safety comes at a price, which lower-income families are less able to afford. Thus, tougher regulations create winners and losers—potentially pitting the interest of children whose families can afford the care against children whose families cannot.[28]

Finally, a fourth way in which preschool settings could potentially affect child health has to do with child abuse. During the 1980s, there were a series of well-publicized cases in which it was alleged that preschool-age children had been abused in day care settings. Many of these allegations turned out to be false, and it is now thought that the incidence of child abuse in day care settings is rare.[29] Nationally, some seven thousand children are found to be abused or neglected in day care settings each year, fewer than 1 percent of all victims of child abuse or neglect.[30] Given that there are some 12 million children in some form of nonparental child care each year, this means that the incidence rate of abuse in day care is extremely low, roughly 0.6 per thousand. By comparison, the overall incidence rate for children being abused by parents or other caretakers is about 12 per thousand, or twenty times higher. Thus, statistically, a child is much more likely to be abused in his or her own home than in a day care setting.[31] There is also some evidence that preschool-age children may be less likely to be physically disciplined at home if they are enrolled in Head Start or a center-based child care program.[32] This protective effect may come about because child care providers keep an eye on children (child care providers report some twenty thousand cases of abuse each year), which deters parental abuse, or because child care providers offer advice and support to parents, which makes parents more likely to use alternative modes of discipline for their children.[33]

Cognitive Development

The evidence that high-quality preschools can promote children's cognitive development is very strong. This does not mean that all preschool experiences promote children's learning. But the best-quality programs certainly do.

The strongest evidence comes from a series of randomized experiments, which offered high-quality preschool programs to one group of children and then compared their outcomes to a comparable group of children who had not been offered the program. Most of these experiments involved disadvantaged children or children who were identified as high risk because of low birth weight or other factors. For instance, the Carolina Abecedarian program provided five years of high-quality center-based care (from age zero to five) to children from families identified as high risk. The Infant Health and Development Program provided three years of high-quality center-based care (from age nine months to three years), with a curriculum similar to the Abecedarian one, to low–birth weight children. Other programs, such as the High Scope Perry Pre-School Program (serving low-IQ and low-income children aged three to five in Ypsilanti, Michigan) or the Early Training Project (serving low-income children aged four to six in Murfreesboro, Tennessee) were less intensive, providing only part-day preschool, but again they were of high quality. Uniformly, the evidence from these experiments points to substantial gains in cognitive achievement for children who had the chance to participate in high-quality preschool. Gains tended to be the largest for the most intensive programs and those that started earliest, but gains were evident even when programs were only offered on a part-day and part-year basis and even when they did not begin until age three or four. Another finding across studies is that the most disadvantaged or at-risk children tended to reap the largest benefits from these programs. For instance, in the Infant Health and Development Program (IHDP), children of mothers who had not completed high school themselves gained the most on IQ tests, relative to children of more-educated mothers.[34]

The evidence from these experimental studies and a host of observational studies supports the view that high-quality preschool care can compensate for what may be a lack of cognitive stimulation in disadvantaged children's homes and thus boost the school readiness and achievement of disadvantaged children. This view led to the establishment of the Head Start program in 1965 and a host of other early childhood intervention programs since that time. Unfortunately, however, these programs have not always lived up to the promise of the early experimental programs. It is difficult to take model programs and turn them into larger-scale programs. It can also be expensive. The Carolina Abecedarian program cost about $15,000 per child per year (in 1999 dollars) and served children for five years; IHDP also cost about $15,000 per child per year and lasted three years. The typical Head Start program spends only a quarter or a third as much, $4,000 to $5,000 per child per year, and serves children for one to two years. It should not be surprising that the quality of Head Start is not as high and that the program does not deliver benefits as large as the experimental programs. Thus, although observational studies have found some benefits of Head Start in terms of cognitive development, these benefits have often been modest and have not always been long lasting. A 2005 random assignment evaluation finds significant gains in reading and vocabulary for children after one year of Head Start attendence. However, we do not yet know if these gains will be lasting.[35]

In terms of other types of center-based care programs serving a wider range of children, a host of observational studies find that center-based care for preschool-age children does seem to promote children's cognitive development and school achievement. Although not as enriched as model programs like Abecedarian or IHDP, center-based care programs do tend to have more-educated staff and to offer more educationally oriented programming and more-structured activities than family day care centers, in-home child care providers, or other forms of child care, and children who attend center-based care tend to score better on cognitive assessments than children attending other forms of nonparental child care.[36] In a study looking specifically at the preschool years and assessing changes in children's cognitive performance, children who attended center-based care between the ages of twenty-seven months and fifty-four months showed greater gains in cognitive development than otherwise comparable children who did not attend center-based care.[37]

The evidence on the cognitive benefits of prekindergarten programs is also positive. These programs, which now serve about one in six American children, provide a year (or two) of publicly funded education to children before they start kindergarten. In some states, prekindergarten programs are delivered by local public schools; in others, programs may be delivered by public schools or community-based agencies, as long as they meet the standards set out by the local school department or state department of education. Evidence from the ECLS-K, for a sample of children who started kindergarten in the fall of 1998, indicates that children who attended prekindergarten the year before kindergarten come into school with better reading and math skills. The gains are particularly large for disadvantaged children (children from low-income families, single-mother families, families where the mother has less than a high school education herself, or families where a language other than English is spoken at home).[38] There is also evidence on the cognitive benefits of prekindergarten programs from evaluations in two states—Georgia and Oklahoma—that have pioneered these programs (this evidence is discussed further later in this chapter).[39]

Of course, the quality of center-based care programs varies widely, and not all programs are equally beneficial. As we have learned more about children's development in the preschool years, we have also made progress in identifying what type of child care best supports children's learning. The key in this area, as in other areas, is for the care to be sensitive and responsive to the child. Preschool-age children learn best when they have the opportunity to tackle tasks and activities that are challenging but not beyond their capabilities and when they have the support of a teacher with whom they have a close relationship. This kind of tailored learning happens most often when teachers are well-educated and trained and when children are in small groups so that they can receive individualized attention.[40]

The experimental evidence on measures to improve quality in child care centers is limited, but the evidence that does exist, from the National Day Care Study conducted in the 1970s, indicates that when children are assigned to teachers with more education and training and when they are in smaller groups, they gain more in school readiness than other children.[41] Quasi-experimental evidence from Florida also points to the importance of teacher education and adult-to-child ratios.[42] Observational studies have also documented links between higher-quality centers, whether measured by structural characteristics (such as teacher education or group size) or process characteristics (such as the sensitivity and warmth of teacher-child interactions), and better cognitive and language outcomes for preschool-age children.[43] Of course, as I discuss later in this chapter, not all center-based programs provide care that is of high quality. Nevertheless, on average, children tend to benefit cognitively from participating in center-based care.

The evidence also indicates that although disadvantaged children may benefit the most, children from advantaged homes also gain from high-quality preschool programs. This perceived benefit probably helps explain why the most educated parents are the most likely to send their children to center- or school-based preschool programs. Such families tend to place a high value on education and cognitive development and to seek out opportunities for their children to make gains in that domain. And since more educated parents usually have higher incomes, they are better able to afford center-based care, which is typically more expensive than other forms of care (such as babysitters or family day care). Similarly, children from more-advantaged families are the most likely to attend high-quality child care. Again, this reflects their families' greater ability to pay, as higher-quality care tends to be more expensive than other care.[44]

Social and Emotional Development

The conclusion that quality matters also applies to the social and emotional arena. Numerous observational studies have found that preschool-age children who are in higher-quality care are more socially competent and have fewer behavior problems in their interactions with other children and adults, with the strongest effects found for process measures of quality, such as the warmth and sensitivity of caregivers' interactions with children. The quality of current settings matters more than the quality of past settings, but the quality of preschool settings does have lasting effects, with children who attended higher-quality care in the preschool years having fewer problem behaviors and more social competence in elementary school.[45]

These results make intuitive sense: warm and sensitive caregivers, like parents, can go a long way toward helping children learn how to regulate their own emotions and behaviors and to get along with others. But in observational research, it is always hard to establish causality: it may be that children who attend higher-quality care are more socially competent and have fewer behavior problems because of something external to the child care (like good-quality parenting at home), which might have existed prior to their entry to good-quality care and even influenced their being placed in that care. Experimental evidence on this point is fairly slim. We have few child care experiments that randomly exposed children to care of different levels of quality—for the very good reason that such experiments would be unethical. The one experiment referred to earlier, the National Day Care Study, which did assign children to classrooms with different teacher education and training levels, found that children assigned to more highly educated and trained teachers did show more cooperative behavior and more task persistence at the end of the year than the comparison-group children.[46]

A different question is how preschool-age children's social and emotional development is affected by participating in nonparental child care versus being cared for exclusively by a parent. Experimental studies of model interventions can tell us what happens when children are randomly assigned to care of high quality. Although these interventions have had as their main goal boosting cognitive achievement and have not always measured effects on social and emotional development, when those effects have been assessed, they have tended to be positive. Indeed, the Perry Preschool program, which provided part-day preschool care for three- to five-year-old year old children with low IQs and from low-income families, had its largest and most lasting effects on social outcomes, reducing crime and delinquency and welfare participation for participants up to the age of forty.[47] There is also evidence from a quasi-experimental program, the Chicago Child-Parent Centers, which provided disadvantaged children in selected school districts with a high-quality preschool program starting at age three and then compared their school readiness and school progress to children in similar school districts who did not receive the program. Children in the program not only had better school achievement at age fourteen, they also were less likely to have repeated a grade, to be placed in special education, and to be involved in crime or delinquency. An important element of this program, and one that likely contributed to its long-run effects, was that children continued to receive extra support in kindergarten and in the primary grades.[48]

So the experimental evidence indicates that high-quality center-based care in the preschool years can improve children's social and emotional outcomes. But what about run-of-the mill preschool care? The question is important because, unfortunately, not all care that preschool-age children attend is as good as the care in the model interventions. Given the current quality mix in the United States today, it is not obvious whether children spending time in care during the preschool years would have better or worse social and emotional outcomes than children remaining home with their parents. The research for infants and toddlers shows that children who spend more time in care in those years, particularly if they began care in the first year of life, tend to have more behavior problems than other children. Is the same true for children who spend more time in nonparental care in the preschool years?

Recent work by the NICHD Early Child Care Research Network attempts to answer this question, but as the researchers note, this is challenging, since many of the children who are in care at ages three, four, or five were also in care prior to age three, making it hard to disentangle the effects of later versus earlier care. The Network researchers try various approaches to this question and find that the answer depends on the approach: in some analyses, the strongest links between child care and social or emotional problems are found when that care occurs in the first year of life, but in one analysis, more time in care at age two is linked with more behavior problems in kinder-garten, while in another analysis, more time in care between age three and four and a half is linked to poorer social competence at age four and a half. Thus, whether more time in child care or education at age three or later leads to more behavior or other problems is not clear.[49] Simi-larly, in analyses of children entering kindergarten in the ECLS-K study, children who had attended more hours of center- or school-based care in the year prior to kindergarten do have more behavior problems and less self-control, as reported by their teachers in the fall of kinder-garten. However, whether this association is due to their experiences at age four or earlier in life is not clear, as the data do not identify pre-cisely when children started and stopped particular forms of care. Thus, teasing out the effects of child care at specific ages is difficult.[50]

A further caveat to any strong conclusion in this area is that the effects of child care on children are not uniform. As we saw earlier, the quality of the care matters enormously. Thus, before concluding whether child care or education has positive or negative effects, we need to know what type of care it was and its quality. There may also be important differ-ences between children, depending on their temperament, gender, and so on. Some children have temperaments that lead them to find being in group care more stressful than others find it. And many, although not all, studies have found that boys' behaviors are more affected by child care than girls'. These differences make it difficult to draw global conclusions: a setting that is healthy for one child may lead to behavior problems for another.[51]

᠄᠉ As we have seen, establishing the effects of child care on preschool-age children's health and development is complex. We can-not draw sweeping conclusions about whether child care in these years is helpful or harmful. The answer on most points is "it depends." It is evident that quality matters a great deal. So too does the particular type of child one is talking about and the outcome that one cares about. For instance, center-based care in the preschool years is clearly associated with better learning outcomes, particularly for disadvantaged children, with the strongest effects when care is of high quality. But when it comes to social and emotional outcomes, the average effect of the care available today on children's behavior, compared to the care parents could provide themselves, seems to be negative, particularly if children are in care for long hours. Yet when care is of high quality, children do better in the social and emotional arenas, as well as the cognitive domain. So again, quality is crucial. In the health domain as well, nonparental care can have a range of effects, in some instances positive and in some instances negative—again, the net effect depends more than anything else on quality.

Current Care and Education Arrangements

It is clear from the research that what matters most about the care that children receive in the preschool years is its quality. Unfortunately, we do not know as much as we would like about the quality of the arrangements that preschool children currently attend while their parents work. The data we have on quality tends to be from small samples or from children observed some time ago. Reviewing the state of the evidence, the National Academy of Sciences Committee on Family and Work Policies in 2003 called for a new nationally representative study of child care quality.[52] Until such a study is carried out, we have to make do with the data that are currently available.

Care and Education Arrangements

Although limited in terms of information on quality, nationally representative surveys can tell us what type of care preschool children are in while their mothers work. These survey data, summarized in Table 3.1 (page 105), show that the pattern of care arrangements is different for preschool-age children than for infants and toddlers. The biggest difference is in the greater use of center-based care. Center care is the dominant form of care for preschool-age children: it is the primary arrangement for 27 percent of children of working mothers at age three, 42 percent at age four, and 51 percent at age five. The share of preschool-age children of working mothers using any center-based care is even higher, because a substantial share, while primarily in care with another type of provider, use center-based care as a secondary arrangement.[53] Children of single parents are slightly more likely to use center-based care than children of married mothers. Table 3.2 (page 106) shows that among single-parent families in which the mother works, 29 percent are using center care as a primary arrangement at age three, 44 percent at age four, and 54 percent at age five.

It is worth noting that center-based care is also common among children whose mothers do not work. Over the past thirty-five years, for as long as the Current Population Survey (CPS) has been gathering data on school enrollment for children aged three and up, enrollment rates in center- or school-based care have been nearly as high for children whose mothers do not work as for children whose mothers do work. In the fall of 2000, these data indicated that about 40 percent of three-year-olds and about 65 percent of four-year-olds were in some from of preschool (while nearly 100 percent of five-year-olds were in preschool or kindergarten), whether or not their mothers worked.[54] These enrollment patterns suggest that parents view center-based care as a form of education for their preschool-age children and not just as a form of day care. However, in practice, the curriculum offered in center-based care varies widely, and some settings offer a more educationally oriented experience than others.

What do we know about the quality of care provided in centers? The Profile of Child Care Settings, which assessed centers in 1990, found that on average centers serving three- to five-year-olds had a group size of seventeen children, and a child-to-staff ratio of ten to one. Such large group sizes and high child-to-staff ratios may make it difficult to provide care that is responsive to individual children's needs. However, a more positive factor is that teachers in centers serving children in this age group are well educated, with about half having a college degree and another 40 percent having at least some college.[55]

A small number of centers have been assessed using observational measures of process quality. The Cost, Quality, and Outcomes Study assessed centers in four states (California, Colorado, Connecticut, and North Carolina) in 1993 on the seven-point Early Childhood Environment Rating Scale (ECERS) (where 1 represents inadequate, 3 represents minimal, 5 represents good, and 7 represents excellent). This study found that on average the quality of care in centers serving preschool-age children was better than in centers serving infants and toddlers but was still not rated good on average in any of the four states. Quality tended to be higher in nonprofit centers and ranged from a low of 3.3 (just above minimal) in for-profit centers in North Carolina to a high of 4.7 (nearly good) in nonprofit centers in California.

The National Child Care Staffing Study, which assessed centers in Atlanta, Boston, Detroit, Phoenix, and Seattle in 1989, found a similar pattern of results, with centers serving preschool-age children rated more highly than those serving infants and toddlers, and nonprofit programs generally rated higher than for-profit programs. Overall, most programs serving preschool-age children were rated better than minimal but less than good, with scores ranging from a low of 3.3 (just above minimal) in for-profit centers in Seattle and Atlanta to a high of nearly 4.7 (nearly good) in nonprofit centers in Boston and Phoenix.

Further information on the quality of care provided in centers comes from the NICHD-SECC, which assessed centers attended by the children in its sample (who were all born in 1991), using the Observational Record of the Caregiving Environment (ORCE), an instrument designed to assess the sensitivity of different types of child care settings to the needs of individual children. Because of this emphasis on individual sensitivity, the ORCE tends to produce lower-quality ratings for centers than for other settings, where children are cared for individually or in smaller groups. With this caveat in mind, it is nevertheless of concern that the NICHD Study found that the quality of care provided by centers to three-year-olds was low. The NICHD Study rated settings on a four-point scale, based on whether positive caregiving was "not at all characteristic," "somewhat uncharacteristic," "somewhat characteristic," or "highly characteristic" of the care researchers observed. I will refer to these categories as poor, fair, good, and excellent, respectively. Only 30 percent of centers were rated good, while 62 percent of centers were rated fair. In the remaining centers, care was either excellent (3 percent of centers) or poor (4 percent of centers).

Within the category of center- or school-based care serving preschool-age children, there are two publicly funded programs that deserve special mention. The first is Head Start, the federally funded program for children from families in poverty and children with disabilities. Head Start funding increased sharply over the 1990s, and the program now enrolls about 10 percent of preschool-age children nationwide, reaching an estimated 60 percent of the low-income three- and four-year-olds who are its main target population. In principle, Head Start has all the right elements to be a high-quality program: it provides a host of services to families and children, in the areas of health, nutrition, family support, and so on, as well as education. However, in practice, Head Start programs face many challenges. Their staff tend to be less well educated, and less well paid, than staff in other center- or school-based settings and yet are expected to work with the most disadvantaged children. As we saw earlier, the evidence from research as to lasting positive impacts of Head Start on children's outcomes is mixed, but the results from the 2005 random assignment evaluation are encouraging, providing evidence of at least short-run gains in child health and cognitive outcomes, reductions in child behavior problems, and improvements in parenting.[56]

The other public program for preschool-age children is prekindergarten, a program that is operated by public schools and that provides a year or two of publicly funded preschool education to children before they enter kindergarten. Prekindergarten has expanded rapidly and now serves about one in six four-year-olds. Depending on the state, these programs may be housed in public schools or in a mix of schools and other community-based settings, but all programs must conform to specific standards set by the state or local education funding body. In contrast to Head Start, prekindergarten teachers are well trained and relatively well paid. About 86 percent have a college degree, and on average they earn about as much as kindergarten or primary school teachers.[57] As we saw earlier, prekindergarten programs have been found to have positive effects on children's reading and math at school entry, although, like other preschool programs, they have in some cases been linked with more behavior problems.

The second most common form of care for preschool-age children with working mothers is care by a grandparent, although this form of care becomes less common as children age. As shown in Table 3.1, grandparents are the primary child care provider for 23 percent of three-year-olds with a working mother, but this share falls to 18 percent for four-year-olds and 14 percent for five-year-olds. Care by other relatives (this category includes relatives other than grandparents or parents) as a primary arrangement also declines as the children age, falling from 11 percent of children of working mothers at age three to 5 percent by age five. Care by grandparents or other relatives is more often used by single parents than by married parents (Table 3.2).

We do not know much about the quality of care provided by grandparents or other relatives. In the NICHD-SECC, on average grandparents were rated as providing better quality care to three-year-olds than did centers, but their quality ratings were still not very high: 37 percent were rated good (and 8 percent excellent) but 53 percent were rated fair (and 2 percent poor).[58]

Parental care also becomes less common as children age but is nevertheless the primary arrangement for 20 percent of three-year-olds with working mothers and for 15 percent of four- and five-year-olds (see Table 3.1). For the most part, when a family with a working mother reports using parental care, they are referring to care by the father while the mother is at work (less frequently, what is being referred to is the mother caring for the children herself while she works, either because she is bringing them along to work or because she is working from home). Thus, it is not surprising that parental (father) care constitutes a much larger share of care arrangements if we look only at married couple families: in these families, 24 percent are using parental care as a primary arrangement for children aged three and 18 percent for children aged four and five (Table 3.2). Also not surprisingly, father care is particularly popular in families where mothers work a nonday shift.[59]

Fathers are not usually included in studies of child care providers, but the NICHD-SECC did include them and assessed them on the same rating scale that was used for centers, relatives, and other types of child care. On this scale (which, as noted earlier, emphasizes sensitivity and responsiveness and thus tends to produce higher-quality ratings for providers who care for children one-on-one or in small groups), fathers scored about as well on average as grandparents and slightly better than centers. At the upper end of the scale, 10 percent of fathers provided care rated excellent and 37 percent good, while at the other end of the scale, 5 percent provided care rated poor and 48 percent fair. How this care compares to the quality of care the mothers would have provided, if not working, is unknown, because mothers were not rated on the child care scale (they were rated on a parenting scale, but scores across the two scales are not readily comparable).

Somewhat less frequently used for preschool-age children is family day care, the primary form of care for 12 percent of children of working mothers at age three, 10 percent at age four, and 7 precent at age five (Table 3.1). Family day care tends to be used more often by married-couple families than by single-parent families (Table 3.2).

As with other forms of care, there is tremendous variation within this category, with some settings looking like small in-home day care centers, while others operate more informally. The Profile of Child Care Settings Study, in 1990, found that on average regulated family day care homes serving three- to five-year-olds had a group size of eight and a child-to-staff ratio of seven to one. In contrast to centers, family day care homes are staffed by less-well-educated providers, only 11 percent of whom have a college degree, with another 44 percent having some college.[60] In the NICHD-SECC, the quality of family day care was rated about the same as center care and lower than other forms of care: 63 percent of family day care providers were rated as fair (and 2 percent poor), while only 29 percent were rated as good (and only 5 percent excellent).

Finally, a small share of preschool-age children of working mothers (between 7 percent and 9 percent of three- to five-year-olds) have as their primary arrangement an individual provider who is not a relative (Table 3.1). This nonrelative could be a friend, neighbor, babysitter, or nanny providing care in the child's home or in another setting. Nonrelative care is used about as much by married-couple and single-parent families (Table 3.2). We know least about this type of care, but it is likely that its quality ranges very widely. The NICHD-SECC found that one subset of this category—in-home care—was of fairly high quality; indeed, it was the most highly rated form of care for three-year-olds,

Table 3.1. Primary child care arrangements of preschool-age children with working mothers: Percentage of each age group in various forms of care

	Age 3	Age 4	Age 5
Center	27	42	51
Grandparent	23	18	14
Other relative	11	7	5
Parent	20	15	15
Family day care	12	10	7
Other nonrelative	8	9	7
Total	101%	101%	99%

Source: Data from the Survey of Income and Program Participation 1996 Panel, wave 10 (spring 1999), as shown in Smolensky and Gootman (eds.) (2003), Table 3-1. Data refer to primary child care arrangements for children who are not yet in school and whose mothers are employed. Percentages in columns do not always sum to 100 due to rounding.

Table 3.2. Primary child care arrangements of preschool-age children with working mothers, by family type: Percentage of each age group in various forms of care

A. Children with married parents	Age 3	Age 4	Age 5
Center	26	41	50
Grandparent	20	14	12
Other relative	9	6	6
Parent	24	18	18
Family day care	13	12	7
Other nonrelative	8	9	7
Total	100%	100%	100%
B. Children with single parents	Age 3	Age 4	Age 5
Center	29	44	54
Grandparent	28	26	19
Other relative	14	8	4
Parent	12	8	8
Family day care	9	7	9
Other nonrelative	8	7	6
Total	100%	100%	100%

Source: Author's calculations using data from the Survey of Income and Program Participation 1996 Panel, wave 10 (spring 1999). Data refer to primary child care arrangements for children who are not yet in school and whose mothers are employed.

with 45 percent of providers rated as good (and 12 percent excellent). These high ratings are in part a reflection of the measure used in the assessment, which produces higher-quality ratings for individual providers, but also may suggest that many of the in-home providers in this sample were highly qualified nannies rather than babysitters. Other surveys that have included informal providers (such as friends or neighbors or nonrelative babysitters) have tended to find that they provide lower-quality care than more-formal providers (such as family day care or center-based care).[61]

The Cost of Care

An important factor related to both the type and quality of care for preschool-age children is its cost. Formal center- or school-based care tends to be more expensive than family day care or care by a relative or other informal provider. And within a given type of care, higher-quality care tends to be more expensive than lower-quality care. It is therefore not surprising that there is a very strong income gradient in the use of formal center- or school-based care and in the quality of care. Three-year-olds from the highest-income families (the top quarter of the income distribution) are nearly twenty-five percentage points more likely to be enrolled in a center- or school-based preschool than are children from the lowest-income families (the bottom quarter of the income distribution); the two groups' enrollment rates are about 50 percent and 25 percent, respectively. A similar gap exists among four-year-olds (with enrollment rates of 75 percent and 50 percent for the highest- and lowest-income children, respectively).[62]

Moreover, children from higher-income families tend to be in higher-quality care. For instance, among families using child care for their four-and-a-half-year-olds in the NICHD-SECC, 56 percent of children from high income families were in excellent- or good-quality care, and 44 percent in poor- or fair-quality care; these figures were reversed for children from low-income families, 56 percent of whom were in poor or fair care and 44 percent in excellent or good care. If we consider just those using center-based care, the pattern is similar, with 59 percent of the high-income children in excellent- or good-quality care (and 41 percent in poor- or fair-quality care), as compared to 47 percent of low-income children in excellent or good care (and 53 percent in poor or fair care). Children from moderate-income families also fare worse in terms of quality of care than children from higher-income families and only slightly better than children from low-income families. Among moderate-income families using care for their four-and-a-half-year-olds in the NICHD-SECC, 53 percent were in poor or fair care and 47 percent in excellent or good care; among those in center-based care, 50 percent were in poor or fair care, and 50 percent in excellent or good care.[63]

Of course, some of these income-related differences may have to do with families' preferences. Working-class families may be less likely to use center-based care and more likely to split shifts and care for their preschool-age children themselves, both because this arrangement is more affordable and because they prefer to do their child rearing themselves. But economic constraints surely play a role. Research shows that when low-income families of preschool-age children are given the means to pay for it (through increased subsidies or free or low-cost slots), they tend to make more use of center-based care and higher-quality care.[64] Kindergarten provides a powerful example. Although as we have seen there are large gaps in enrollment between higher- and lower-income three- and four-year-olds, these gaps do not exist for five-year-olds, nearly all of whom are now enrolled, regardless of their family income.[65] The fact that kindergarten, while not compulsory in all states, is provided universally and free of charge clearly plays an important role in influencing parents' decisions about using it.

Implications for Policy

The statistics on the quality of care in which preschool-age children are placed are sobering. As we have seen, the quality of care is not very good on average, and large disparities exist in children's experiences in preschool care and education. But fortunately, we can do something about this problem. Indeed, we can take many steps to improve the quality of care that preschool-age children experience and to even out the disparities in that care. We can draw inspiration from the advances made in several states and communities. We can also build on examples from other countries. These examples point to three particularly promising options for improving the quality of care for preschool-age children: improving care in the private market through quality-related rating and payment systems and tighter regulations; building on the most popular War on Poverty program, Head Start; and moving to universal preschool or prekindergarten.

Improving Care in the Private Market

The system of early childhood care and education that currently exists in the United States is distinctive in its reliance on the private market. Parents for the most part choose arrangements themselves and pay for them out of pocket, although costs may be offset by subsidies or tax credits or may even be fully subsidized in the case of public programs such as Head Start or prekindergarten. Relying on the market has tremendous advantages. Most importantly, it gives families choice. However, this choice is constrained for many families by issues of affordability. And the downside of leaving preschool care and education to the market is that we end up with low levels of quality. High-quality preschool programs are expensive, and most families cannot afford to pay what high-quality care would cost.[66]

Is there a way to keep preschool programs in the private market but improve their quality? Increasing the amount of child care subsidies or credits would allow families to spend more money but does not guarantee that the money would be spent on higher-quality care. For this reason, many experts in the field have advocated for two further steps: establishing tiered rating and payment systems and tightening up regulations.[67] Although some experts advocate for one and not the other, I think there is a useful role to be played by both.

The idea of quality-related rating and payment systems is simple. Several states (such as North Carolina, Pennsylvania, and Tennessee) already use star-rating systems, whereby providers receive more stars and are eligible for higher reimbursement if they deliver care of higher quality; another thirty states and the District of Columbia (as of 2003) have other forms of tiered reimbursement systems, paying a higher rate to programs that are accredited or meet other defined quality standards.[68] When subsidy systems for low- and moderate-income families are linked to these rating systems, preschools meeting the highest standard can be subsidized at a higher rate than preschools meeting lower standards. Families are still able to choose whichever form of preschool they prefer but receive less in subsidy if they choose a provider that is rated lower in quality.

Tighter regulations provide an additional check on the quality of care provided in the market. Although it is always possible that some providers could operate illegally, tightening regulations would force at least some providers to either raise the quality of their care or go out of business. Regulations may also serve an information function, communicating to parents as well as preschools what is minimally expected of a child care provider. This could be particularly important in the area of health and safety. As we saw earlier, research has shown that when regulations are tighter, children have fewer injuries. This safety does come at a price, which some parents may not be able to afford. For this reason, we have to think about expanding subsidies tied to quality and tightening regulations as a two-part strategy. Otherwise, we run the risk of pricing families out of care altogether.

North Carolina provides a good example of this kind of approach.[69] In 1990, North Carolina had one of the poorest-quality child care systems in the country. With the backing of the legislature and the governor, the state began taking steps to improve the system. Licensing standards were raised, and in 2000 North Carolina instituted a new "star-rated" licensing system, whereby participating child care providers receive from one to five stars, indicating the quality of the care and education they offer in terms of program standards, staff education, and their compliance history. The new system, which is voluntary but tied to higher reimbursement rates, gives providers a chance to receive credit for operating a higher-quality program and also provides more information to parents than a licensing system that simply indicates whether a provider meets minimum standards.

Recognizing that improving quality can be costly, North Carolina has greatly expanded its investment in child care subsidies and has also set up several programs to help offset the costs to providers of improving quality. The Teacher Education and Compensation Helps (T.E.A.C.H.) program, which began as a pilot in 1990 and is now available statewide, provides scholarships for child care workers who wish to complete further course work to increase their level of training and education and also provides funds to help pay them higher salaries. The Smart Start program, established as a pilot program in 1993 and extended statewide in 1998, provides quality-improvement grants to programs. These grants are only one element of Smart Start, a comprehensive early childhood development reform program that includes a host of initiatives to increase access to high-quality early childhood care and education.

These quality-improvement initiatives have raised the quality of care and education that preschool-age children in North Carolina receive. The share of children attending high-quality centers has increased, as has the share of children attending centers with more-educated providers.[70] North Carolina's reforms have been used as models by other states seeking to improve the quality of their preschool care and education, and Smart Start now operates a National Technical Assistance Center, which provides intensive assistance to states looking to replicate its model.

Looking beyond our own boundaries, Australia provides another good example. Australia, like the United States, has traditionally had a market-based child care system, with little governmental involvement. However, with increased numbers of women working when their children are young, the government decided to get more involved in subsidizing care and in making an effort to improve the quality of care. Thus, alongside expanded funding for child care subsidies in the 1990s, Australia also introduced a new Quality-Improvement and Accreditation System (QIAS) in 1994, whereby early childhood education and care providers must meet specific quality standards to be eligible for government subsidies. The QIAS standards are based on the guidelines for developmentally appropriate practice set out by the National Association for the Education of Young Children (a U.S.-based organization of child care experts) and emphasize process aspects of quality. Child care and education providers first conduct a self-study to see the extent to which their practice conforms to the QIAS standards and are then rated by a peer reviewer. Providers who do not pass the peer review are encouraged to develop a plan to come into compliance and are censured only if they fail to participate, or if they fail to pass after three tries.[71]

Another example of tighter regulation and standards comes from the United Kingdom, which, like Australia, has greatly expanded its involvement in early childhood care and education while building on a largely private market system. The United Kingdom has a very tight system of standards and monitoring for primary and secondary schools but traditionally did not apply that system to pre–primary education and care. As part of its National Childcare Strategy, introduced in 1998, the government tightened standards for preschools, setting out a recommended curriculum and learning goals for the early years. At the same time, it moved responsibility for monitoring preschool programs' compliance with the standards to the same body that monitors primary and secondary schools. The result has been that preschool curriculums have become more uniform and more educational in focus.[72]

An important element of the reforms in North Carolina, the United Kingdom, and Australia is that they have aimed not at punishing poor-quality providers but rather at helping them improve the quality of the care and education they offer. By setting out clear standards, providing support for teachers to receive additional training, involving providers in the assessment of their program quality, and providing technical assistance and curriculum materials as well as enhanced subsidies, these reform efforts not only set out higher standards but also support programs in meeting those standards.

Building on Head Start

Another way to improve the quality of preschool care and education is to build on the Head Start program, which since 1965 has provided preschool to low-income and disabled children. In principle, Head Start has many of the elements that a high-quality program should have. In particular, its emphasis on the whole child and on health and nutrition as well as learning and behavior is laudable. However, in practice Head Start has not always lived up to the hopes its founders had for it. Careful observational studies, while finding some positive effects of Head Start on children's outcomes, have also found that effects are not always lasting. Evidence from the 2005 random assignment evaluation shows that children benefit from Head Start after one year in the program, but we do not know yet whether those gains are lasting.

A major concern about Head Start has been the quality of its programming, particularly with regard to promoting children's academic school readiness. In 2003, President Bush proposed heightening Head Start's emphasis on reading and other aspects of academic school readiness and also initiated a program to test Head Start children to see how much they were learning while in the program. Bush also proposed allowing at least some states to experiment with taking their Head Start funds and using them to serve low-income or disabled children in other settings. Critics of these proposals feared that such experiments would dilute Head Start's traditional focus on the whole child and would lead programs to emphasize basic skills at the expense of other aspects of health and development; they also worried that, as is always a risk with more-flexible funds, money might be shifted to serve other children.

I think both sides in the Head Start debate have some merit. Defenders of the program are right to applaud its whole child focus and are right to fear that block-granted funds could be diverted to inappropriate programs or even to serve other children. And surely there is no need to test each and every Head Start child to find out what the program is teaching. However, critics of the program are also right to point out that it has probably not done as much as it could to prepare children academically.

Head Start programs have many good features. They involve parents, and they aim to deliver services to the child and family. When observers have gone out to rate the quality of care in Head Start centers, as compared to other centers serving disadvantaged children, they have found that Head Start compares favorably in terms of process quality. Compared to other centers, Head Start centers look equally good in terms of overall classroom climate, teacher warmth and sensitivity, and so on. However, when we recall that the average quality of center care has been found to be just mediocre, it is worth asking whether we would want Head Start to be better than the average, particularly since it is serving such disadvantaged children.

Moreover, there is no denying that the quality of Head Start programs, measured in terms of structural elements that matter for learning, is often low. The average Head Start teacher does not have a college degree (only about one quarter do), is paid about $16,000 per year, and has responsibility for a group of twenty-three children at one time. Teachers in private preschools are about twice as likely to have a college degree, are paid more, and have responsibility for fewer children (ten to twenty, depending on the state and setting). Children attending prekindergartens have teachers who are even better educated and better paid—86 percent have a college degree, and 82 percent are paid the same rates as elementary school teachers, whose average salary was $42,000 in 2001—although their class sizes tend to be high as well (on average, twenty to twenty-five children).[73]

A further concern is that not all Head Start programs emphasize academics. Programs vary widely in terms of the curriculum they use, with only some using the curriculum from the Perry Preschool program that was to serve as their model.[74] Yet, we know from research that curriculum matters: too little emphasis on academic instruction can leave children ill prepared for school, while too much teacher-directed instruction can decrease their motivation and lead to behavior problems. The key is having a curriculum that is tailored to the interests and abilities of the child.

It is no wonder that children in Head Start programs do not always gain as much in terms of reading and math readiness as children in other preschool settings. The world has changed since Head Start began, and Head Start may need to change to keep up. When Head Start first started back in the 1960s, few three- and four-year-olds were in any form of preschool, and the little bit of academics that children got from Head Start went a long way. But in today's world, with 40 percent of three-year-olds and 60 percent of four-year-olds in some form of preschool, Head Start needs to do more. Yet Head Start programs are poorly funded relative to other types of preschool programs. Research shows that when Head Start programs spend more money, Head Start children do better—they have higher reading scores and are less likely to be held back in school.[75]

So, I think a case can be made for spending more money on Head Start programs but on condition that they meet specific standards, such as hiring more-qualified teachers and adhering more closely to academically oriented preschool or prekindergarten curriculums that have been demonstrated to be effective with preschool-age children. Essentially, this is analogous to spending more money on subsidized care but tied to higher quality and tighter regulations. Both pieces (higher funding and higher standards) are needed.

I would also advocate taking a closer look at Head Start budgets and seeing if there is a way to spend the money more wisely. The average Head Start program spends only about 40 percent of its budget on education. When programs spend a larger share of their money on education, children have fewer behavior problems and are less likely to be held back.[76] These findings suggest it would be worth looking at shifting some money within Head Start budgets to increase spending on education-related items such as teacher salaries.

Moving to Universal Preschool or Prekindergarten

Another way to approach the problem of poor and uneven quality in preschools is for government to play a more active role in providing that care and education. A number of experts in the United States have called for universal preschool or prekindergarten for three- and four-year-olds, as a way to ensure that children receive preschool of higher quality and more uniform quality prior to entering kindergarten at age five. Many of those who advocate universal provision point to the example of other countries, who have increasingly moved to provide preschool to all children in the year or two prior to school entry and in some cases even earlier. A number of states and localities are moving in this direction as well.

The experience of other countries in this area is illustrative. It is striking that, although countries are very diverse in terms of care and education arrangements for younger children, they are much less diverse when it comes to provision for preschool-age children. For children age three and older, there is growing convergence across countries on two key points: the importance of children being in high-quality care and education, and the responsibility of government (rather than parents or the private market) to provide or fund that care. Across countries, preschool is increasingly seen as education and is coming to be universal, particularly in the year or two immediately prior to formal school entry. As a result, the public role in preschool care tends to be larger in many other countries than in the United States, enrollment rates for preschool age children tend to be higher, and the enrollment gaps between children from low- and high-income families (which are so striking in the United States) tend to be smaller.

How this move to universal preschool is being accomplished and how the experience of other countries differs from that of the United States, can be seen in a set of in-depth studies, conducted for the Organization for Economic Cooperation and Development (OECD), of early childhood care and education provision in twelve advanced, industrialized countries.[77] The countries included (Australia, Belgium, Czechoslovakia, Denmark, Finland, Italy, the Netherlands, Norway, Portugal, Sweden, the United Kingdom, and the United States) have differing approaches to social policy provision (representing three distinct types of social welfare regime: the continental European, Nordic, and English-speaking), and different levels of wealth.[78] Yet, most are moving in the direction of providing a free or low-cost preschool place, on at least a part-day basis, to all children aged three and older. As a result, their preschool enrollment rates tend to be high, particularly in the year prior to school entry and sometimes earlier (see Table 3.3).

Some of the highest enrollment rates are seen in the continental European countries. In Belgium and Italy, as shown in Table 3.3, preschool enrollment is universal starting at age three, with virtually all children enrolled in a preschool or kindergarten for the three years from age three until age six, when formal school begins. France, not included in the OECD study, also follows this pattern, with universal enrollment in preschool starting at age three and continuing until school entry at age six (indeed, France is extending its preschools to reach two-year-olds, about a third of whom were enrolled as of 1998).[79] Two other

Table 3.3 Share of children in preschool or school, by country and age, in 1999 (in percent)

	Age 3	Age 4	Age 5	Age 6	School starting age
Australia	26	43	82	100	6
Belgium	98	99	99	99	6
Czech Republic	47	82	93	100	6
Denmark	67	91	94	100	7
Finland	32	40	48	72	7
Italy	95	100	98	100	6
Netherlands	0	98	100	100	5
Norway	70	77	81	100	6
Portugal	56	68	74	100	6
Sweden	64	69	75	100	7
United Kingdom	52	95	100	99	5
United States	35	59	79	98	5–7 (depends on state)

Source: Figures on enrollment from Organization for Economic Cooperation and Development, 2001, p.188, Appendix table: "Data from Figure 3.2, Net enrollment rates by single year of age in pre–primary and primary education, 1999 (%)." Figures on compulsory school starting age from OECD, 2001, p. 46, Table 3.1: "Terms and organization of main forms of ECEC provision."

continental European countries in the OECD study (the Czech Republic and Portugal) have lower enrollment rates but are moving to catch up (the Netherlands follows a slightly different pattern, with universal enrollment at age four and school at age five).

Enrollment rates are also high in the Nordic countries, although here comparisons are more difficult, since formal school tends to start later. Among the Nordic countries, Denmark stands out as having the most widespread provision, with near-universal enrollment in the three years prior to school entry at age seven, but enrollment rates are very high in Sweden and Norway as well. Finland has the lowest enrollment rate in this group.

The OECD study also included three English-speaking countries, the United States, Australia, and the United Kingdom. In the United States, where formal school usually begins at age five (although some states do not require school attendance until as late as age seven), the OECD study found 35 percent of children enrolled at age three and 59 percent at age four. This 59 percent figure is the lowest rate of enrollment in the year before formal school entry among the twelve countries in the OECD study. Of course, the United States does have an early school-starting age, but even if we restrict the comparison to the three countries where school starts at age five, the United States stands out as having the lowest enrollment the year before. Australia, which as noted earlier, has a market-based system like the United States, also has low rates of enrollment relative to the continental European and Nordic countries.

The United Kingdom provides an interesting point of comparison. As Table 3.3 indicates, the OECD study found that nearly all four-year-olds, and about half of three-year-olds, were enrolled. However, until very recently, the picture for the United Kingdom was quite different. Historically, the United Kingdom had a system (like the Australian and U.S. systems) that relied primarily on the private market, with limited subsidies for low-income families and limited direct provision targeted to disadvantaged or at-risk children. In 1991, only 30 percent of British three-year-olds and 54 percent of four-year-olds attended a nursery class or school, and most of these attended part-time.[80] It was not until 1996 that the government, under the Conservative Party, took the first steps toward wider provision for preschool-age children, with the introduction of a nursery voucher scheme for four-year-olds. When the Labour Party came into office in 1997, it replaced this scheme with one of its own and went on to guarantee at least a part-time preschool place to every four-year-old whose parents wanted one. This pledge was soon fulfilled and was followed by a pledge to make similar provisions for three-year-olds by 2004. Thus, in the last decade, the United Kingdom went from having one of the lowest preschool enrollment rates among OECD countries to having a universal entitlement to a free part-time preschool place for all three- and four-year-olds.

Of course, figures about enrollment do not tell us about the quality of the preschools that children are attending. What do we know about the quality of care being provided to children in these universal programs? Not surprisingly, quality varies across countries. In several countries, quality seems to be uniformly high; in others, quality is lower or more varied.

With regard to child-to-staff ratios, for instance, experts recommend a ratio of not more than fifteen children to one teacher for children in the age three-to-six range.[81] Of the twelve countries in the OECD study, eight have regulations that set child-to-teacher ratios this low or lower (Australia, 10:1; Czech Republic, 12:1; Denmark, 6:1; Finland, 7:1; Norway, 14:1–18:1; Portugal, 15:1; Sweden, 6:1; and the United Kingdom, 8:1–13:1), with Denmark, Finland, and Sweden standing out as having particularly favorable ratios. Four countries in the OECD study, including the United States, set ratios above the standard (Belgium, 18:1–19:1; Italy, 20:1–28:1, the Netherlands, 20:1; and the United States, where ratios range from 10:1 to 20:1, depending on the state).[82]

With regard to teacher training and education, standards vary a good deal across countries. Again, Denmark, Finland, and Sweden stand out from the rest, requiring all child care or education teachers (except family day care providers) to have a three- or four-year university degree. Italy is also moving in this direction, requiring that in future, all teachers in its preschools for three- to six-year-olds will have a university degree. But in other countries, the level of staff training and education depends on the sector. So, for instance, in Australia, Belgium, the Netherlands, and Portugal, teaching staff in preschool settings must have a three- or four-year university degree, but staff in other child care settings are less highly trained and lower paid. Differences by sector are a particular problem in the United Kingdom, where as in the United States, a large divide exists between teachers working in child care or preschool settings, who tend to have low levels of training and pay, and teachers in school-based programs, who tend to have university degrees and to be paid on a par with primary school teachers.[83]

As noted above, the United Kingdom has recently moved to a system of universal provision for three- and four-year-olds, and how to ensure that the care is of good quality has been a major concern. The United Kingdom has tightened up standards for preschool programs, insisted that they follow a recommended academic curriculum, and begun monitoring them on the same terms as primary and secondary schools. The United Kingdom has also invested in research on what constitutes quality child care. A large-scale observational study of the Effective Provision of Preprimary Education (EPPE) has shown that some existing preschool programs—in particular, those that integrate services and education, those that have more-highly educated staff, and those that provide more sensitive and responsive care—are more effective than others in preparing children for school, in terms of cognitive attainment and social and emotional development.[84] These lessons are now informing government policy. The government's ten-year child care strategy, announced in December 2004, draws on the findings from EPPE to set the goal of all preschools being led by a university graduate, alongside a host of other quality-improvement initiatives. Recognizing that improving quality will not occur overnight, the ten-year strategy set up a series of milestones—interim steps to be taken by specific dates to show that progress is being made on the road to higher quality.[85]

So what can we take away from the experience of other countries? I see two lessons as being particularly relevant for the United States at this juncture. The first is that it is possible to provide universal early childhood care and education and to have that programming be of high quality. The second is that there are steps that government can take to improve the quality of programming and to close the divides between different sectors or different programs.

As informative as the European cases are, we can also see cases of universal provision even closer to home. Although less heralded, states and localities in the United States have embarked on their own efforts to provide universal preschool.

The first such effort involved kindergarten. As recently as 1964, only 58 percent of American children attended kindergarten.[86] Then, as now, primary school began in first grade, when children were age six. Over the course of the past forty years, kindergarten has become universal. Although kindergarten is still not compulsory in all states and is provided on only a half-day basis in about half the schools, nearly all children attend it. Essentially, schooling now begins with kindergarten, at age five. It is important to recall, however, that kindergarten is not technically school—it is pre-primary school or preschool. So, if we want to look for evidence as to whether universal preschool is feasible in the U.S. context and could provide good-quality early childhood education, kindergarten is a useful case study.

The evidence on kindergarten answers two important questions about universal preschool. First, elementary schools can expand their provision to include preschool classrooms. Second, these classrooms appear to be of fairly high quality, relative to the quality of other preschool provision available in the United States. Kindergarten teachers are generally on a par with other elementary school teachers in terms of their training, education, and pay and thus are more highly qualified and paid than most preschool teachers. And although class sizes tend to be large, curriculums have been developed that are tailored to the learning needs and styles of five-year-olds, although these are now being affected by a push for more academic instruction in many schools. It is hard to judge the effects of kindergarten, now that all children attend. We do know that children tend to lose ground over the summer, suggesting that they learn something in school they do not get otherwise. We also know that children who have the opportunity to attend full-day kindergarten learn more than children who attend only part-day programs. This evidence suggests that, although there is room for improvement, children are learning in kindergarten.[87]

However, there is one major weakness in kindergarten programs when it comes to meeting the needs of children of working parents. Whether full-day or part-day, few programs are linked with out-of-school programs specifically designed to provide developmentally appropriate care for kindergarteners whose parents work and who need care for them before or after the start of the school day. With most mothers of five-year-olds working, many of them full-time, a substantial share of kindergarteners are in some form of child care before or after school. Yet few of these child care programs are located at children's schools. Among children attending kindergarten in 1998, only 4 percent were in a before-school program located at their school, and only 10 percent were in an after-school program at school.[88] This means that the majority of children who use before- or after-school care are with providers or programs located elsewhere in the community and must be transported between several different locations during the course of the day.

We do not know much about the quality of out-of-school care for kindergarteners, but the evidence we do have is not encouraging. Controlling for a host of other characteristics, kindergarteners who spend time in center- or school-based out-of-school programs are rated by their teachers as having more behavior problems and showing less self-control; they also score more poorly in reading and math.[89] It may be that these effects are a reflection of poor-quality care, or that they indicate that regardless of quality, too many hours of center- or school-based care are difficult for some children at this age. If poor quality is the problem, further attention to raising the quality of these programs is needed. Keeping in mind that these out-of-school programs are technically child care programs, we can see how quality-related rating and payment systems and tighter regulations could both play a role here.

The second move toward universal preschool in the United States involves prekindergarten. Prekindergarten programs provide a year or two of publicly funded part- or full-day preschool education to children prior to kindergarten, effectively extending public schooling to four- and sometimes even three-year-olds. Depending on the state, prekindergarten programs may be located in a public school or in an approved community-based setting (such as a child care center). As of 2003, a total of thirty-nine states had established prekindergarten programs, although only six had made a substantial investment in them. These programs served about 14 percent of all four-year-olds in 2003. The average cost per child of prekindergarten is $4,400 for a part-day program, and $8,800 for a full-day program.[90]

Although the numbers enrolled are still small, these programs look very promising. In analyses of children in kindergarten in the fall of 1998 (from the Early Childhood Longitudinal Study, Kindergarten Cohort), children who had attended prekindergarten the year before kindergarten entered kindergarten scoring better on reading and math than children who did not attend preschool that year, even after controlling for a host of child, family, community, and school characteristics. These effects are especially large for children from disadvantaged families (families with low incomes or low parental education) or families where a language other than English is spoken at home. As might be expected, the reading and math gains are less apparent by first grade, as the children who had not attended preschool start catching up.[91] Nevertheless, other research analyzing math achievement for fourth-graders has found lasting gains in states that had a higher share of children enrolled in prekindergarten.[92]

One concern that early childhood educators have raised about formal programs like prekindergarten is whether the curriculum would be too academically oriented and not sufficiently attuned to children's social and emotional needs. As we have seen, there is a pattern of results in the research literature showing that center- or school-based care is associated both with greater learning gains and with the development of more behavior problems, for at least some children. Unfortunately, this may be the case with at least some prekindergarten programs as well. In the 1998 kindergarten cohort, although children gained academically from attending prekindergarten, they were also rated by their teachers as having worse behavior and less self-control. However, these problems were found only for children attending prekindergarten in a setting other than the school where they attended kindergarten, suggesting that when children move directly from prekindergarten to kindergarten in the same school, such problems do not occur, presumably because these programs are of higher quality or because they fit better with the kindergarten programs.

It is hard to tell how these two sets of effects balance out. The fact that children attending prekindergarten are, if anything, less likely to repeat kindergarten and more likely to be promoted to first grade suggests that perhaps the academic gains outweigh any behavior problems. Moreover, the behavior problems do not seem to have much effect on children's school achievement in first grade.[93] But ideally we would like to see a program that boosts learning without creating behavior problems. So as the states expand prekindergarten programs to serve more children, they will want to be careful about the design of these programs and will want to be sure that they meet children's social and emotional needs as well as their learning aims.

However, the evidence to date suggests that prekindergarten initiatives can do this. As of 2004, two states—Georgia and Oklahoma—had implemented universal prekindergarten programs (New York had also passed universal legislation but had yet to implement it fully while Florida did not enact its program until the following year). The prekindergarten initiatives in both Georgia and Oklahoma have been evaluated, and the results are very encouraging.[94]

Georgia has since 1995 offered a free, full-day prekindergarten place to all four-year-olds. The program is directed by the state, which sets out minimum standards for quality, but is then delivered by a range of local providers. As of 2003, private for-profit providers and local public school systems operated 88 percent of classes (46 percent and 42 percent respectively), with the remainder provided by Head Start programs

(1 percent) and programs located within faith-based organizations (10 percent). Each program must use a state-approved curriculum and meet staffing and class-size requirements, which include teachers having an associate's or college degree, and classes having no more than twenty students and being staffed by a teacher and teacher's aide.

Just over half (54 percent) of Georgia four-year-olds attended a prekindergarten program (as of 2003), with another 9 percent in Head Start. The remainder attended private preschools, participated in other types of early childhood care and education, or were at home with their parents. Because families are able to select whether to participate, it is difficult to tell what effect prekindergarten attendance has on children's school readiness. However, analyses taking into account children's prior scores suggest that both prekindergarten and private preschool programs lead to gains in children's academic performance.

The variety of prekindergarten programs in Georgia has allowed evaluators to compare outcomes for children in different types of programs. This comparison has suggested that particular types of curriculum may be more effective than others. For instance, children whose teachers used a more adult-directed rather than child-directed style of instruction showed less task persistence, were less positive about learning, and behaved worse in class. It is interesting, however, that no systematic differences have emerged between the programs provided in public schools and those offered by private providers. Thus, public school programs seem to do as good a job as the private providers in boosting school readiness.[95]

Oklahoma has since 1998 offered a free prekindergarten place to all four-year-olds. Oklahoma's program differs from Georgia's in that school districts deliver the program directly to students, although some do collaborate with Head Start or other day care programs in doing so. Quality as measured by structural indicators is high: all teachers have a college degree, their starting salary is $27,060, and classes are capped at twenty children and child-to-staff ratios capped at ten to one.

Participation in Oklahoma's program is voluntary, but about two-thirds of families (as of 2002) take up the offer. Families can only enroll their child if the child meets the birthday cutoff for that year. An evaluation in Tulsa, the state's largest school district, took advantage of this quasi-experiment, comparing outcomes for children who were eligible for the prekindergarten program with those who just missed being eligible (because of their birth date), and found positive effects of the program on children's scores on language and cognitive tests but no effects on behavior problems or other measures of social and emotional development. Gains were particularly large for minority and disadvantaged students, especially if they attended full-day programs (as 42 percent of children overall did). In the words of the evaluators, these results "lend support to the proposition that the public school system is a viable and effective vehicle for delivering educational services to young children."[96]

᠊ᢌ᠊ PERHAPS THE SINGLE biggest challenge lies in implementation. We know what children need in these years and what types of programs best meet those needs. The challenge is in getting programs to provide what we know to be good-quality care.

Given their promising track record, expanding prekindergarten programs seems to me a very promising way to improve the quality of care for three- and four-year-olds. And if combined with the other two approaches—improving the quality of market care and improving and expanding Head Start—expanding prekindergarten programs would give families real choices as to good-quality care for their preschool-age children. If, as I expect, prekindergarten proved to provide good-quality care, families would move their children there, and market care for three- and four-year-olds would gradually disappear. In the same way, prekindergarten would provide competition for Head Start programs, or the two could collaborate in creative ways, as they already are beginning to do in some states and localities. It is exciting to think of a world in which a low-income family would have a choice of sending their child to the local Head Start program or prekindergarten—or of sending their child to prekindergarten or kindergarten in the morning and to a Head Start wrap-around center or another high-quality child care program in the afternoon.

Looking Ahead

It is tempting to think that meeting children's needs when parents work becomes considerably easier when children start primary school, at age six. But, as any working parent can attest, that is not necessarily the case. While it is true that parents need to arrange and pay for fewer hours of care—because children are in school for a good share of the hours that parents are working—that care is often harder to come by and often of poor quality. And as children enter the school-age years, they increasingly want to, and should, have a voice in deciding what type of care they will be in. Yet school-age children are not old enough to care for themselves for substantial lengths of time or to get themselves to activities on their own, so transportation to and from school, home, friends, and various programs is a further challenge. In short, as we shall see in the next chapter, finding, coordinating, and paying for care that is healthy and developmentally appropriate for school-age children while their parents work is easier said than done.

4

School-Age Children

CHILDREN AGED SIX TO TWELVE, and how they fare when parents work, have received much less attention from researchers and policy makers than younger children, in part because middle childhood has been seen as a less dramatic period of development.[1] But, as parents can attest, the school-age years are a time of tremendous growth and development and a key period for health, as patterns established in these years set the stage for a lifetime of healthy or unhealthy behaviors.

Another reason for the relative neglect of school-age children is the assumption that children this age are in school while their parents are at work. However, schools cover only about half the hours that full-time employed parents are at work or commuting to work during the year. So unless parents work only part-time, part-year, and on a school schedule, schools do not cover all the hours they work. And most school-age children cannot just be left on their own for extended periods of time.

So the need for child care does not end when children enter school. Yet what parents quickly discover is that the system of child care for school-age children is more haphazard and more difficult to navigate than for younger children. This mismatch between the needs of children and the system that does exist has spurred efforts to expand after-school programs and other programs to care for children during their out-of-school time.

Drawing on evidence from developmental research and analyses of longitudinal data sets such as the National Longitudinal Survey of Youth Child Supplement (NLSY-CS), this chapter considers what children aged six to twelve need to promote healthy growth and development and how that care can be provided in their out-of-school hours—before school, after school, and during summers and school vacations. The chapter also reviews what we know about how parental employment affects school-age children and who currently cares for them while their parents are working. Drawing on this evidence, the chapter concludes by considering what additional steps schools and other community-based organizations should take to meet the needs of school-age children.

What School-Age Children Need

Early psychoanalytic thinkers, led by Sigmund Freud, tended to dismiss the school-age years as a "latency period" when not much happened developmentally. Erik Erikson was the first to highlight the specific developmental tasks associated with middle childhood.[2] Erikson's theory of life cycle development identifies challenges and milestones that individuals face in each stage of their lives. According to this theory, children in the school-age years are primarily grappling with the challenge of developing a sense of industry, figuring out what they are good at and how they will fit into society. Children who successfully master this task will move into adolescence with a sense of self-confidence that will equip them to face and surmount new challenges; those who do not will leave these years with a sense of inferiority that will handicap their future success.

This process is a highly differentiated one, as children begin to see themselves as individuals and identify the specific things they are interested in or good at. If you ask five-year-olds if they are good at something like math or puzzles, most will say yes, regardless of their actual ability. But school-age children will answer differently, depending on how good they actually are at the task.

In virtually all cultures, children aged five to seven begin formal schooling and begin to learn reading, writing, and arithmetic. This period has been called the "age of reason," and indeed children's reasoning does become substantially more advanced, as they make gains in being able to reflect on their own and others' thinking, plan ahead, and predict what will happen next.[3]

Paralleling the increasing sophistication of children's thinking is a growing social and emotional maturity. Children increase their self-regulation, becoming more able to control their emotions and behaviors and to take responsibility for them. They are also more able to understand how another person thinks and feels. This growing capacity to relate to others underpins another key change—the growth in the importance of peers. School-age children increasingly value the time they spend with peers and develop closer and more differentiated friendships than they had in early childhood. They also become more attached to their peer group and more susceptible to its influence.

At the same time, children are growing physically and, in many cases, are beginning to experience the hormonal changes that precede puberty. The average age of menarche (first menstruation) for American girls is now twelve and a half years, which means that hormonal changes are beginning for the average girl around age ten or eleven, and for some girls considerably earlier (age at puberty ranges from about eight to fourteen for girls, and about nine to fifteen for boys). By the end of the school-age years, both boys and girls are anticipating adolescence and beginning to think about how they will handle dating and all the other challenges that lie ahead. The fact that school-age children are thinking about sexual relationships but have for the most part not yet begun to engage in them (fewer than 10 percent of ninth-graders say they had sexual intercourse before the age of thirteen), makes this an opportune time to educate them about healthy relationships and about such issues as partner violence and safe sex.[4]

The school-age years are also an opportune time for health promotion.[5] Lifestyle choices—in areas such as exercise, nutrition, and the use of alcohol and tobacco—begin to be established in the school-age years, and these choices go on to have major implications for health in adulthood.

Again, there is tremendous scope for individual differences. Some children exercise regularly in school and outside school and are physically fit. But a worryingly large share do not get regular exercise and spend long hours in sedentary activities like watching television or playing computer games. In 1984, the National Academy of Sciences panel on school-age children raised the concern that "for most children age 6–12 in the United States, television viewing constitutes the largest single portion of free time on a typical weekday," with children watching three to four hours a day, and eleven- and twelve-year-olds, particularly boys, watching even more.[6] Although the number of hours of TV that children watch has declined somewhat in the intervening twenty years, this decline has been more than offset by the increase in time that children spend sitting at computers.[7] Time on a computer may well be more educational than time in front of a TV, but both are sedentary activities that do not contribute to physical fitness.

A related area of concern is nutrition. Rates of obesity among school-age children have skyrocketed, with approximately 15 percent of school-age children overweight in 2000 compared to only 4 percent thirty years earlier, placing children at elevated risk of adult obesity and all the illnesses and problems that go with it.[8] Although the primary determinant of obesity is eating more food than needed, the amount of physical activity a child engages in will obviously affect his or her weight as well. Children who spend more time watching TV or on the computer and less time engaged in physical activity will be at higher risk (unless they cut back how much food they eat), simply because they burn off fewer calories.

Another important set of health-related attitudes and behaviors has to do with the use of tobacco, alcohol, and drugs. Although we may think of school-age children as being too young to use these substances, over a third of ninth-graders report that they had drunk alcohol before the age of thirteen, while 19 percent say they had smoked a cigarette and 10 percent say they had tried marijuana.[9]

In sum, the school-age years, rather than being a latency period, are in fact a period of dramatic growth and development. They are also a "window of opportunity."[10] In the best of circumstances, children emerge from the school-age years with a sense of self-confidence and a sense of how they relate to peers that will have lifelong consequences for how they view themselves and their place in the world. The school-age years are also an opportune time for parents and others to help children develop healthy attitudes and behaviors.

The Role of Parents

Parents of school-age children influence their health and development in a myriad of ways.[11] The care that parents provide and the warmth and sensitivity of their interactions with their children and with each other influence children's view of themselves and the way they will interact with others. Parents also continue to be an important source of cognitive stimulation and can exert a strong influence on the way children approach learning and school. Parents set standards for children's behavior and enforce those standards, through monitoring and discipline. More generally, parents serve as role models, across domains—parents can model (or not model) healthy nutrition and behaviors, good mental health, and a commitment to work and career. And through family routines and traditions, parents can transmit a broader set of values having to do with manners, culture, and ethics, as well as social skills.

Parents also influence their children indirectly—through their role as family managers or gatekeepers—and as children get older and spend more time out of the home, in school, and with peers, this aspect of parents' influence on children's development becomes increasingly important.[12] Family management or gatekeeping refers to the arrangements parents make that affect children's environments and activities. By choosing where they live and what schools and services they use within those locations, parents affect whom their children are with day to day and the care and education they receive. Of course, parents' influence extends only so far—it is up to the children to decide how hard to work in school, what subjects and activities to focus on, and which friendships to cultivate. And, for many families, choices as to where to live and what schools and services to use are severely constrained by low income, limited choice in their areas, or other factors.

As children move through the school-age years, they begin to form relationships with other adults who they can turn to as sources of advice, inspiration, and role modeling. The growing importance of these relationships reflects children's increasing maturity and ability to engage with adults. It also reflects the expansion of children's networks to a host of adults beyond their classroom teachers—coaches, music instructors, Sunday School teachers, scout leaders, Big Brothers or Sisters, as well as adult relatives, such as grandparents, aunts, or uncles. Parents often play a key role in setting up and facilitating these relationships.

Thus, parents affect their children in many ways, and parental employment could too. At the same time, we would not expect parental employment to completely determine children's outcomes or to have a unitary set of effects. Parents and children adjust when parents go to work or work different hours, and if these adjustments are successful, we might observe few strong effects of employment on children's outcomes.[13] And as we have noted above, parents are not the only influence on children's outcomes—school-age children increasingly exert an influence on their own outcomes (through the choices they make and through their interactions with peers) and are influenced by adults other than parents.

Effects of Parental Employment

What does the research conclude about how parental employment affects school-age children's outcomes? What do parents and children say? Although the research base on school-age children is not as strong as it is for younger children, the research that does exist points to some interesting similarities and differences.

Health

The area of health is a good example of the interplay between parents, the child, and other adults in the school-age years. Parents, of course, have primary responsibility for children's health. However, as children get older, they become more active agents in their own health—choosing whether to eat the healthy lunch their parents have packed for them or whether to take part in the swimming class their parents want them to take. They also take on a more active role in their encounters with health care providers. When a six-year-old is taken to the doctor, much of the conversation is between the doctor and the parent, and the parent is seen as having primary responsibility for carrying out the doctor's instructions. But as the child gets older, increasingly the conversation is between the child and the doctor. Other adults also play an expanded role in promoting children's health. Teachers, coaches, and other adults can motivate school-age children to exercise, eat well, and make healthy choices about tobacco, alcohol, and drugs.

Given these multiple influences, what do we know about the effects of parental employment on children's health in the school-age years? Here, as elsewhere, I turn first to the evidence from experimental studies, although, unfortunately, these have been limited to low-income families.

As we saw in the prior chapter, experimental studies of welfare-to-work programs have found that programs that increased employment and income were neutral or improved child health, while programs that increased employment but not income were neutral or worsened child health. For the most part, this pattern of results holds in middle childhood, although school-age children have not often been analyzed separately from preschoolers.[14]

Turning to observational studies, the studies reviewed in the prior chapter found few effects of parental employment on young children's health, with the exception of a finding that preschoolers whose mothers work are more likely to be overweight. This finding seems to be replicated in the school-age years. A study examining children aged three to eleven from the NLSY found that children whose mothers had worked more hours to date were more likely to be overweight, with these effects tending to be strongest in families with the highest incomes.[15] However, another study from the NLSY focusing specifically on ten- and eleven-year-old children found that, although there was a tendency for children whose mothers worked more hours when the children were aged three to nine to be more likely to be obese or at risk of obesity, these differences were not statistically significant.[16] Thus, it appears that the effects of parental employment may be stronger before children reach the ages of ten or eleven. Perhaps parents exert more influence on children's nutrition (or exercise levels) earlier in childhood, with other factors (school meals and children's eating and activities with friends) playing a more important role in the later school-age years.

There may well be other effects of parental employment on child health, but these have not been as extensively studied. For instance, parental employment can affect the availability of a parent to stay home when a child is sick. The medical literature suggests that children recover more quickly if a parent is present and involved in their care.[17] Yet, as we saw in chapter 1, few American employees have the right to take paid time off from work when a child is sick, and low-income workers are the least likely to have such rights.[18]

Cognitive Development

Parents' role in cognitive development in the school-age years also reflects the growing interplay between parents, other adults, and the children themselves. During the school-age years, teachers take on increasing responsibility for children's learning, but parents continue to play an important role.[19] Parents influence children's learning indirectly through their choice of schools or neighborhood, interactions with teachers, and, in some cases, arranging and paying for outside tutoring, lessons, or courses. Parents also influence children's learning more directly, by setting expectations for their children and monitoring homework, school attendance, and school progress. Parents also provide instrumental support, in the form of computers and learning materials as well as a structured time and a quiet place for children to study and get homework done. Some parents help with homework, read books, or work with children on research, art, or science projects. Parents also play an important role in motivating children to work hard and do well in school, whether by setting an example, showing that they value schoolwork and expect their child to excel, or providing praise and encouragement. Conversely, parents can also undermine children's motivation, by conveying the message that they do not value success in school or that they believe their child is not capable of achieving it.

Given these multiple ways that parents affect children's cognitive development and school achievement, what do we know about the effects of parental employment in these years? As we saw in the prior chapters, children's cognitive development may be adversely affected when mothers work in the first year of life, particularly if that employment is full-time, but not thereafter. In particular, experimental studies of welfare-to-work initiatives carried out by the Manpower Demonstration Research Corporation (MDRC) showed that low-income preschoolers whose mothers were exposed to welfare-to-work reforms fared no worse than other children and actually had better cognitive outcomes if their mothers' programs included earnings supplements that boosted family incomes along with employment. But this pattern of results does not hold up in the school-age years.

Detailed analyses of the MDRC data suggest that the effects of maternal employment vary a good deal, depending on the child's age. The same types of programs that had positive effects on school achievement for children who were aged two to five at the time of the experiment turn out to have no effect on school achievement for children who were aged six to nine when their mothers were encouraged to work and negative effects on school achievement for children who were aged ten to eleven. These adverse effects for ten- to eleven-year-olds may reflect the more difficult school situation that they are in (since many of them are making the transition from elementary to middle school) or may reflect different demands placed on them within the family (if for instance they are being asked to babysit younger children or help with work around the house).[20]

Observational studies examining the effects on children's cognitive development of parental employment in the school-age years typically find no significant effects.[21] For instance, a study of children from the NLSY-CS examined cognitive outcomes (math, vocabulary, and reading scores) at age ten and eleven and found negative effects of full-time maternal employment that occurred in the first three years but no effects of maternal employment that occurred from age three onwards.[22] This absence of effects may indicate that parental employment in the school-age years does not matter or that it has countervailing effects that offset each other. That is, parental employment might benefit children's school achievement by raising family income and resources available to support the child's learning, but it might also reduce the time parents have available to monitor or help with homework, particularly if parents are working during the evening or at night.[23] Thus, the net effects could be zero.

It is also possible that parental employment is beneficial for some groups of children but not for others, and that these effects offset each other. Some support for this conclusion is found in studies that analyze children separately by gender. Such studies have tended to find that school-age girls have higher aspirations and do better in school when their mothers are working, in contrast to school-age boys, who often do worse in school when their mothers work.[24] The study discussed above, of ten- and eleven-year-olds in the NLSY-CS, found such gender differences: boys whose mothers had worked full-time during the first nine years of their life scored significantly lower on both reading and math, but girls did not.[25] We do not know what explains these gender differences. It may be that boys are more affected by their mother not being available after school or that girls are equally affected but also gain (in a way that boys do not) by having a working mother as a role model or by having their father (when present) more involved.[26]

Social and Emotional Development

As we saw in the prior chapters, externalizing behavior problems have been linked with full-time maternal employment in the first year of life as well as with long hours in low-quality child care. However, this finding is specific to the early childhood years. Studies of school-age children have generally not found links between parental employment and more externalizing behavior problems or have found that such links are due to the effect of maternal employment earlier in the child's life.[27] Some studies have found that parental employment is associated with better behavior. For instance, among ten- and eleven-year-olds in the NLSY-CS, those whose mothers worked when they were aged three and older had significantly fewer behavior problems (and on this outcome, there were no significant differences in effects between boys and girls).[28] One possible explanation is that working mothers may parent their children differently than stay-at-home mothers. For instance, one in-depth study of third- and fourth-graders found that employed mothers were less coercive and more openly affectionate than stay-at-home mothers and that these aspects of parenting were linked to their children's better social adjustment.[29]

Observational studies have also examined the links between parental employment, parental mental health, and children's social and emotional adjustment. These studies tend to find that parents who are working are in better mental health, are less harsh, use more effective types of discipline in their parenting, and have children who are rated by teachers as being better adjusted and better behaved.[30] However, it is difficult to ascertain from these studies whether parental employment is causing the improved child outcomes or whether the causality goes in the other direction (since parents who are in better mental health or have children who are better-adjusted may be more likely to work) or whether they are due to some other factor that is not controlled for in the study design.

There has also been a good deal of research on parental stress and on the extent to which stress or satisfaction at work "spills over" to affect families at home.[31] Although this literature finds that parents are affected by how stressful or satisfying their jobs are, these effects do not always spill over to children. Where effects are found, they seem to work through parents' interactions with their children and, in particular, through the warmth or harshness of those interactions. For instance, one classic study of air traffic controllers with four- to ten-year-old children found that on the days when work was more stressful, these fathers were more withdrawn and less warm with their children.[32] There is also evidence that parents who have more complex and challenging jobs and jobs that offer more scope for autonomy interact in a more positive way with their children.[33]

What Parents and Children Say

Another way to assess the effects of parental employment is to ask parents and children what they think about parents' working. There are, of course, many problems with this approach—parents and children may be reluctant to say they are unsatisfied with their current arrangements or may, on the contrary, be unrealistic and say they want something that is not attainable. Nevertheless, parents' and children's reports can tell us something about what goes on within families when parents work and how parents and children feel about that.

Do parents and children wish they had more time together? Surveys dating back to the 1970s do find working mothers and their school-age children complaining that they do not get to spend enough time with each other.[34] Fathers are not always included in these surveys, but when they are, fathers and their children also say they don't get enough time together. Indeed, working fathers if anything are less satisfied with the time they have for family than working mothers are, with 64 percent of fathers of children aged eight to twelve in a recent nationally representative survey conducted by the Families and Work Institute saying they have too little time together, compared to 31 percent of mothers. Children in the same survey report lower levels of dissatisfaction but also are more dissatisfied about time with fathers, with 29 percent saying they have too little time with their fathers, compared to 24 percent saying they have too little time with their mothers.[35] These differences make sense, given that children really do spend less time with their father: among eight- to twelve-year-olds, 40 percent spend two hours a day or less with their father; 31 percent, three or four hours a day; and only 30 percent, five or more hours a day—versus 29 percent spending two hours or less a day with their working mother; 23 percent, three to four hours; and 45 percent, five or more hours.[36]

It is also clear that time matters. Children whose parents spend more time with them rate their relationship more positively.[37] But this does not mean that children wish their parents would not work or see work as harmful. When children are asked what one thing they would like to change about their parents' work, having their parents cut back is not the first answer they give. Children wish their mothers and fathers could earn more money and be less stressed and tired by work. Only 15 percent wish their father would alter his work to spend more time with them, while 10 percent wish their mother would.[38]

Although it may seem puzzling that children would like more time with parents but don't wish for parents to cut back on work, the answer may lie in the fact that children wish for more time with parents even when parents do not work. The share of children who say they have too little time with their mother is the same whether or not the mother works.[39] And according to children's reports, whether their mother works does not affect how close they feel to her. When children are asked whether their parents make them feel important and loved, spend time talking with them, or know what is really going on in their lives, the replies do not differ according to whether the mother works or whether she works full-time or part-time. Whether the father works does make a difference, with children feeling closer to fathers who do work.[40] This latter finding is consistent with prior research showing that when fathers are unemployed, their relationships with their children are poorer.[41]

Children's reluctance to suggest that their parents cut back may also reflect their acceptance of parental work as a reality and, in most families, a financial necessity. Children do express concern about their parents being stressed and tired. It is telling that when children are asked to grade their parents, they give them the lowest grades on how well they are able to control their tempers—giving 41 percent of mothers and fathers a grade of C or lower.[42] Parents concur that they have trouble controlling their tempers, and some also report problems with feeling stressed, rushed, or unfocused in their interactions with their children; indeed, among employed parents of eight- to twelve-year-olds, 38 percent say the time they spend with their child is typically rushed.[43] Parents who report having problems with feeling rushed or stressed also report that their children have more behavior problems.[44]

The share of parents who feel stressed or rushed may be rising over time, as parents increasingly are juggling other tasks while spending time with their children. In 1975 parents reported doing something else for about a third of the time they spent with their children, but nowadays that share is closer to two-thirds.[45] The share of parents who feel they are working too many hours is also increasing. In the 1997

Families and Work Institute survey, more than 60 percent of parents said they would like to cut their work hours, compared to fewer than 50 percent in 1992; over the same time period, the number of hours that the average parent wanted to cut back rose from five hours per week to nine or ten.[46]

The parents who are most likely to report feeling rushed or stressed are those who work long hours but also those who work nonstandard hours (hours that include evenings, nights, or weekends) and those who do more work at home before and after their regular work day. This group is not necessarily in the worst jobs—indeed, those who find their jobs particularly rewarding and challenging and who report having the most autonomy are among the most likely to bring work home and to report feeling pressured at home. To the extent that more parents fit into these categories—as more parents are working in long-hours jobs, working nonstandard hours, and bringing work home—these results suggest that family life is becoming increasingly pressured for families with school-age children and that this may be particularly problematic in families where parents work in professional jobs to which they are highly committed. Indeed, these parents may experience some of the most stressful situations, as higher standards for parenting in middle-class families conflict with higher standards for commitment to professional jobs.[47]

꘍ IN SUM, the research on school-age children suggests that the effects of parental employment may be very different in these years than in early childhood. In the health area, we find few effects of parental employment on school-age children, with the exception of an elevated risk for obesity, but this risk may be stronger earlier in childhood than in the later school-age years. In the cognitive area, the main finding is the lack of overall effects in the observational literature, although with some evidence of adverse effects for older school-age children in the welfare-to-work experiments; however, when boys and girls are analyzed separately, it appears that boys but not girls may be at risk of poorer school achievement when their mothers work full-time. In the social and emotional area, we find no overall effects of parental employment, for boys or girls.

When we look at what parents and children say, we find both parents and children saying they wished they had more time together and families feeling stressed and rushed. However, children whose parents do not work wish for more time with them too. And on the plus side, children whose parents work also report benefits; they recognize the economic value of work and the other benefits it brings. There is no evidence in children's or parents' reports of major concerns about parents' working, although it is notable how many parents, and in particular fathers, wish they could spend more time with family.

The absence of strong effects of parental employment in the school-age years should perhaps not be surprising. Families actively adapt to parents' employment, adjusting their other activities and bringing in extra resources to compensate for the things that working parents cannot do themselves.[48] It is also likely that whatever effects parental employment does have will vary, depending on who is caring for the child while the parent is at work and the quality of that care. We turn to that question next.

Current Care Arrangements

Although schools provide a substantial amount of care and supervision for children while their parents are working, schools do not cover all the hours that parents are at work. If parents work nine to five, and commute an hour each way, the school session covers roughly six of those ten daily hours, but that leaves four hours uncovered before or after school every day, plus uncovered school vacations and summers. If parents work nonstandard hours—during evenings, nights, or weekends—schools cover an even smaller share of their work time. So who is caring for school-age children during the hours when they are not in school and their parents are working?

Self-Care

The best source of data on children's care arrangements comes from the Survey of Income and Program Participation (SIPP). These data, shown in Tables 4.1 and 4.2, indicate that the out-of-school care arrangements of school-age children are very different from those of preschool-age children and become progressively more so as the children age. The most striking change is in the share of children spending any time in self-care—a category that is used to denote a child spending time without adult supervision. The share of six- and seven-year-olds whose parents report that they spend time in self-care is very low—between 1 and 3 percent—whether or not the mother is working. However, the share of children in self-care increases very dramatically as children age, and this increase is faster if mothers are working. On average, children whose mothers are employed enter self-care about a year earlier (as shown in Table 4.1, the rates for children of working mothers at each age are comparable to the rates for children of non-working mothers who are a year older). As a result, overall rates of self-care are higher when mothers work.

As might be expected, rates of self-care are also higher when mothers are working full-time as opposed to part-time, and when they are working a day shift as opposed to an evening or night shift; rates of self-care are also higher when the mother is divorced, separated, or widowed.[49] However, perhaps contrary to what we might expect, self-care is more common among more affluent families. The share of school-age children of employed mothers spending time in self-care rises from 5 percent in families with incomes below $18,000 to 14 percent in families with incomes above $54,000.[50] Self-care is also more common in rural or suburban areas than urban areas.[51] These patterns suggest that families are more likely to use self-care when they feel their neighborhoods are safe.[52]

These figures probably understate the numbers of children who spend at least some time on their own after school.[53] Parents are understandably reluctant to tell an interviewer that their child spends time home alone. Parents may also forget what arrangements they used or may not view self-care as a regular arrangement that should be mentioned. Surveys that ask children directly if they have spent any time on their own that day find much higher rates of self-care. One such study

Table 4.1. Percentage of children in "self-care," by age of the child and employment status of the mother

Age:	6	7	8	9	10	11	12
Mother employed	2	2	5	8	13	18	29
Mother not employed	1	3	3	4	7	12	17

Source: Author's calculation, using data from the Survey of Income and Program Participation 1996 Panel, wave 10 (spring 1999), as shown in Blau and Currie (in press), Table 4. "Self-care" refers to children who spend any time without adult supervision during their out-of-school hours during a typical week.

Table 4.2. Primary out-of-school care arrangements of school-age children, by employment status of the mother: percentage of each age group in various forms of care

A. Mother employed	Age:	6	7	8	9	10	11	12
Parent		36	36	39	38	41	37	38
Relative		27	32	32	33	32	38	44
Center or organized activity		21	20	17	15	18	17	13
Nonrelative		16	12	12	14	9	8	5
Total		100%	100%	100%	100%	100%	100%	100%

B. Mother not employed	Age:	6	7	8	9	10	11	12
Parent		71	77	70	75	69	68	65
Relative		15	12	14	14	18	20	24
Center or organized activity		12	9	14	10	12	10	9
Nonrelative		2	2	2	1	1	2	2
Total		100%	100%	100%	100%	100%	100%	100%

Source: Data from the Survey of Income and Program Participation 1996 Panel, wave 10 (spring 1999), as shown in Blau and Currie (in press), Table 2. Data refer to primary child care arrangements for children whose mothers are employed (Panel A) or not employed (Panel B). Parent refers to care by the mother or father, or no regular child care arrangement. Relative refers to care by a grandmother, sibling, or other relative. Nonrelative refers to care by a babysitter, nanny, or other person not related to the child. Center or organized activity includes child care centers and after-school programs.

found that 26 percent of third-graders (eight- and nine-year-olds) and
54 percent of fifth graders (ten- and eleven-year-olds) were alone at
some time after school on the day of the survey.[54] Similarly, a study that
asked both about regular self-care and occasional self-care found that
although only 8 percent of third-graders were in self-care on a regular
basis, 49 percent were on their own occasionally.[55]

Is self-care at this age a good thing? Children in this age group increasingly want independence and enjoy spending time on their own or
with peers, and they may balk at attending activities that they find boring or childish. Parents also want children to become independent and,
as a practical matter, may not be able to arrange or afford supervised activities that cover all of a child's out-of-school time and that are interesting and age appropriate.

Yet parents also worry about their children taking on too much responsibility too soon or getting into trouble if they are left too much on
their own or with friends. Experts worry too. Many make a connection
between children being unsupervised after school and the jump in juvenile crime rates in the after-school hours.[56] Unsupervised children
may also be at higher risk of experimenting with drugs, alcohol, tobacco, and sex, particularly as they approach the teen years.[57] And there
may be consequences for children's school achievement, particularly in
this era of increased accountability and high-stakes testing, if they do
not receive adult supervision and help with their homework.[58]

What does the research tell us about the effects of self-care on children's outcomes? Observational studies tend to suggest that children are
more likely to get into trouble if left on their own and are more likely to
have behavior problems, but such studies cannot tell us whether self-
care is causing the problems or is just associated with them (perhaps because the children had more problems to start with or are experiencing
other problems in their families or schools).[59] One study that addresses
the causality question by using family fixed effects (comparing siblings
who have been in self-care to those who have not, in analyses of ten- to
fourteen-year-olds from the NLSY-CS) still finds that children in self-
care get into more trouble (e.g., are more likely to skip school, use alcohol or drugs, or have stolen something or hurt someone).[60] Results for
children's cognitive outcomes have been less consistent. Although some
studies have reported poorer grades or school achievement for children
who spend time in self-care, others have found no effects.[61]

It is important to keep in mind that self-care includes two different types of arrangement. One is allowing children to stay home alone (or with siblings), perhaps with a parent checking in by phone and often with strict instructions as to what they may and may not do. The other is allowing children to "hang out" with peers, whether at someone's home or in the neighborhood. It stands to reason that the effects of self-care would vary depending on whether a child is at home, possibly under some form of monitoring or supervision even if only by phone or whether the child is spending unsupervised time with peers, who may offer inducements to get into trouble. And in fact, the research finds just such differential effects. For instance, one study found that children had more behavior problems if they spent more unsupervised time with peers after school, particularly if they were not closely monitored by parents and lived in risky neighborhoods but not if children spent time alone (or with siblings) after school or spent supervised time with peers.[62] Another study found that children who spent more time alone after school were more likely to develop depression, while children who spent time unsupervised with peers were at risk of lower grades and more behavior problems.[63]

So there are clearly costs associated with children caring for themselves, particularly if they are spending unsupervised time with peers. But parents and children also benefit. For parents, self-care may be the key to being able to hold down a full-time job without facing prohibitively high child care costs. Children may enjoy being able to fend for themselves and not having to be picked up by a babysitter or to participate in a boring after-school program. We need to learn more about these costs and benefits before we rush to judgment about whether too many children are in self-care too early and whether they would be better off in some other form of care.

The evidence we do have on the effects of self-care, particularly when it involves young children spending unsupervised time with peers, is worrying. But it is also likely that the effects of self-care will depend on what the alternative is—that is, on the type and quality of the care or activities the child would have been in if she or he had not been in self-care.

Parents as Caregivers

So what are the options for supervised out-of-school care for school-age children, and how widely used are they? If we use the SIPP data to identify whether children's primary care arrangement in their out-of-school time is with a parent, relative, or nonrelative or in a center or organized activity, we find that for most of the school-age years, parents are the single most important form of care for children with working mothers, identified as the primary form of care for roughly 40 percent of children (see Panel A, Table 4.2). We need to view these numbers with a bit of caution, because they do not tell us how actively involved parents are with their children during these hours and also because parental care includes children whose parents reported no regular child care arrangement, but nevertheless these numbers suggest that parents play an important role in out-of-school care in families where mothers work, although not as important as in families where the mother does not work (see Panel B of Table 4.2). More detailed data (not shown in Table 4.2) indicate that parents are most likely to provide care themselves when two parents are present and can share care or when one parent is working part-time.[64]

Theory and research on the importance of parental involvement and monitoring suggests that there would be benefits to children of having a parent home with them after school. However, there is little direct evidence on this point. There are also costs associated with parents' providing care themselves, and parents pay those costs, by shifting their work hours or reducing their time at work. Currently, there is no subsidy for the cost of that care.

Relatives as Caregivers

Relatives (whether grandparents or other relatives, including siblings) are another important source of care for school-age children with working mothers, serving as the primary form of care for roughly 30 percent of these children between the ages of six and ten, and 44 percent by age twelve. Relatives are also involved in caring for children whose mothers are not employed, but to a much lesser extent. More detailed data (not shown in Table 4.2) indicate that grandparents' role declines as children age, while other relatives, such as siblings, become more important.[65] Care provided by grandparents or other adult relatives may be subsidized for low-income families, so long as the relatives meet all applicable requirements, but care by siblings is not.

We know relatively little about the impact of care by grandparents or other relatives on children's outcomes in the school-age years. (Care by siblings is often included in studies of self-care.) The impact of relative care is likely to depend a good deal on the kind of care that the relatives are providing—whether they are taking children to softball practice or piano lessons, providing supervision and a healthy snack while children do homework, or letting them watch TV and eat junk food. Relative caregivers of school-age children have not been studied in the same way that caregivers of younger children have, so our knowledge of the quality of the care they provide is even more limited.

Nonrelatives as Caregivers

Nonrelatives (babysitters, nannies, and other nonrelated adults) play a fairly small role in caring for school-age children of working mothers and an even smaller role in caring for children when mothers are not employed. Care by nonrelatives, like care by adult relatives, may be subsidized if the family is eligible and if the provider meets the requirements. We know little about the effects of this type of care on school-age children's outcomes. As with relatives, the effects are likely to be dependent on the quality of the care provided, but we know little about the quality of care currently on offer.

Centers and Organized Activities

In recent years, there has been a good deal of interest in formal after-school programs. Yet centers and organized activities, a category that includes after-school programs as well as child care centers, are the primary form of care for a surprisingly small share of school-age children in their out-of-school hours, and this share declines as children age.[66] In families in which the mother is employed, this category is the primary form of care for 20 percent of six- and seven-year-olds, between 15 and 18 percent of eight- to eleven-year-olds, and only 13 percent of twelve-year-olds. Nevertheless, children whose mothers are employed are more likely to have a center or organized activity as their primary form of care than children whose mothers are not employed (see Panel B of Table 4.2). Children whose mothers work also spend more hours in that care, an average of sixteen hours per week as compared to seven hours per week for children whose mothers do not work.[67]

These figures do not capture all the children who participate in a center or organized activity in their out-of-school time. Some children who have another form of care as their primary arrangement also participate in a center or organized activity at least part of the time. This is particularly true for children of employed mothers: in this group, 20 to 30 percent of those with another primary arrangement (parental care, relative care, or nonrelative care) also spend at least some time each week in a center or organized activity, in contrast to only about 10 percent for children of nonemployed mothers.[68]

The fact that so few children are in centers or organized activities is a function of several factors. One is cost. Most families whose children participate in after-school programs pay for those programs (roughly 75 percent of parents pay a fee when their children participate, and these fees typically cover roughly 75 percent of program costs), and these costs may be prohibitive for low- and even moderate-income families.[69] A related issue is ease of access. Programs may be located in different settings, and parents may not be available or may not have the transportation to bring children from place to place.

Another factor is children's preferences. One common finding in research on after-school programs is that by the age of eleven, children become less interested in the kinds of after-school programs they formerly attended and less willing to participate on a regular basis.[70] How much this is due to children's increasing maturity or to a mismatch between the programs offered and children's interests is not entirely clear. Many after-school programs are designed for younger school-age children (ages six to ten) and offer toys and materials (like Legos) most appropriate for that age group. Fewer programs offer activities designed to appeal to older children (activities like sports, theater, field trips, or science).[71]

Children participate at higher rates when programs offer them more choice and more grown-up activities. But, if programs are boring or pitched to younger children, school-age children will vote with their feet and spend more time at home, with family, or with friends. And, as children age, their parents are increasingly willing to let them do so. As we saw in Table 4.1, there is a steady increase in self-care as children age, as well as an increase in children being at home with parents or other relatives.

However, the fact that children stop attending formal after-school programs does not mean that they stop participating in activities. Rather, children increasingly participate in more individualized lessons or activities—like music or swimming lessons, individual tutoring, or sports teams.[72] The 2001 National Household Education Survey found that 31 percent of children in grades kindergarten to grade two participated in some kind of activity after school, with sports being the single most popular item (taken by 20 percent of children); this share rose to 41 percent of children in grades three to five, and grades six to eight, again with sports being the single most popular item (taken by about 30 percent of children). Nearly half of these activities are provided by children's schools, and the share of activities provided by the school rises with age—23 percent of participating children from kindergarten to grade two said the activity was provided by their school, as compared to 42 percent of children from grades three to five, and 66 percent of children from grades six to eight.[73] Thus, for many children, schools are an important provider of activities, above and beyond formal after-school programs.

It is also true that many activities are offered outside school, on a privately paid basis, and more-affluent children are much more likely to take part in such activities than low-income children, whose parents are less likely to be able to afford them or to be available to take their children to them.[74] More-affluent families are also more likely to sign their children up for a large number of activities, again because they are more able to afford it but also because they are more likely to see a full set of activities as important for children's development.[75] Although some private programs do offer scholarships or sliding scale fees, the majority do not. The 1991 National Study of Before and After-School Programs found that only 15 percent of for-profit providers set lower fees for low-income families, and even among nonprofit providers, only 30 to 40 percent did so.[76]

What do we know about the quality of after-school programs and their effects on child outcomes? Although we lack current, nationally representative data, the research we do have suggests that program quality varies widely, with staff tending to be poorly-paid and turnover rates tending to be high. Reflecting this varying quality, the research on the effects of after-school programs provides somewhat mixed results. Nevertheless, one generally consistent finding from observational studies is that school-age children who attend after-school programs tend to have better behavioral outcomes, particularly compared to children who spend time in self-care and particularly when children are from higher-risk groups (i.e., lower-income children, younger children, or those from urban or high-crime neighborhoods). Some studies have also found that boys seem to benefit more than girls.

These observational studies have not been able to control for the possibility that the children who participate may be different from those who do not; thus, the children may have had different outcomes even if they had not attended after-school programs.[77] More recent evaluations of specific programs, discussed later in this chapter, make some efforts to address this problem. Also noteworthy is a recent study of Canadian children that attempts to control for this selection problem by using family fixed-effects models, which compare outcomes for siblings who did or did not participate in programs.[78] This study found that low-income children benefited both academically and behaviorally when they participated in structured out-of-school activities, with the greatest gains for children who participated in a mix of sports, clubs, and lessons, although other combinations of after-school activities were also beneficial. The key element seemed to be participation in a team sport, which provides children a sense of athletic competence, skills in regulating their behavior and emotions, and links to peers and adult mentors.

After-school programs are funded with a variety of mechanisms. Funding has increased in recent years in response to growing concern about what children are doing in their after-school time and growing awareness of the role that after-school programs might play in boosting student achievement and preventing risky behaviors.[79] One of the largest funding streams is the 21st Century Community Learning Centers (21st CCLC) program, funded by the U.S. Department of Education, which began as a demonstration program with $1 million in federal funding in 1997, grew to $40 million in 1998, and was funded at a level of $1 billion in 2002. Programs funded by 21st CCLC dollars are located in elementary and middle schools and must include an educational component, such as providing space and support for children to do homework or to receive extra tutoring.

There are also numerous state-funded and locally-funded after-school programs, and these programs too are growing rapidly. California's Proposition 49, for instance, increased funding for out-of-school programs by over $400 million in 2004, while an earlier initiative by the city of Los Angeles (begun in 1988) devoted $10 million to after-school programs, including the highly rated LA's BEST (Better Educated Students for Tomorrow) program.[80] The city of Chicago has also invested heavily in after-school programming, opening programs that served close to one hundred thousand students in over three hundred schools in the late 1990s.[81] Foundations and nonprofit organizations have long played a major role in after-school provision, and they too have stepped up their efforts in recent years. For instance, the Soros Foundation committed $125 million over five years to The After-School Corporation (TASC) in New York City, while the DeWitt–Reader's Digest Fund spent $13 million on after-school programs in three major cities (Boston, Chicago, and Seattle).[82]

With these expansions in funding, after-school programs have become more widely available. There has been a particularly sharp growth in programs based at schools. The share of public schools that offer an extended day program—a program operated at the school that provides services to children before or after the regular school day—increased from 16 percent in 1988 to just under 30 percent in 1994 to nearly 50 percent in 2000; over the same time period, the share of private schools offering extended-day programs grew from 33 percent to 48 percent to 65 percent.[83]

The community sector continues to be actively involved in after-school programs. Many after-school programs (about 75 percent, as of 1991 when the last national study of before- and after-school programs was conducted) are not located in schools but elsewhere in the community. And many programs at schools are operated by, or in partnership with, community-based organizations (in the 1991 national study, this was the model used in about half the school-based programs). These programs often go beyond after-school programming to offer more comprehensive services to children and families. The well-respected New York City Beacon Schools, for instance, offer a host of activities and services for children and their families. These "lighted schoolhouses," which are often open thirteen to fourteen hours a day, seven days a week, are designed to be a safe haven and resource to families well beyond school hours.[84]

Evaluations of school-based programs are often very encouraging. The Chicago schools that expanded their after-school programming, for instance, saw improved scores in math (in thirty-nine of forty schools) and reading (in thirty of forty schools).[85] The LA's BEST program has been linked with better academic outcomes for children who participated the most actively.[86] Similarly, New York City's TASC program saw improved math scores for children who had participated the most over a two- or three-year period.[87] But in the absence of a controlled experiment, it is difficult to prove that the improved outcomes were caused by an after-school program and not by some other changes happening within schools or by other differences between participating students and those who did not participate at comparable levels.

The recent evaluation of the expansions of the 21st CCLC program is one of the few that has used a random assignment design.[88] Regrettably, however, this evaluation used random assignment for only a portion of the evaluation—the part studying elementary school-age children, but not middle school children. Moreover, there were several problems with the study that limited its ability to answer all the questions we might have hoped it would address. Most importantly, the survey questions about children's after-school care arrangements were not as detailed as they should have been.

Nevertheless, the results of the 21st CCLC elementary school random assignment evaluation offer some useful lessons. The first important—and surprising—finding is that the program did not substantially alter the share of children spending time on their own after school. Comparing children who were offered the program to control group children who were not offered a slot, the program increased the share of children being cared for at school by 10.5 percentage points, but it did so mainly by reducing the share of children being cared for by a parent (down by 7.4 percentage points). The remaining increase was accounted for by a decrease in children being cared for by a sibling (down by 2.7 percentage points). However, as mentioned earlier, the measures used in the evaluation were not sufficiently detailed, and some of the children reported to be in care with a parent or a sibling may have spent at least some time on their own, so the decrease in self-care could be larger than it appears to be.

The second important and surprising finding from the elementary school random assignment evaluation is that the 21st CCLC program increased parents' involvement with their children's schooling, as measured by attendance at school events and help with homework. This was not an intended outcome of the program and thus was an unexpected benefit. A third finding is a positive impact of the program on some but not all measures of student achievement. Students offered a chance to participate in a program had better grades in social studies and history. There was also a tendency for students to have better grades in math, English, and science, although these differences were not statistically significant. Teachers also reported that children were more likely to be trying hard in reading and math. However, on other academic outcomes, the evaluation found no significant differences.

So how should we read these results? My view is that given that the programs evaluated were in operation for a relatively short time, and that children attended on average only two days per week, the results are pretty encouraging. However, the programs did not achieve all the goals that we might have wished them to achieve. We need to keep in mind that the programs were mainly educational in focus. Thus, it is good news that they were at least somewhat effective in boosting student achievement and parent involvement in schooling. Whether they altered youths' risky behaviors is unknown. Nor is it clear whether these programs substantially altered the likelihood that children were on their own after school or with peers. The evidence suggests that the programs did not—rather, they got children to spend more time at after-school sessions, rather than at home with parents or siblings, and as educators had predicted, this did lead to better school achievement on some measures. The fact that the programs led to more parental involvement as well is an unexpected and important additional outcome. It may be that seeing their children be offered a special program and seeing their children put more effort into their school work in turn motivated parents to help out more.

Implications for Policy

Despite recent increases in interest and funding, a surprisingly large share of school-age children with working parents are not participating in out-of-school programs. Although children enjoy and benefit from having some unstructured time, whether on their own, with parents, relatives or other caregivers, or friends, children also benefit from having some involvement with after-school programs and activities, if those are of good quality and are pitched to their level and interests. Programs give them a chance to pursue and develop interests, to form relationships with supportive adults outside their family, or to get extra help with homework if needed. Programs can also be a place where children get important health-related information and support in making healthy decisions about sex, tobacco, and other substances.

Why don't more children participate? As we have seen, one hurdle is the often poor quality of after-school programs. In particular, there is often a lack of fit between school-age children's interests and the activities offered in programs. This mismatch results in low attendance rates, reducing the ability of programs to make a difference for children. A second hurdle is the difficulty that parents face in paying for care. Most programs rely heavily on parent fees, and these can be prohibitive for low- and even middle-income families. A third barrier is lack of access. Many communities do not have enough programs, and in others activities are often located outside school, which makes it difficult for children whose parents are at work and cannot transport them to attend.

Americans resoundingly support after-school programs, with 90 percent or more telling pollsters they think there should be organized activities or places for children and teens to go to every day that provide opportunities to learn. And 50 percent or more say they think there are not enough programs currently and that they would be willing to pay more taxes to support such programs.[89] Given this public support, what are the most fruitful directions for policy?

To address the three problems highlighted above and increase school-age children's access to high-quality out-of-school programs, I would recommend three steps: increasing quality of programs to better fit the needs of school-age children, providing further subsidies for programs for low- and middle-income families, and expanding programs located at or near public schools. However, these policy solutions take for granted that the current school calendar will remain the same. But is that the right assumption to be making? I would argue that we should also consider policies to extend the school day and year, as way to better meet the needs of children with working parents and other children as well. I discuss each of these policies below.

Improve Quality

As after-school programs have expanded, so too has interest in improving their quality. But efforts to improve quality face many challenges.

In some ways, after-school programs are like the elephant in the Indian fable, with some seeing the elephant as a trunk, others seeing a leg, and still others a tail. After-school programs, too, have many aspects. Some see these programs as educational, others see them as a forum for youth development, while still others see them as child care for children with working parents.

If we come back to the most important aspect of quality—whether care is sensitive and responsive to the needs of the child—we can see that some or all of these views could be correct, depending on the particular child. Some children need help with homework or extra tutoring several days a week, some want a safe and fun place to "hang out" from time to time or on a more regular basis, and others need extended care and a snack every day while their parents are at work. Whatever their needs, children will want a program that is not babyish or boring and that is safe and friendly. After school programs must be flexible enough to meet these varied needs.

Fortunately, there are many resources available to help states and localities looking to improve the quality of their after-school programs. Successful programs exist and can be used as models by other programs. The National Governors Association has a technical assistance project to help states develop higher quality.[90] The National School-Age Care Alliance has developed quality standards and an accreditation system as part of its efforts to improve quality.[91] And several research groups provide information about evaluations of after-school programs and best practices.[92]

Increase Subsidies

School-age children must compete with younger children, not just for the attention of their parents and policy-makers, but also for funding. Although federal and state child care subsidy dollars can be used to cover the costs of care for low-income children up to the age of twelve, the majority of those dollars go to cover the costs of care for children under the age of six.[93] Parents looking for help paying for after-school programs or activities encounter a bewildering array of programs, each of which has its own rules about subsidies and financial aid, with some offering no aid at all. Low-income families' interest in using programs is sensitive to how much programs cost.[94] Experiments with low-income families have shown that if families are given vouchers or other forms of assistance, they use them to sign their children up for out-of-school programs and activities, and their children benefit as a result.[95] Middle-income parents too say they would like more help covering the costs of out-of-school child care programs. If subsidies are flexible enough to allow families and children to choose the programs that best meet their needs and if they are tailored to quality programs, expansions would be worthwhile. In particular, expanded subsidies would help narrow the gap that currently exists between affluent children and low- and middle-income children, with the most well-off currently benefiting from private lessons and activities that other children cannot always afford.

There are two main ways to expand subsidies for out-of-school programs for school-age children. The first would be to increase funding through existing low-income child care subsidy programs, in particular the Child Care Development Fund. Such funding, however, would not help families above the cutoff for child care subsidies (typically, around 185 percent of the federal poverty line). Thus, to reach middle-income families, we should increase the amount that families can subtract from their taxes through the Child and Dependent Care Tax Credit. In 2003 a family could claim a maximum of $1,050 for one child or $2,100 for two children.[96] Raising the amount that families could claim would increase the resources that families have available to pay for out-of-school programs. As with child care for younger children, higher subsidies or credits could be provided for families using care of higher quality.

Locate Programs Strategically

Locating more programs at or near public schools is the surest way of enabling all students to attend them, whether or not their parents work or have a car or are available to chauffeur them after school. If programs are on school grounds (or within easy reach of school grounds, with transportation provided), children can go directly from school to program. This does not mean that programs have to be run by schools. On the contrary, many school-based programs are operated by community-based organizations, which use the school's space and run the program themselves. Locating programs at or near schools also does not mean that programs have to be primarily educational in focus. As we have seen, a good-quality program should offer lots of choice, including some activities that are educational, some that are more youth development oriented, and others that are more health or recreation oriented. There is also the question of how these strategically located programs should be funded. If they are dependent on parent fees, even their convenient location will not make them accessible to low- or moderate-income families. So expanded funding through direct funding sources such as the 21st CCLC program and state-funded after-school programs makes sense.

Extend the School Day and Year

American school children typically attend school for about six hours a day, 180 days per year. This schedule has not changed since public schools were founded nearly two hundred years ago. But the world has changed greatly in that time. We no longer live in a primarily agricultural society, and children no longer need to be home after school and in summers to help their families with the harvest. Nor do most families have stay-at-home parents who can care for children after school and during school vacations. At the same time, the material that children need to master to be full participants in society has grown exponentially.

A typical school in the United States is open thirty hours per week. Other nations tend to keep their schools open longer—thirty-seven hours per week in Luxembourg, forty-four in Belgium, fifty-three in Denmark, and sixty in Sweden.[97] And many countries have a longer school year. Children in Canada, the United Kingdom, Finland, and Norway go to school ten more days per year than children in the United States—an additional two weeks. Children in Denmark, Germany, and the Netherlands are in school twenty more days than the United States—an additional month. Children in Luxembourg have the longest school year—thirty-two days (more than six weeks) longer than in the United States. These countries tend to have shorter school vacations and, in particular, shorter summer holidays. We know from research that children lose ground over the long American summer holiday and that children from the lowest-income families lose the most ground.[98]

So there are good reasons to extend the school day and year. But is this really feasible? The many extended-schedule schools that exist already suggest that keeping schools open for longer days is workable. For instance, the City of San Diego has a "6 to 6" program "providing a safe place for children during the hours most parents work."[99] This extended–school day program, available to every elementary and middle school child in the city, includes activities such as tutoring, mentoring, and homework assistance, arts and crafts, performing arts, music and drama, sports, recreation, and snacks. Some school districts have also begun experimenting with longer school years. About a dozen states have passed legislation extending their school year, and others are developing year-round schooling models.[100] These are promising experiments and worth watching closely.

Looking Ahead

As we have seen, the school-age years are a time of fundamental growth and development and a window of opportunity—when children can flourish, gaining a sense of themselves and their place in the world, or flounder, starting to fail in their schoolwork or their lives outside school. The care they receive in these years will help set the stage for how they will do in adolescence and in their adult lives. Fortunately, the importance of the school-age years has now come to be more widely recognized, as has the need of school-age children for good-quality out-of-school programs. In this area, at least, the public is willing to spend more money on programs, and there are many examples of good programs to draw upon.

But what of adolescence? If the school-age years are a window of opportunity, the adolescent years are often viewed as just the opposite. What do adolescents need from their parents, and what can parents and others do to meet those needs when parents are working? Can teenagers just fend for themselves when parents work? If not, what kinds of programs make sense for them? We turn to these questions in the next chapter.

5

Adolescents

YOUTHS AGED THIRTEEN to eighteen become increasingly independent from their families but still need adult guidance, support, and monitoring. The notion that adolescents care only about themselves and their peers is a myth. Adolescents know what is happening with their parents and are influenced by it. When parents work, or change work, adolescents are affected—not only in terms of the supervision they receive but also in terms of what they may be asked to take on in the household. Adolescents are also affected by the emotional climate in the home and are keenly aware of financial stress.

Although adolescents spend increasing amounts of time on their own, with peers, or at their own jobs, they will also engage in school- or community-based programs if those programs are sufficiently tailored to their interests. Out-of-school programs can have important effects on outcomes for adolescents. Well-designed programs can promote school achievement and college enrollment and deter teen pregnancy and drug use. Poorly designed programs can actually lead to worse outcomes for youths. So getting programs right matters a lot. There is also now a substantial body of evidence about the effects of adolescents' own employment on their success in school and later life. We now have a clearer sense of when work is good for teens and when it is not.

This chapter considers the evidence on what adolescents need to support their healthy growth and development and successful transitions to adulthood, what parents can provide, and what others can and should provide. Policies considered in this chapter include school- and community-based activity programs as well as mentor programs.

What Adolescents Need

The adolescent years stand out as the period when humans grow and change more visibly than in any other period, except perhaps early childhood. The physical changes are very striking, as girls and boys go through puberty and are transformed into young women and men. The biological changes associated with puberty prepare youths to be sexually active and are also linked to changes in cognition and social and emotional development.[1]

Adolescence is also a period of tremendous psychosocial growth and change. In the life cycle model of Erik Erikson, the developmental task for adolescence is to develop a sense of mastery, identity, and intimacy.[2] Thus, adolescence is a time when young people are thinking not just about relationships but about their competence on a number of dimensions and about their future place in society. Through their studies in school and their experiences outside school adolescents have the opportunity to master new skills and to identify a future career path.

Adolescence is a period of opportunity but also of risk.[3] In the health domain, behaviors adopted in the adolescent years can influence the course of health for many years to come. Nutritional habits set in adolescence can lay the groundwork for a lifetime of healthy eating or poor nutrition and obesity. It is of concern that nutritional habits seem to worsen in adolescence. The number of youths eating five or more servings of fruit and vegetables a day declines from ninth to twelfth grade, as does the number drinking three or more glasses of milk.[4]

Likewise, patterns in exercise in adolescence can lay the groundwork for levels of physical activity in adulthood and later life. Here, as well, healthy behaviors decline in these years, with the share of youths who participate in vigorous physical activity three or more days per week falling from 69 percent in ninth grade to 55 percent in twelfth grade.[5] The combined effects of poor nutrition and too little exercise can be seen in the record-high rates of obesity, with 30 percent of high schoolers either being overweight or at risk of becoming overweight.[6]

Among the risky behaviors that become particularly salient in adolescence are smoking, use of alcohol or drugs, sexual activity, criminal involvement, and injury or suicide. Half of all adolescents try smoking cigarettes at least once by ninth grade and a quarter are currently smoking in twelfth grade.[7] Taking up smoking after adolescence is rarer— so in this sense, adolescence is a particularly risky period. The use of alcohol or illicit drugs follows a similar pattern, with many youths trying alcohol or drugs at least once by high school and a substantial number using alcohol or drugs heavily or on a regular basis. Two-thirds of ninth-graders have tried alcohol, and a fifth have had at least one episode of heavy drinking (defined as five or more drinks in a row) in the prior month; these figures rise to 83 percent and 37 percent by twelfth grade.[8] Nearly a third of ninth-graders have tried marijuana, with nearly 20 percent having used it in the past month; these figures rise to one-half and one-quarter respectively by twelfth grade.[9] Youths who have not used alcohol or drugs by the age of eighteen are much less likely to do so in adulthood than youths who used these substances before the age of eighteen. And youths who use alcohol or so-called soft drugs (such as marijuana) are more likely to go on to use harder drugs in adolescence or later years.[10]

Alcohol and drugs not only pose a direct risk to health and development but also are associated with higher rates of other risky behaviors. Although it is hard to know which causes which (or whether in fact some third factor causes both), it is known that youths who use tobacco, alcohol, or drugs are also more likely to be sexually active, to be involved in crime, and to be at risk of injury or suicide. In some cases, the direction of causality is clear. For instance, drinking is linked to higher injury rates in large part because of the risks associated with drinking and driving, which a worryingly large share of youths engage in, with a third of twelfth-graders saying they have been in a car with a driver who has been drinking and a fifth saying they have driven after drinking themselves.[11]

Early sexual activity is risky for adolescents' health in that it may expose them to sexually transmitted diseases, including HIV infection, and also carries with it the risk of teen birth, which is associated with worse outcomes for the resulting child as well as the teen parents themselves. One-third of ninth-graders report that they have had sexual intercourse, with this proportion rising to 62 percent by twelfth grade.[12]

Rates of condom use are high, with 60 to 70 percent of youths who are sexually active saying they used a condom the last time they had intercourse, but more worryingly, some youths report using no form of birth control or having had multiple partners.[13]

Criminal involvement too, although primarily of concern because of its social consequences for the youth and his or her victims, is also of concern on health grounds, because of the risks it poses to the youth and the victims. Criminal involvement escalates sharply in early adolescence, as does possession of weapons. By ninth grade, a quarter of boys report that they have carried a weapon at least once in the past month, and 10 percent report having carried a gun.[14]

Adolescence is also a period of heightened risk for mental health problems, including suicide. Rates of depression are sharply higher in these years than earlier in childhood, with nearly 30 percent of high schoolers saying they have felt sad and hopeless for two or more weeks and 15 percent saying they have seriously considered suicide in the past year.[15] Later adolescence (and young adulthood) is the time when schizophrenia and other major mental illnesses first appear, although thankfully these affect only a small number of youths.

Cognitive development in adolescence has, until fairly recently, received less attention than in the earlier parts of childhood. However, we now understand that adolescence is a period of rapid and important cognitive development, in particular with regard to higher-order thinking and abilities related to inhibition and control.[16] We also know that there are some cognitive tasks that can rarely be done before adolescence—thus, there is a reason that higher-order math is almost never taught before these years. We also have come to understand that brain development underlies some of what are seen as the developmental challenges of adolescence. Youths at this age are famous for ignoring the potential consequences of their actions and seeing themselves as invulnerable. We now know that the capacity to see and understand risks and to inhibit behavior to take them into account grows during these years; in this sense, the brain of a twenty-one-year-old really is different than the brain of a thirteen-year-old.

As in other parts of childhood, but perhaps to an even greater extent, in adolescence there are many links among the three domains of development. As already discussed, there is a fairly close link in adolescence between health behaviors and outcomes and social and emotional ones.

Health and social and emotional development are in turn linked to cognitive development and in particular to success or failure in school. Youths who are involved with alcohol or drugs are less likely to keep up with their schoolwork and are more likely to drop out. But, again, teasing out what came first is challenging. So too in examining the links between whether adolescents work and how they fare in other domains. Adolescents who commit long hours to work tend to be less engaged in school, to be at greater risk of behaviors such as smoking, drinking, and using drugs, and to have poorer relationships with their parents—but sorting out whether the employment is causing the problems or vice versa is difficult.[17]

The Role of Parents

Many parents of adolescents feel that they have little influence over their children, but the evidence strongly suggests otherwise.[18] What parents do matters. Across a host of domains, the evidence is clear that youths fare better when they have a close relationship with their parents and feel they can talk with them openly.[19] Young people do spend less time with their parents in these years and their relationship changes, as youths become increasingly independent and autonomous. But time together still matters.

For example, youths do better when they live in families who have meals together on a regular basis.[20] Analyses of seventh- to twelfth-grade students (ages twelve to nineteen) from the National Longitudinal Study of Adolescent Health find that the share of youths who have dinner with their parents at least five times a week declines from 74 percent at ages twelve to fourteen to 61 percent at ages fifteen to sixteen and 42 percent at ages seventeen to nineteen. But for each of these age groups, having dinner together mattered: youths who ate dinner with their parents at least five times a week did better across a range of outcomes: they were less likely to smoke, to drink, to have used marijuana, to have been in a serious fight, to have had sex, to have thought about or attempted suicide, or to have been suspended from school, and they had higher grade point averages and were more likely to say they planned to go on to college. These differences held up even after controlling for other differences among families.

Why is having dinner together so important? Eating together is probably a pretty good indicator of a family in which parents and children talk to each other on a regular basis. The timing and location of those conversations are not written in stone—what is key is that parents are checking in with their children most days and allowing unstructured time to talk. Having the conversation over a meal helps but is not essential.

The research is clear that adolescents do better across a range of outcomes when parents are aware of their activities and keep tabs on them.[21] Parents are not the only influences, of course. During these years, other adults, such as teachers, coaches, and mentors, play an increasingly important role as sources of support and advice.[22] Parents and other adults also serve as role models; their choices about smoking, nutrition, exercise, or alcohol or drugs influence children's choices.[23]

Another important factor for adolescent outcomes is money. Youths who live in families with higher incomes have better outcomes on a host of dimensions, while youths fare less well on average if they live in families with low incomes or financial hardship.[24] Money matters in part because it allows families to buy more things for their children—better schools, better neighborhoods, more enriching activities, and so on. But it also matters in terms of the home environment. When money is tight, parents may be harsher or less engaged with their children, may argue more with each other, or may be more anxious or depressed, all of which can have adverse effects on the children. In addition, adolescents are more aware than younger children of their family's financial situation and may feel that strain and react to it.[25]

Effects of Parental Employment

The above discussion suggests that parental employment could matter a lot to adolescents, to the extent that it affects the time parents have for them, the quality of the relationship parents and children have, the quality of the home environment, and also the financial resources available to the family. Clearly, there will be trade-offs. A parent working longer hours will bring in more money, which could reduce stress and financial hardship and also could be used to pay for a move to a better neighborhood or school or to enroll the adolescent in beneficial programs; but this parent will also be away from home longer hours and possibly be less available to talk with the youth and monitor his or her progress in school and other activities. Adolescents whose parents work long hours may be called on to take on more adult responsibilities, which can help them become more mature and independent but which can also interfere with their schooling. So what does the research find?

Health

Studies of parental employment have tended not to focus on adolescent health, and so we know relatively little about the effects of parental employment on adolescent health. Studies that have looked at health-related outcomes such as drug or alcohol use or early sexual activity have tended to not find differences between adolescents whose parents work or do not work.[26] What seems more important to these outcomes, as we shall see later in this chapter, is what adolescents are doing while their parents are working and the extent to which their parents are monitoring their activities.

Cognitive Development

Here, as for other age groups, the strongest evidence comes from experimental evaluations of welfare-to-work reforms and low-income families. A series of such studies carried out by Manpower Demonstration Research Corporation (MDRC) has found generally positive effects of parental employment on cognitive outcomes for preschool-age children when that employment is accompanied by income gains, but some negative effects on school achievement for children aged ten to eleven.[27]

A comprehensive analysis by MDRC focusing specifically on adolescents (youths aged ten to sixteen at the time of the intervention and followed up to ages twelve to eighteen) found a pattern of significantly poorer school outcomes for youths whose mothers were exposed to the welfare-to-work reforms.[28] The most negative effects were found for adolescents who had younger siblings. These adolescents experienced the largest negative effects on school performance and receipt of special education services and were also more likely than youths from the control group to be suspended or expelled from school or to drop out of school. The fact that negative effects are strongest for adolescents with younger siblings suggests that these adolescents may be taking on more responsibilities, which in turn interfere with their schoolwork. Indeed, these youths were more likely to be babysitting younger siblings and less likely to be enrolled in after-school programs and activities themselves. They were also more likely to be employed and to work for longer hours. These additional responsibilities may not be harmful in and of themselves, but in these families who were moved from welfare to work, the responsibilities may be taken on to a greater extent and at an earlier age than they otherwise would have been, resulting in a developmental "mismatch," a case of too much, too soon.[29]

Observational studies of mostly middle-income families, in contrast to these experimental studies of low-income families, have tended not to find large negative or positive effects of parental employment on adolescents' school achievement. This absence of effects may reflect the fact that in most observational studies, parents have moved into employment voluntarily and, in many cases, have already been working for some time, so that their families have had time to adjust. As is the case in middle childhood, however, there is some evidence that mothers' employment is more beneficial for adolescent girls than for boys.[30]

Social and Emotional Development

The MDRC studies of welfare-to-work reforms did not collect as extensive data about youth behavior as they did for school performance, and results on the outcomes they did collect were mixed.[31] Of the six welfare-to-work programs for which data were available on adolescents' behavior problems, only two led to significant increases. Of the two programs with data on police involvement, one led to a significant increase. The only program that collected data on delinquent behavior and substance use found increased minor delinquent activity (like skipping school) and drinking once a week or more but no increase in major delinquent activity (like using drugs or weapons). So the effects here were smaller and less consistent than the effects on cognitive outcomes.

Observational studies too find mixed and not always strong links between parents working and socioemotional outcomes. Studies that compare adolescents with working parents to those whose parents do not work often find no significant differences in behavior problems or social adjustment.[32] However, adolescents have been found to be affected by problems associated with their parents' employment, such as work interruptions, job losses, changes in employment, or financial strain. A large amount of research dating back to the Great Depression has found that parents' problems associated with work can affect the way they parent their adolescents and can in turn affect the adolescents' adjustment.[33] And, like school-age children, adolescents may be affected by the nature of their parents' work and its influence on parents' interactions with them.

What Adolescents and Parents Say

Another way to approach the question of how parental employment affects adolescents is to ask adolescents and their parents directly, as researchers from the Families and Work Institute did.[34] As we saw in the results for school-age children in the preceding chapter, surprisingly few children in this nationally representative survey say they wish their parents would work less and spend more time with them, and children generally report feeling as close to parents who work as they do to parents who do not work. If we narrow the focus to adolescents, these results do not change. Adolescents give their parents poorer grades than younger children do, but those grades are not affected by whether their mothers work or work full-time, and fathers who work are actually rated higher than fathers who are not employed.[35]

Nevertheless, adolescents' reports do point to some potential problem areas. As we have seen, family meals have been found to be an important protective factor for a host of adolescent outcomes. Yet, only a third of adolescents aged thirteen to eighteen say they eat dinner with a parent every day.[36] Similarly, many schools expect parents to be involved with their children's homework, yet only a third of adolescents say their parents ever do homework with them.[37] We should note that, in this survey, whether a mother or father worked did not affect the likelihood that they ate meals with their child or did homework together. Children whose mothers worked full-time did report that their mothers spent less time with them on weekdays, but working full-time did not affect the specific activities the mothers and children engaged in.[38]

Like younger children, adolescents report being concerned about their employed parents being tired or stressed and their lives being rushed. Nearly half also report feeling that children have to grow up too fast because of the pressures of parents' work and family lives; this sentiment is shared by their parents, who are even more likely (70 percent) to feel this way.[39]

* * *

ॐ THE EVIDENCE on the links between parental employment and adolescent outcomes suggests that these associations are likely to be complex. Adolescents are affected by what their parents do, and so to the extent that employment affects what parents do with their children, it will matter for their outcomes. Parental employment in the adolescent years has some effects on both socioemotional and cognitive outcomes. We know least about the links between parental employment and adolescent health.

The evidence we have reviewed suggests that to the extent parental employment does affect adolescents, these effects probably work through parents' interactions with their children and also through what adolescents are asked to take on while their parents are at work. But clearly adolescents' outcomes will also depend on what they do in their out-of-school time. We turn to that subject next.

What Adolescents Do in Their Out-of-School Time

Adolescents engage in a wide range of activities during the hours when they are not in school. What do we know about those activities and how well they meet adolescents' needs when parents are working? Here we will consider three major categories of activities: spending time alone or "hanging out" with peers; participating in extra-curricular activities (such as sports, music, or drama) at school- or community-based programs; and having paid employment.

Time Alone or with Peers

Estimates for the amount of unsupervised time that adolescents spend on their own or with peers vary. One recent report suggests that adolescents typically spend some twenty to twenty-five hours per week on their own.[40] Are adolescents with employed parents more likely to spend time on their own? The Survey of Income and Program Participation (SIPP) asks parents of children up to the age of fourteen about their care arrangements for out-of-school time, and those data suggest that children are more likely to be on their own if their mothers are employed. As we found for school-age children in chapter 4, adolescents enter self-care—unsupervised time on their own or with peers—at a younger age if their mothers work (see Table 5.1). Thus, 37 percent of thirteen-year-olds with employed mothers are in self-care versus only

23 percent of those with nonemployed mothers. The gap is narrower at age fourteen, suggesting that as children age, these differences fade.

Is self-care at this age harmful? Are adolescents spending too much unsupervised time on their own or with peers? These are hard questions to answer. Young people enjoy time on their own and with peers and do need some unstructured time to relax. However, too much unsupervised time can be harmful. Observational studies have found that adolescents who are on their own during the out-of-school hours are more likely to be sexually active, use alcohol and drugs, smoke, and be involved in violence or gangs.[41] They also have poorer diets, are less active, and are more likely to be lonely or bored, although other studies have found that they are on average as well-adjusted as youths who do not spend as much time alone.[42] However, given that these studies are observational, we cannot know for sure whether spending time in self-care is causing problems or whether the problems come from some other source.

Similarly, observational studies have found that children who spend more unsupervised time with peers are at higher risk of antisocial behavior, criminal involvement, use of drugs or alcohol, and early sexual activity.[43] Unsupervised time with peers is especially problematic when the peers are themselves involved in problem behaviors such as criminal involvement or drug or alcohol use.[44] But again, as these are cross-sectional studies, they cannot tell us the extent to which the problems are caused by too much unsupervised time with peers or other factors.

One finding that is clear from the research on adolescents' spending time alone or with peers is that even in these circumstances parents can make a difference, by knowing what their children are doing, where they are, and who they are spending time with. Parental monitoring is beneficial across all contexts but is especially important in high-risk environ-

Table 5.1. Percentage of 13- and 14-year-olds in "self-care," by employment status of the mother

	Age 13	Age 14
Mother employed	37	45
Mother not employed	23	40

Source: Author's calculation, using data from the Survey of Income and Program Participation 1996 Panel, wave 10 (spring 1999), as shown in Blau and Currie (in press), Table 4. "Self-care" refers to children who spend any time without adult supervision during their out-of-school hours during a typical week.

ments, where young people are exposed to more risky behaviors and more problematic peers.[45] Thus, youths whose parents work may be more at risk if they spend time on their own or with peers—and if their parents monitor them less closely. Parents' relationships with their children matter as well. Youths are more susceptible to being led astray by their friends if they have a poor relationship with their parents.[46]

Extracurricular Activities

As much as adolescents value time on their own or with friends, they will also spend time in structured activities if those activities are sufficiently tailored to their interests. When surveyed, adolescents say they want programs and activities that give them a chance to spend time in constructive activities with adults and other youths.[47] They also value programs that give them opportunities for leadership, community service, and links to paid employment.[48]

Estimates of youth participation in extracurricular activities at school- or community-based programs range widely, but recent surveys tend to find that half or more of youths participate in an out-of-school activity, whether based at school or in the community.[49] Youths are more likely to be involved in such activities when they come from higher-income families and live in more affluent communities.[50] One activity that seems to be particularly widely engaged in is sports. Half of high school girls (51 percent) and nearly two-thirds of high school boys (64 percent) say they have played on one or more sports teams in the past year. However, girls' participation declines over the high school years, from 55 percent in ninth grade to 46 percent in twelfth grade.[51]

Data from the SIPP, shown in Table 5.2, suggest that adolescents with an employed mother are more likely to be in a formal center or organized activity as their primary out-of-school arrangement than children whose mother is not employed. Nevertheless, few children in either group have a center or organized activity as their primary arrangement. This makes sense, since children in these years more typically do a variety of things in their out-of-school time, rather than attending the same program or activity every day.

Programs serving youths in their out-of-school time are very diverse, ranging from well-known community-based programs such as the Boy and Girl Scouts, Boys and Girls Clubs, and the YMCA and YWCA

Table 5.2. Primary out-of-school care arrangements of 13- and 14-year-olds, by employment status of the mother: Percentage of each age group in various forms of care

A. Mother employed	Age 13	Age 14
Parent	39	36
Relative	48	50
Center or organized activity	11	14
Nonrelative	2	2
Total	100%	100%
B. Mother not employed	Age 13	Age 14
Parent	61	60
Relative	31	32
Center or organized activity	7	7
Nonrelative	1	1
Total	100%	100%

Source: Data from the Survey of Income and Program Participation 1996 Panel, wave 10 (spring 1999), as shown in Blau and Currie (in press), Table 2. Data refer to primary child care arrangements for children whose mothers are employed (Panel A) or not employed (Panel B). Parent refers to care by the mother or father, or no regular child care arrangement. Relative refers to care by a grandmother, sibling, or other relative. Nonrelative refers to care by a babysitter, nanny, or other person not related to the child. Center or organized activity includes child care centers and after-school programs. Percentages do not always sum to 100 due to rounding.

to smaller, local programs. Some programs are based in schools, others in the community. Some serve youths in groups; others, such as Big Brothers Big Sisters, provide one-on-one mentoring. Programs also differ in their aims: they may be educational, recreational, oriented toward prevention of specific risky behaviors, or oriented toward positive youth development.[52]

The varied nature of programs makes it difficult to generalize about program effects. But looking across programs, a host of observational studies have found links between participation in extracurricular activities at school or in community-based programs and better outcomes for youths, such as positive identity, better relationships with peers and adults, better school performance, and reduced rates of dropping out, teen pregnancy, delinquency, drug use, and cigarette use.[53] However, sorting out the real effects of programs from differences that simply reflect the type of youths who participate is always a challenge. Not all programs are equally effective, and some programs actually lead to worse outcomes. In particular, if programs bring youths together with others who have antisocial values, and if youths with problem behaviors dominate the group, the end result can be to increase problem behaviors, not decrease them.[54] Thus, programs need to be careful about which youths they bring together and what norms the group communicates.

In recent years, as interest in out-of-school programs for youths has grown, so too has funding.[55] Funding for youth programs is provided by an array of federal agencies, including the Department of Labor (which primarily supports employment and training programs), the Department of Agriculture (which supports the 4-H program and also programs to provide meals and snacks to youths in other programs), the Department of Justice and Department of Health and Human Services (which primarily support prevention programs), and the Department of Education (which funds both educationally oriented and prevention programs). States and localities also spend substantial amounts on programs for youths, although the bulk of the after-school programs they support are targeted to elementary and middle school students, not adolescents. Foundations, as well as some private businesses, are also active in this area.

There has also been an expansion in program evaluation. We now have experimental evaluations on several youth programs—Big Brothers Big Sisters, the Quantum Opportunities Program, the I Have a Dream Program, and the Teen Outreach Program—and the results are encouraging.[56]

The Big Brothers Big Sisters program, as its name implies, assigns an adult to be a Big Brother or Big Sister to an at-risk youth. Big Brothers and Big Sisters act as mentors, meeting regularly with the youths, spending about a half day together three to four times a month. A random assignment evaluation found that youths who had been given a Big Brother or Big Sister when they were aged ten to sixteen had better school attendance and higher grades, were less likely to be involved in violence, were less likely to start using drugs or alcohol, and were more likely to trust and not lie to their parents. The largest impacts were seen for young people who had lower grades, poorer school attendance, or less family support to start with.[57]

The Quantum Opportunities Program offered ninth-grade students from low-income families a chance to participate in after-school educational and community service activities during the four years of high school, paying them for each hour they participated. Compared to the control group, youths who were randomly assigned to the program were more likely to complete high school and go on for further education. They also had fewer children and were less likely to be involved in crime.[58] Along similar lines, the I Have a Dream Program randomly selected low-income youths and offered them support to finish high school and go on to college. An evaluation of this program found that it too increased rates of high school completion, compared to schools not offered the program.[59] The Teen Outreach Program, a random assignment experiment that enrolled ninth- to twelfth-grade students in a program of volunteer service as well as weekly small class discussions, led to lower rates of school failure, school suspensions, and teen pregnancy.[60]

These experimental evaluations indicate that high-quality programs can improve outcomes for adolescents. And they indicate that there is not just one model that is effective. Successful programs have ranged from one-on-one mentoring to programs that focus on keeping youths on track academically to service-oriented programs that aim to improve social as well as educational outcomes. One likely mechanism through which these programs operate is helping young people develop positive relationships with trusted adults (as well as peers). Young people who have a good relationship with an adult (a mentor, coach, teacher, activity group leader) are less likely to develop problem behaviors. And having a good relationship with a mentor can help young people develop a better relationship with their parents as well (as the evidence from Big Brothers Big Sisters indicates).

Parents can make a real difference here. Parents can help guide and encourage their children to be involved in extracurricular activities and programs. Parents can also be involved in the programs themselves. When parents are involved with what their children are doing outside school, communication and trust between them are better.[61]

Paid Employment

Most adolescents work at least part-time during their out-of-school hours. Three-quarters of seventeen-year-olds have worked during the prior year; this percentage rises to 80 percent among eighteen-year-olds.[62] These youths are working pretty steadily, averaging thirty-three weeks a year among those both working and attending school.[63]

It is perhaps surprising that adolescents are more likely to work if their parents work.[64] This may be because parents who are working provide a role model or give adolescents access to contacts that help them find work. Or it may be that in communities where jobs for adults are scarce, there are fewer jobs for youths as well.

There has been an extensive debate about whether adolescents' working interferes with their school performance or leads to poorer outcomes in other domains.[65] Answering this question is difficult because the adolescents who work may be different than those who do not—they might be less engaged in school to start with, or, conversely, they might be better students. If studies simply look at the association between working and other outcomes and do not take this selection into account, results could be biased. Recent studies that have used more rigorous methods have tended to find negative effects of longer hours of work on school performance. For instance, one recent study, which used variation in child labor laws to adjust for selection, found that students who worked more hours in twelfth grade had worse math scores.[66]

If there are negative effects of adolescents' working on their school performance, these seem to be primarily for youths who work long hours—more than twenty hours per week. For these youths, the hours at work may directly compete with hours students could be spending on schoolwork. Studies have found that youths who work long hours in high school spend less time on homework, are more tired in school, and are more likely to be absent from school.[67]

At the same time, however, if employment is not for excessive hours, it can give adolescents valuable work experience as well as a chance to grow and mature, particularly if their job is a good one that offers a chance to develop valued skills.[68] In this respect, adolescents whose parents work may be advantaged, in that these young people may be more likely to get help from their parents to obtain good jobs. Working parents can also exert a positive influence on their adolescents' career choices, values, and attitudes toward work.[69]

Implications for Policy

We saw in the prior chapters that there have been expansions in recent years in programs that provide care, education, or activities for preschool and school-age children while their parents work. However, the same is not true of programs for adolescents. In part, this reflects the fact that adolescents are not seen as needing child care. For this reason, child care monies can, for the most part, not be used to offset the costs of programs serving youths aged thirteen or older. Youths in this age range, whether or not their parents are working, are served through a different set of school- and community-based programs.

The evidence we have reviewed suggests that adolescents would benefit from expanded access to high-quality out-of-school programs, whether or not their parents work. However, youths whose parents work may benefit to a larger extent than youths with a stay-at-home parent. As we saw, youths whose parents work spend more time on their own or with peers. If their parents continue to closely monitor their activities and maintain a close relationship, this unsupervised time will not pose a risk, but if youths are spending more time unsupervised and their parents are too busy to keep tabs on them and spend time with them, increasing access to structured activities and programs would be helpful. Here, I consider two ways to do so.

Changing the School Calendar

For the most part, efforts to extend the school day or school year are focused on somewhat younger children—children in primary school or middle school. The reform that has been most focused on adolescents has been scheduling the school day to start later in the morning. This reform is prompted not so much by parents' work schedules as by evidence on adolescents' sleep schedules.[70] Adolescents tend to stay up later and sleep later in the morning than younger children do, and some schools have begun experimenting with a later start to the school day to better capitalize on the hours when adolescents are most awake and ready to learn.

However, more dramatic changes to the school day could well be beneficial. American adolescents have more out-of-school time than youths in other countries and do not seem to spend it in a very productive manner, devoting relatively little time to completing homework and a more substantial amount of time to watching television.[71] Television watching peaks early in the high school years, with 41 percent of girls and 47 percent of boys saying that they watch three or more hours a day in ninth grade, but as late as twelfth grade, about 30 percent of boys and girls are still watching three or more hours a day.[72] This is a lot of time for young people to be sitting around, watching shows that typically have little educational content and that often feature heavy doses of sex and violence.

Adolescents could benefit from more time in school. In tests administered in thirty-nine countries in 2003, American eighth-graders were outscored in math literacy by students in twenty of the other twenty-eight advanced industrialized countries from the Organization for Economic Cooperation and Development (OECD) and three of ten non-OECD countries, and American eighth-graders were outscored in science literacy by students in fifteen OECD countries and three non-OECD countries. American eighth-graders scored even more poorly— outscored by students in twenty-two OECD countries and three non-OECD countries—in problem solving, an area that requires students to apply skills in reading, math, and science to solve real-world problems.[73] These gaps, if anything, widen during adolescence. In tests administered in the United States and sixteen other countries in both 1995 and 1999, American fourth-graders tested in 1995 scored at the international average in math and above average in science, but by 1999, when students were tested in eighth grade, their performance had fallen to below average in math and to just average in science.[74] In today's increasingly technological and global economy, such low levels of math and science attainment will place American youths at a disadvantage.

Any changes in the school day or year for adolescents would have to be coordinated with changes for younger children, so as not to disrupt families' schedules, particularly around the long summer vacation. But it may well be worth experimenting on a districtwide basis with having schools stay open for two to four additional weeks each year or for an additional half hour or hour each day.

Extending Access to High-Quality Programs

Ten years ago, when the Carnegie Council on Adolescent Development reviewed the evidence on programs serving youths, they lamented the state of the research on programs and called for more rigorous evaluations. Experimental evaluations, using random assignment methods, have now been conducted, and as we saw earlier, the evidence is encouraging. High-quality programs serving youths in their out-of-school time can be effective in promoting their development and in preventing them from engaging in problem behaviors. But as we also saw, access to such programs still varies, with higher-income youths more likely to participate in activities and programs after school. Thus, as we expand our investments in after-school and summer programs for school-age children, we should not forget the teens, who could benefit from these programs as well.

We should also bear in mind the evidence on teens' working, which suggests that work after school or in the summer can provide valued work experience, if the job provides an opportunity to learn skills and make productive connections with peers and adults and if the hours are not so long that they interfere with school. Many schools and communities already offer programs to help teens connect with good jobs, and these programs should continue to be supported. Programs that link teens with part-time jobs or summer internships that relate to their schoolwork and allow them to explore careers are likely to be particularly valuable.[75]

Looking Ahead

As we have seen, the needs of children change dramatically as they move from infancy and the toddler years, through the preschool years, and into middle childhood and adolescence. So too do the policies that would help meet their needs when parents are working. How do those pieces of the policy puzzle fit together? What would a package of supports to meet the needs of children when parents work look like? And what would it take to put such a package of supports in place, if not for our children, then for the children of tomorrow? The next chapter takes up these questions.

☞ 6

Where Do We Go from Here?

IN PRIOR CHAPTERS we have reviewed the evidence on how children fare when parents work and identified policies that would better meet their needs. Grounded in a developmental perspective, many of these policy recommendations are specific to particular age groups. But children, of course, do not come in just one age, nor do they stay that age forever. Families need a package of supports that meets the needs of children from birth onwards. In this chapter, we consider what such a package of supports would look like, how politically feasible it is, and what its costs as well as benefits would be. First, however, it is useful to reiterate the key values and principles that must be taken into account in formulating policy in this area.

Fundamental Values and Principles

As we saw in the Introduction, three core principles underlie our thinking about children, families, and parents working. The first is respecting choice. Because Americans value choice, particularly when it comes to the family and child rearing, policies should to the extent possible support families making their own choices about work and care arrangements. The second core principle is promoting quality. Americans care deeply about the well-being of children, but many children are in arrangements that are not of good quality. So raising the quality of care must be a priority. The third core principle is supporting employment. Not only is the work ethic a widely shared American value, but work is a financial necessity for most parents. In addition, supporting work is central to ensuring that women and men have equal opportunities. So policies to meet the needs of children should not discourage parents from working. Satisfying all three principles simultaneously can be difficult, and often trade-offs must be made. But it is crucial that we keep all three principles firmly in mind.

We also must be sure that the policies we select are a sound investment. There are really two issues here. The first is efficiency—making sure that policies represent a good return for our investments. The second is equity—making sure that policies promote equal opportunities or outcomes. Sometimes efficiency and equity are at odds, and policymakers will have to choose which to give more weight. In many cases, we lack hard evidence as to how the costs and benefits of programs stack up. But it is nevertheless important to keep these values and principles in mind, so that where there are trade-offs or uncertainties, the implications are considered.

A Package of Supports

The analysis in the preceding chapters led to a set of policy recommendations, some of which applied to families overall, others to families with children of a specific age. Can these policies be folded into a package of supports to better meet the needs of children when parents work? And can this be done in a way that satisfies our key principles—respecting choice, improving quality, and supporting parental employment—while at the same time improving efficiency and equity?

Policies for Children of All Ages

As we saw in chapter 1, dramatic changes in families have affected the availability of parents to meet their children's needs. More children are living with parents who work—whether these are single working parents or working couples—and fewer children have stay-at-home parents. However, our policies have not kept pace with these changes.

Employer policies make too little provision for workers who need flexibility to take care of family responsibilities, while public policies provide too little support for parents seeking to balance work and family.

In light of these changes in families, two key policy reforms would better meet the needs of children—across age groups—when parents work.

The first is giving parents more flexibility to take time away from work to take care of family responsibilities, through expanding family and medical leave rights and introducing the right to request part-time and flexible working. The 1993 Family and Medical Leave Act (FMLA) broke new ground by giving employees in medium- and large-sized firms the right to take up to twelve weeks of job-protected leave a year for urgent family or medical needs. However, the FMLA is limited in several respects: it covers only about half the private sector workforce, excluding those in firms with less than fifty employees; it makes no provision for paid leave and is thus unaffordable for lower-income workers; and it covers only a subset of the situations when parents need to take leave. To better meet the needs of children, the FMLA should be extended to cover all workers and to cover a broader range of family situations. In addition, a mechanism to provide paid leave for at least a portion of the twelve weeks should be identified, by requiring firms to provide pay or by establishing a social insurance fund. As discussed in chapter 1, I favor establishing a social insurance fund rather than requiring employers to replace wages, because a social insurance fund would impose fewer costs on employers (for whom even unpaid leave would require some adjustments, particularly in the case of small firms) and would also pose less risk of hurting the employment prospects of groups that employers think would be most likely to take such leave.

Expanding the FMLA would help parents meet the needs of children in emergencies, but parents also need more flexibility on an ongoing basis. For some families, the best way to meet a child's needs is for a parent to work part-time or on a flexible schedule. A resounding majority of employees—about 80 percent—say they would like to have more flexible work options and would use them if there were no negative consequences at work.[1] Yet such flexibility is not available in all jobs or to all workers. Although there may be limits to what can reasonably be offered, particularly in small firms, we have probably not yet reached those limits.

Instituting a right to request part-time or flexible hours, as European

countries have done, would help support parental employment while respecting families' choices about what mix of care is best for their children
and also respecting employers' right to refuse such arrangements if they
are not practicable in a given setting. However, if part-time and flexible
working is to be a real choice for parents, it must be compensated on an
equitable basis. In particular, part-timers should receive the same pay per
hour as full-time workers do, and employer benefit plans should not dis-
criminate against part-time workers but rather should provide prorated
time off, pensions, and other benefits as a function of the hours worked.

Such reforms would impose some costs on employers, but those
costs would be balanced by benefits in terms of increased employee satisfaction and productivity and long-term workforce stability. And the
reality is that the firms with which American companies are competing—in Europe and elsewhere—are already providing these types of
flexibility and benefits. This makes it hard to argue that American firms
would lose out in the global marketplace if they had to do so.

The second policy reform that would benefit working families with
children of all ages is breaking the link between work and essential family benefits, by providing some core benefits such as health insurance
through a social insurance program like Medicare rather than through
employee benefits. A parent's work choice should not be constrained by
the fact that cutting back hours, changing jobs, or taking a period of
time at home to care for a child will mean losing the family's health insurance coverage (or paying exorbitant fees on the private market).
Moreover, the current system is inefficient, since some families end up
with too much health insurance if both parents work. It is also inequitable, as dual-earner couples often have a choice of health plans,
while at the other end of the spectrum, single working parents and others in low-wage jobs struggle to afford premiums and co-payments and
worry about losing coverage if they change jobs.

Although low-income children are now guaranteed coverage in most
instances through public child health insurance programs, applying for
coverage and maintaining eligibility is hard for working parents, and
often the parents themselves are not covered. Yet when parents are not
covered, they are less likely to bring their children for needed care,
even if the children are covered. So, leaving parents uncovered or leaving their coverage to the whims of the private market is not only inequitable, but it also poses risks to children's health.[2]

A more sensible system would cover all children and parents through a social insurance program like Medicare and would remove the burden of health care coverage from employers and employees. Doing so would be more equitable and would also help make American firms more competitive in today's global marketplace, where they are competing with firms in other industrialized countries who do not have to pay the costs of private health insurance for their workers but rather can rely on the public safety net.

Another important missing piece in the United States is a basic income support for families with children. It was not until 2001 that the U.S. child tax credit was made refundable, so that it would be available to families with children even if they did not owe taxes, but the earnings threshold means that the lowest-income families are still not eligible. At the same time, the value of the credit was doubled, to reach $1,000 per child by the year 2011, but this amount remains very low relative to the costs of raising children and relative to what other countries provide. In my view, the child tax credit should be raised this year to at least $2,400 per child for all low- and moderate-income families (and raised regularly thereafter in line with inflation). This would provide a minimal amount of support—enough to replace what a parent would earn in six weeks if she or he worked forty hours per week at $10 per hour—to protect children from extreme hardship if a parent loses a job, leaves work, or cuts back on hours; at the same time, the support would not be so generous as to erode parents' incentives to work. As such, it would strike a balance between supporting employment, parental choice, and quality of care.

Policies for Families with Infants and Toddlers

The tensions between respecting choice, promoting quality, and supporting employment are higher in the first few years of life than at any other period. Infants and toddlers are uniquely vulnerable, and their parents face hard choices about working, using child care, or caring for the children themselves. Reflecting these tensions and what we know from research about how best to meet the needs of infants and toddlers when parents work, chapter 2 identified two priorities for policy reform.

The first is giving parents the option to spend more time at home in the first year of life. There are three key policies in this area: instituting a parental leave program that offers all new parents who worked prior to the birth a year of paid leave through the social insurance system, giving new parents the right to request to return to work part-time or to work flexible hours, and providing an at-home infant child care subsidy for low-income parents who do not qualify for parental leave.

Together, these supports would give parents the option to stay home for up to a year after the birth of a child but would not require anyone to do so; they would also give parents the option of part-time or flexible hours. As detailed in chapter 2, they would not place an undue cost burden on employers or society. A social insurance program similar to the one that went into effect in California in 2003 (but providing up to a year of paid leave rather than six weeks as in California) would cost $100 to $200 per year in additional payroll taxes per employee, a modest amount when compared to the benefits that would accrue to society in terms of child health and development. Giving parents the right to return to work part-time or to work flexible hours does not impose onerous costs on employers (who may refuse if the costs would be too high). Part-time work does, of course, impose costs on parents, who would forgo income, but at least some parents would prefer to have this option. And an at-home infant child care subsidy, if pegged to out-of-home child care subsidy amounts, does not cost any more than subsidizing a child being in out-of-home care but again may produce substantial gains in child health and development.

Another policy option for families with infants is an early childhood benefit, payable to all low- and moderate-income families with a child under age one. Such a benefit could be used to offset the cost of a parent staying home or the cost of purchasing high-quality child care and thus would respect parental choice and would not discourage employment, while allowing families to arrange higher-quality care. An early childhood benefit is a straightforward way to provide support to families with a young child, analogous to the child benefit or child allowance that many advanced industrialized countries provide to all families with children. In the U.S. context, such a benefit would be most similar to the child tax credit and would need to be coordinated with it, as well as with other cash benefit programs for children. If coordinated with other benefits, the cost would be relatively modest, on the order of about $225 million per year if limited to low- and moderate-income families with a child under one.[3]

A second priority is providing better-quality care for children whose parents work. Here, the most promising options are providing more support for parents to use high-quality care, tightening state regulations for infant and toddler care, and expanding the Early Head Start program. These steps would raise the quality of care without substantially limiting parental choice or discouraging employment. Indeed, these steps would help educate parents on standards for quality child care, so that they can choose wisely and see that the standards are met. Each of these options would raise the costs of care, whether those costs are paid by parents, subsidies, or direct government expenditures on programs such as Early Head Start. As we saw in chapter 2, these options would also yield benefits in improved child health and development.

These investments would be a more worthwhile way to spend child care dollars than the policies in place currently, which often result in parents and the government paying top dollar for care that is of poor or merely adequate quality. When we ask the question in this way—not just whether we should be spending money on child care for infants and toddlers but also how we should best invest the money that we are already spending on care for that age group—the conclusion that we should make sure we are investing in good-quality programs is clear.

Early childhood benefits, extended beyond the first year of life to children up to the age of three, are also an option here. The advantage of early childhood benefits is their simplicity and their support for parental choice. However, early childhood benefits are not the most direct way to improve child care quality for infants and toddlers. These benefits would have to be paired with other policies, such as tightening regulations, if we want to be sure that they affect quality of care; otherwise, parents might spend the benefits on more care or higher-priced care but not necessarily care of higher quality. Thus, although early childhood benefits for children beyond the first year of life may be justified on other grounds (i.e., as a form of income support for low- and moderate-income families), they are less advantageous than the other policies listed above, if our primary aim is to raise child care quality.

Policies for Families with Preschool-Age Children

As we saw in chapter 3, the major challenge in meeting the needs of three- to five-year-olds when parents work has to do with the uneven and often poor quality of care currently available to them. Thus, the key policy priority for this age group is improving the quality of care and education. This involves three key steps.

The first is improving care in the private market. This can be accomplished through quality-related rating and payment systems (that recognize and pay a higher price for higher-quality care) and through tighter regulations (that signal to both parents and providers what levels of care should be provided). So long as subsidies cover the cost of the higher-quality care for low-income families, these two policies together would not place unnecessary limits on families' choices but would raise the level of quality.

The second way to raise quality is to improve Head Start. As with improving care in the private market, this will require both raising standards and investing more money to allow programs to meet those standards. Investments to raise the educational level of teaching staff in Head Start and to expand health and education programming would be particularly worthwhile.

The third promising option to improve quality is to expand prekindergarten. These programs are proving to be some of the best-quality programs on offer, but only serve about one in six American preschoolers (as of 2003). Now is the right time to build on the lessons learned in the states that have pioneered these programs and expand them to serve more preschoolers. We can also build on the experience of other countries, such as Denmark, England, France, Italy, and Sweden, where publicly provided preschool is the norm. These programs, if voluntary, do not interfere with parental choice; on the contrary, they expand parents' choice set by giving them a high-quality option that may not currently exist in their community.

Good-quality care does not come cheaply. In this area, as in others, you get what you pay for. Center-based preschool costs families with working parents on average about $4,100 per year, but the price of care ranges widely, with prices as high as $20,000 a year or more in some urban areas.[4] State child care subsidy programs typically reimburse parents for a much lower amount (since they reimburse only a portion of costs and only up to a market rate that may be well below the true private market cost).[5] The average Head Start program costs about $5,000 per year per child, only slightly more than the typical preschool program, reflecting the fact that many programs operate only part-day and part-year and that program staff are not highly paid.[6] Prekindergarten programs, if they operate full-day for the nine-month school year, cost more, about $8,800 per year, about the same as a year of elementary school education, but they pay for themselves in terms of their benefits to school readiness.[7] High-quality intensive interventions cost even more, on the order of $15,000 per child for a full-time year-round slot, but also yield the largest and most lasting benefits.[8]

Policy makers will have to decide how much they are willing to invest in quality preschool programs. I think a reasonable decision would be to use school-age programming as a guide and invest as much in preschoolers as we do in school-age children. This would allow states and localities to offer full-day prekindergarten and kindergarten programs for all children aged three, four, and five. The evidence is strong that investments in quality preschool programs more than pay for themselves. Indeed, they may yield a larger return than investments in school-age programs, because children's outcomes are more readily influenced in the preschool years and because gains made in these years will set children on the pathway to success in school and later years.[9] Investments in preschool programs also promote equity, since they typically raise school readiness more for disadvantaged children than they do for their more advantaged peers.[10]

Policies for Families with School-Age Children

As we saw in chapter 4, there has been a surge of interest in programs to provide care for school-age children during their out-of-school time, but it is still the case that many six- to twelve-year-olds do not have access to good-quality programs, and children whose parents work are more likely than others to be home alone or to spend time unsupervised with friends after school. This chapter highlighted two key policy priorities to better meet the needs of school-age children when parents are working.

The first is to increase children's access to high-quality out-of-school programs. To do so, three steps are needed. The first is to improve the quality of existing out-of-school programs. Programs currently on offer do not do as good a job as they might at meeting children's needs, as evidenced by sometimes weak evaluation results and low attendance rates. States and localities need to draw upon the lessons from the most successful programs to improve their program quality. Doing so will expand children and families' options and give them more access to high-quality care.

A second, complementary, step is to increase subsidies. Programs serving school-age children must compete for funding with programs serving younger children, and many current school-age programs rely heavily on parent fees to cover their costs. As a result, parents often face even higher costs for an hour of after-school care than they do for an hour of pre-school care. Expanded subsidies would give families more choices among programs and would help support parents who are working.

A third, related step is to provide more programs at or near public schools. Even where high-quality and affordable programs do exist, children with working parents will find it almost impossible to attend them if they are not located strategically. Locating programs at or near schools will make them more accessible to children and will also reduce disruptions to parents' work.

The other policy reform that would help better meet the needs of school-age children with working parents is to extend the school day and year. American children attend school fewer hours a day and fewer days a year than children in many other countries. Although it is fashionable to bemoan the state of American public schools, the quality of education they provide has been improving in recent years, as a result of state and federal reform initiatives. Now would be a good time to capitalize on those successes and try some experiments with longer school days and more days in school. The additional time in school could even be offered on a voluntary basis, if there are communities where families might object to their children having to spend more time in school. But chances are good that many families would leap at the chance to have their children spend more time in school, since they know that every hour spent in school is potentially an hour when their child can be engaged in a constructive activity or learning, as opposed to an hour when parents need to arrange care or have their child be on his or her own.

Here too policy makers will have to make choices about how much they are willing to invest in expanding quality out-of-school programs or extending the school day and year. Given the current public willingness to spend more money on out-of-school programs for school-age children, this is a good time to conduct some experiments both with expanding out-of-school programs and with extending the school day and year. The truthful answer is that we do not know, based on current research, what the pay-offs to such efforts will be or whether a dollar is better spent on another hour of school or on an hour of quality out-of-school programming. Now is the time to find out.

Policies for Families with Adolescents

Chapter 5 considered adolescents, aged thirteen to eighteen, and what they need for healthy growth and development when parents work. Two key policy recommendations emerged for this age group.

First, as with school-age children, one useful reform would be to change the school calendar. The rationale for extending the school day or year is much the same as it is for school-age children: adolescents probably do have too much unsupervised time outside school and could benefit from more time in instruction. Moreover, a revised school calendar would better fit the industrial and service economy of 21st century America. If any changes are to be made to the school calendar, it would make sense from the perspective of families to coordinate these changes, so that daily schedules and vacation schedules for school-age children and adolescents do not get out of sync.

A second useful reform, again similar to that proposed for school-age children, would be to expand access to high-quality programs serving adolescents in their out-of-school time. If anything, the research base on what constitutes a high-quality program is stronger for this age group than it is for younger school-age children, with several recent random assignment evaluations identifying successful programs (such as Big Brother Big Sister, Quantum Opportunities, I Have a Dream, and Teen Opportunity Program). We now know what kinds of programs are helpful for adolescents and what kinds of programs are not. Additional investments in high-quality programs would raise the quality of programs on offer and would give adolescents and their families a better set of choices. These programs should include ones that help adolescents get valued work experience. Most adolescents work by the time they finish high school, and under the right conditions—if the job is a good one and does not require an excessive number of hours—working can contribute to healthy growth and development. Part-time or summer jobs that are linked to what teens are doing in school and that help them explore career options are particularly rewarding.

Key Elements

If we put all these policies together, the resulting package has seven key elements that would go a long way toward better meeting the needs of children when parents work. This policy package would include the following seven elements:

1. *Give parents more flexibility* to take time off work to take care of family responsibilities, through expanding family and medical leave rights and introducing the right to request part-time and flexible work hours.
2. *Break the link between employment and essential family benefits,* in particular health insurance, by providing health insurance through a social insurance program like Medicare rather than through employee benefits and by raising the refundable child tax credit to provide an income cushion for families with children.
3. *Give parents more options to stay home in the first year of life,* by providing all new parents a year of parental leave paid through the social insurance system, giving new parents the right to request to return to work part-time or to work flexible hours, and providing an at-home infant child care subsidy to low-income parents or an early childhood benefit to low- and moderate-income families.
4. *Improve the quality of care for infants and toddlers* (aged zero to two), by providing more support for parents to use high-quality care, tightening regulations, and expanding the Early Head Start program.
5. *Improve the quality of care and education for preschool-age children* (aged three to five), by raising the quality of care in the private market, improving Head Start, and expanding prekindergarten.
6. *Increase access to high-quality out-of-school programs for school-age children and adolescents,* by improving the quality of programs, increasing subsidies, and locating more programs at or near schools.
7. *Change the school calendar for school-age children and adolescents,* by experimenting with a longer school day or longer school year.

Looking at these elements, three cross-cutting themes are apparent. The first is the need for more flexibility for parents. Flexibility is key in supporting parental choice and also in enabling parents to provide or arrange high-quality care while continuing to work themselves. A second theme is the need for better-quality care for children across all ages. High-quality care is essential in meeting children's needs and in making parental choice and parental employment a reality. A third theme is the need for some supports to be provided on a more universal basis. Universal provision of high-quality preschool, extended-hours schools, and basic income supports, including adequate health insurance for families with children, must be in place if children are to be protected from fluctuations associated with their parents' moving in and out of the workforce or specific jobs. Whether children have adequate health insurance or a good preschool or an enriching program to go to after school should not depend on their parents' jobs.

This package would be costly, but as we have seen, many of the costs would be offset by savings, in terms of better child health and development, improved school readiness, greater school achievement, and less risky behavior in the school-age and adolescent years. Nor does the entire package need to be implemented at one time. Incremental steps in each of the areas would make a difference for children today and pave the way for progress in the future. The United Kingdom's ten-year strategy for child care nicely illustrates this kind of approach, laying out ambitious ten-year goals along with a set of interim steps to be accomplished along the way.[11]

Moreover, in many cases these policies would not require new dollars but rather would mean investing more wisely the dollars we are currently spending. Although many low-income families don't get help with their child care expenses, the United States now spends much more on child care subsidies and out-of-school child care programs than ever before. In 2000, the federal and state governments combined spent over $20 billion on child care and out-of-school care.[12] And parents spend even more. Public subsidies in the United States cover only about 40 percent of the cost of care for children under five (and a smaller share for school-age children), with parents paying the remainder.[13] Yet the quality of what parents and the government are buying is not as high as it should be. As consumers of child care and out-of-school care, parents and the government should insist that their money is spent wisely. We now have the evidence base to tell us which programs are of good value and promote health and development. It's time to put our money there.

Moving Forward

The policies in this package of supports do not derive from a particular political point of view, whether liberal or conservative, but rather are based on widely shared values and the best available research. Yet the American public does not speak with one voice, particularly on such personal issues as work and care for children. How far apart are Americans on these issues, and how would this kind of policy package fare in state legislatures and in Congress? Are Americans prepared to move forward on this kind of agenda?

There are certainly areas where Americans disagree. The FMLA is a good example. The law was vetoed twice by the first President Bush but was the first bill signed into law by President Clinton in 1993. Since that time, some Democrats and Republicans have proposed extending it in various ways, while others have bitterly opposed any extensions that might raise costs for employers.

The issue of whether and how to provide paid leave is a particular sticking point. It is widely recognized that without pay, family leave benefits are worth little to low-income families, who cannot afford to go without a paycheck. Over 80 percent of employees say the FMLA should be expanded to provide paid leave; a similar or even larger percentage support expanding social insurance programs to provide paid leave.[14] But requiring employers to provide paid leave could place an unfair burden on employers and could lead to discrimination against women.

I think both sides of the argument have merit, and that is why I propose funding paid leave through a social insurance fund rather than requiring employers to pay the costs. In California dropping the employer payments and having employees fund the paid leave was a key step in getting paid family and medical leave enacted.[15] Similarly, in New Zealand dropping employer payments and funding leave through general revenues paved the way for that country to move from unpaid leave to paid leave.[16] Thus, even in an area as contested as this, there is in fact a policy option that could satisfy most parties to the debate while better meeting children's needs.

There are also areas where Americans agree. Indeed, I am encouraged by the high level of agreement among Americans about many of the issues having to do with meeting the needs of children when parents work, in particular, the importance of a good education, starting with preschool, and the importance of good-quality out-of-school care. Large majorities of Americans endorse the view that preschool should be available for all children whose parents want them to attend, and that schools and communities should be providing more out-of-school child care programs. Support for universal preschool is widespread, with business leaders joining in the call for states to provide universal programs.[17] So too is support for after-school care, with 90 percent or more of Americans saying that after-school programs are important and that there should be organized activities for school-age children and teens in every community.[18] Many Americans say they would be willing to pay more in taxes to support such programs. Half of voters would be willing to pay $100 more per year in state taxes to make sure that every child has the opportunity to attend an after-school program.[19]

According to a 2000 survey by Public Agenda, many Americans think it would be best if they could care for their children themselves, particularly when they are young.[20] Fully 80 percent of parents with children under the age of five say they think having a parent at home is the best arrangement for young children. But Americans also recognize that many parents must work and are supportive of efforts to improve the quality of child care and its affordability. Just under 70 percent agree that it is unrealistic for most families to have a parent stay at home, and over 80 percent agree that there is a serious shortage of affordable and good-quality child care. Parents are particularly concerned about the safety of child care settings and the risk of abuse or neglect. A majority support quality-improvement initiatives such as tightening regulations and expanding Head Start.

Americans do hold firm views about the primary role played by a child's own parents. Yet, they also are increasingly open to the idea that parents can't do it all. A resounding majority—nearly 80 percent—agree that it is much harder to be a parent today than in the past.[21] And nearly as many—72 percent—say that "raising children is the responsibility of parents *with the support of others in their communities.*"[22]

⌇ So WHERE DO WE GO from here in moving forward to better meet the needs of children when parents work? In this concluding section, I lay out some next steps for parents, employers, schools and communities, and policy-makers.

What Parents Can Do

As I have emphasized throughout the book, parents are already working hard to meet the needs of their children while they work. No parent should go away from this book feeling that there is one right way to meet the needs of children or that they should follow the research rather than their own best instincts and judgment. Yet, as a parent myself, I do think there are some lessons for parents from the research.

First, parents really do matter a lot, even in the years when children seem to care only for their peers. Being available to talk and listen, keeping track of what the children are doing, and letting them know you care—whether through eating dinner together or through other regular check-in times—these things make a difference.

Second, parents need to be alert and informed consumers. The sad truth is that many child care and out-of-school care programs are not as good as they should be. If parents speak up and demand better-quality programs, this situation can change.

Third, parents need to speak up in the workplace. For too long, working parents have been told that the key to success in the workplace is to not mention family responsibilities. Better to say you have to take the car to the garage, the conventional wisdom goes, than to say you have to take the child to the dentist. But if parents don't speak up and say that they need time off or don't take advantage of time off when it is offered, the workplace culture will never change. Parents who feel that they would like to spend more time with their families are not alone. Today's parents really do view the world differently than their parents' generation did.[23] They are more likely to prioritize family over work and to want to spend more time at home. Yet, like their parents' generation, they fear that expressing those views at the workplace will hurt their careers. Here, the old adage "safety in numbers" really does hold true: if all parents speak up, it is harder for an employer to single anyone out, and it is more likely that the workplace culture will change.

Fourth, parents need to speak up in their communities and in their polling places. Family issues have sometimes become hot political issues and can be again—but only if parents speak up. As I describe later in this chapter, in Florida pressure from parents moved a reluctant leg-islature to enact a universal prekindergaten law, while in California a well-orchestrated grassroots campaign persuaded the governor to sign the nation's first paid family and medical leave law.[24]

What Employers Can Do

Examples abound of employers who are investing in meeting the needs of children when parents work, because doing so helps their employees, their company, and the workforce of tomorrow.[25] There is no one checklist of things an interested employer can do: the right answer will depend on the needs of the employees in that particular workplace. Talking to employees and finding out what they need and would use is always a good starting place. So too is learning about what other em-ployers have done.

It is important to keep in mind that even a small investment can make a difference. Training managers to inform parents of the benefits already available and to encourage parents to use them, implementing flexible hours policies, helping employees with information about child care or out-of-school care—all of these are relatively low-cost measures that can help better meet children's needs.[26] Employers should not feel that this is an all-or-nothing venture. On the contrary, this is an area where small steps can make a big difference.

Employers can play an important role as public advocates. The Com-mittee for Economic Development, a business group, is one of the most prominent and influential advocates for universal preschool education. Corporate Voices for Working Families, another business group, is help-ing to lead the campaign for better-quality child care and out-of-school care.

Employers can also get more involved in public-private partnerships. Currently, only 11 percent of large firms are involved in partnerships in their community.[27] But surely employers will be more effective if they partner with others, and increasingly employers are realizing this. The American Business Collaboration for Quality Dependent Care, for in-stance, has brought together eighteen companies and fifty local part-ners, who invested $100 million from 1995 to 2000 to increase access to high-quality care in local communities.[28]

What Schools and Communities Can Do

As we have seen, schools and community-based organizations (such as nonprofit agencies, churches and synagogues, and local charities) have a potentially very important role to play in expanding access to high-quality preschool and out-of-school care. And they are already doing a great deal to fulfill this role. Given limited resources and the many other demands they face, what more can schools and communities reasonably be expected to do?

One of the most useful roles that schools and community-based organizations can play is to help educate and motivate others—such as parents and employers. Asking parents and employers to donate time and money or to join a task force or working group are ways that schools and community-based organizations can draw on these resources and get them more involved.

Schools and community-based organizations can also provide opportunities for others in the community to help out. The many adults who volunteer as mentors, Big Brothers and Sisters, or soccer coaches are testimony to the willingness of people from all walks of life to donate their time and effort to make a difference for children. Americans are more positive than ever about helping children. More than three-quarters (78 percent) are interested in getting involved in helping kids in their community, and nearly all (97 percent) believe that one person can make a difference in the life of a child.[29] Here again, small steps can make a big difference. Big Brothers and Sisters see the children they work with only a few times a month but have a large impact.

What Policy Makers and the Public Can Do

The challenge for policy makers and the public at large is clear: better meeting the needs of children when parents work will require us as a country to invest additional resources and to spend resources more wisely. Do we have the political will to spend more on meeting the needs of children, and do we know how resources should be spent?

I think the answer to both questions is yes. There is now a greater awareness and understanding than any time in the past of how important investments in children are, and this new recognition has greatly increased the public's support for investments in children—whether in the form of paid leave for new parents or universal preschool or more widely available after-school programs. There is also a much stronger evidence base. Across many of the program areas considered in this book, we really do know what works and what constitutes a sound investment.

These programs will not come easily, but examples from across the country suggest that interest and support are growing. In the parental leave area, although only one state, California, had enacted a paid family and medical leave program as of 2004, paid leave bills were under consideration that year in twenty-one other states and the District of Columbia.[30] Four states (Minnesota, Montana, Missouri, and New Mexico) had piloted or enacted at-home infant child care programs to support low-income parents staying home with their children for the first year of life.

Support for prekindergarten programs is expanding even more rapidly. By 2004, all but ten states had prekindergarten programs serving at least some four-year-olds and in some cases three-year-olds. In spite of tight budgets, fifteen states increased their spending on prekindergarten in 2004, building on a consensus about the value of high-quality preschool that cut across political parties.[31] By 2005, four states (Florida, Georgia, New York, and Oklahoma) and the District of Columbia had universal prekindergarten programs for four-year-olds (although New York's program was not fully funded and Florida's program fell short of what its sponsors had intended).

Support for programs to assist school-age children and adolescents in their out-of-school time is growing as well. Funding from state governments as well as other sources (foundations, localities, and the federal government) increased dramatically in the 1990s. By 2000, nearly 50 percent of public schools had extended-day programming, up from only 30 percent just six years earlier.[32]

In these times of strained state budgets, how did these states (and other funders) decide to make programs for children a priority? In some cases, it was one policy maker—a legislator, mayor, or governor—who got the ball rolling, with the support of parents, employers, schools, and community-based organizations. But in many other cases, parents or other groups led the way.

In California, a strong labor and community coalition led the effort to enact a paid family and medical leave law.[33] The coalition took advantage of the fact that California was one of five states that already had a paid medical leave law on the books (through its Temporary Disability Insurance or TDI program). This made enacting paid family leave somewhat easier, since it would be possible to do so by extending the existing TDI law. The coalition was also able to identify a well-respected legislator, Sheila Kuehl, a California state senator, to take the lead on the bill. And the coalition took advantage of the fact that this bill would be popular with women voters in an election year when Governor Gray Davis faced a tight reelection battle. Getting the bill passed and signed into law was not easy. In the end, the coalition had to compromise, settling for six weeks of paid leave funded by employee contributions (rather than twelve weeks funded by employers and employees). But the law marked the first paid family and medical leave law in the United States, a major accomplishment.

In Florida, the impetus for universal prekindergarten came from a statewide referendum, which passed in spite of the opposition of state lawmakers.[34] The campaign for the referendum was led by an unusual coalition, which included David Lawrence Jr., former publisher of the *Miami Herald*, and the mayor of Miami, Alex Penelas. Even Governor Jeb Bush, who had opposed some earlier education initiatives, came to see the benefit of this one. In the end, support for the program was so strong that the legislature had no choice but to enact it, and Governor Bush was able to use his veto to push the legislature to enact a slightly better version. Although supporters were disappointed that the program the legislators approved still fell short of the quality they had hoped for, the good news is that a universal prekindergarten program is now on the books, and future legislative sessions can work on improving it.

The lesson from these examples is clear—it is not necessary to wait for a majority to begin to move forward with policies to better meet the needs of children when parents work. If policy makers or other individuals are bold enough to take the lead, there are large constituencies out there that will follow that lead. Working parents aren't a special interest group: they are the majority of parents. And there are many others who share their concern—business owners, grandparents, school teachers, clergy, police.

Time to Act

Public opinion polls confirm that Americans care deeply about children and are willing to spend more money on them, but understandably, they want their money to be well spent. I hope the evidence in this book will inform and persuade those who are currently undecided that we do know what will help meet the needs of children when parents work and that we can invest wisely in programs that will benefit our children and our country.

A majority of parents now work, but the issues raised here have implications that go beyond them. We all have a stake in the children of working parents and a vested interest in better meeting children's needs. And we now know better than ever before what programs will help. So there is no excuse for waiting. The time to act is now.

Notes

Introduction

1. This calculation assumes that the typical school is open six hours a day, five days a week, thirty-six weeks a year (taking into account holidays, vacations, and summers), for a total of 1,080 hours per year. For a typical child who starts school at age five (and attends full-day kindergarten that year), schools then provide a total of 14,040 hours of care between the age of five and eighteen (1,080 hours of care a year for thirteen years). Meanwhile, the parent working full-time is at work forty hours a week, plus another seven and a half hours commuting (assuming an hour-and-a-half commute each day, or forty-five minutes each way). If the parent works fifty weeks a year, that amounts to 2,375 hours per year, for a total of 42,750 hours between the child's birth and the child's turning eighteen. If schools cover only 14,040 of those 42,750 hours, that amounts to 32.8 percent, just under a third.

1. Children and Parents

1. According to *Newsweek* "What Matters Most," (special issue, Fall/Winter 2000, 6), parents placed most priority on raising a moral child, a preference followed closely by raising a happy child and raising a smart child. See also Farkas et al. 2002.

2. Sociologist Annette Lareau, in her 2003 book *Unequal Childhoods*, refers to this scheduling of middle-class children's time as a strategy of "concerted cultivation" and contrasts it with the process of "natural growth" seen in lower-income families, where children spend more unscheduled time with family members and peers.

3. Ann Hulbert's history of child-rearing advice in the twentieth century illustrates how the issues about which parents are advised have expanded; see Hulbert 2003.

4. Hulbert 2003, 334.

5. Crittenden 2004.

6. These include William Damon's *The Moral Child* (1988) and James Q. Wilson's *The Moral Sense* (1993) and *On Character* (1995).

7. Hulbert (2003, 172) describes the changes Spock made in the third and fourth editions of his manual, *Baby and Child Care*. She also describes, on p. 283, how Bruno Bettelheim rallied to the defense of working mothers with his article "Why Working Mothers Have Happier Children" and other publications. See also discussion in Hulbert 2003, 286–287.

8. Leach makes these policy recommendations in her 1994 volume, *Children First*.

9. Brazelton and Greenspan 2000, 155. Greenspan, who opposes nonparental day care for young children, does not necessarily advocate a return to the traditional family. He calls for a four-thirds solution—where each parent (of a two-parent family) works two-thirds time (or one parent works full time, and the other one-third time). Others express even stronger views about day care. See, for example, Laura Schlesinger's *Parenthood by Proxy: Don't Have Them If You Won't Raise Them* (2000).

10. Hulbert 2003, 354.

11. "Still Guilty After All These Years" is the title of Susan Chira's review of advice books for working mothers, in the *New York Times Book Review*, May 8, 1994, p. 11.

12. Hays 1996, 4. See also Douglas and Michaels (2004, 4), who refer to these new higher standards for mothers as the "new momism."

13. See Galinksy and Bond (2004), which compares men's and women's time with children in 1977 and 2002. See also Coltrane 1996; Crouter et al. 1999; Furstenberg 1995; Galinsky 1999; Gerson 1993; Jacobs and Gerson 2004; and Yeung 2001.

14. Barnett and Rivers 1996; Deutsch 1999; Hertz 1986; Hochschild 1989.

15. Quote from John Watson's *Behaviorism*, published in 1925, quoted in Ridley 2003, 256.

16. Quote is from Francis Galton's article "The History of Twins, as a Criterion of the Relative Powers of Nature and Nurture," published in 1875 in *Fraser's Magazine* 12: 566–576, quoted in Ridley 2003, 73.

17. *Nature via Nurture*, Ridley 2003.

18. For an overview of behavioral genetics, see chapter 2 in Shonkoff and Phillips 2000. See also Rutter et al. 1999 and Plomin et al. 1997.

19. Duyme et al. 1999.

20. Caspi et al. 2002.

21. Mednick, Gabrielli, and Hutchings 1984; see also Ridley 2003.

22. See Zuckerman and Kahn 2000.

23. Zuckerman and Kahn 2000, 92.

24. For an extended critique, see Bruer 1999. See also Thompson and Nelson 2001.

25. The classic research on critical periods in cats' vision is reported in Wiesel and Hubel (1965). A similar study of monkeys, and the study of binocular vision in monkeys, are reported in Hubel, Wiesel, and Levay (1977) and Levay, Wiesel, and Hubel (1980). For a more detailed discussion of critical periods, see Bruer 1999, chap. 4.

26. See Bruer 1999, chap. 4, and Shonkoff and Phillips 2000, chap. 20.

27. For more detailed discussions, see Bruer 1999, chap. 5, and Shonkoff and Phillips 2000, chap. 20.

28. For an overview of the literature on fathers, see Lamb 1996; Levine and Pittinsky 1997; Parke 1996; and Tamis-Lemonda and Cabrera 2002.

29. Work by Case and Paxson (2001), for instance, shows that mothers play a

more important role than fathers in determining key investments in children's health but that fathers are more important in providing access to health insurance.

30. See Deutsch (1999), who documents how families in her study were working to establish a more equal balance of responsibility, often challenging gendered notions about responsibility for work and family in the process.

31. U.S. Bureau of the Census 2003, Table 84, p. 72.

32. U.S. Bureau of the Census 2003, Table 70, p. 63.

33. See McLanahan and Sandefur 1994.

34. Ellwood 1988, 136.

35. Figure for 1950 from Hulbert 2003, 296. Figures for 1970 onwards from U.S. Bureau of the Census 2003, Table 597, p. 391.

36. Ross Phillips 2004.

37. Galinsky et al. 2004.

38. Heymann 2000.

39. See, for instance, Blank 1998; Ferber and Waldfogel 1998; Tilly 1996.

40. Galinsky et al. 2004, Figures 1 and 2.

41. Galinsky et al. 2004.

42. Kmec 1999; Waldfogel 2001b. See also Crittenden (2001) and Williams (2000), who have written about what employers expect of the ideal worker and how that conflicts with taking care of family responsibilities.

43. For recent proposals along these lines, see Gornick and Meyers 2003; and Jacobs and Gerson 2004.

44. These two programs are described in Smolensky and Gootman 2003, chap. 8.

45. These programs are described in Smolensky and Gootman 2003, chap. 8.

46. Waldfogel 1999.

47. The child tax credit is described in Smolensky and Gootman 2003, chap. 8.

48. Galinsky et al. 2004.

49. For an overview of this program, see Smolensky and Gootman 2003, chap. 8.

50. Waldfogel 1998b.

51. The figure of $2,400 per year is consistent with Duncan and Magnuson (2003), who propose a $2,400 per year benefit for low- and moderate-income children aged one to six. Many analysts have called for universal child health insurance, and it is also widely noted that if children are to be taken to the doctor on a regular basis, it is important that their parents be covered as well (since parents who lack coverage themselves are less likely to take their children to the doctor even if the children are covered).

2. Infants and Toddlers

1. Hrdy 1999.

2. Hulbert (2003) provides an overview of the many childrearing books produced over the last century.

3. Research on the importance of early experiences and on early brain development was summarized in reports by the Carnegie Task Force on Meeting the Needs of Young Children (1994) and the Families and Work Institute (Shore 1997). This research also entered the popular press, with cover stories in magazines such as *Newsweek* in the late 1990s. Although these reports were for the most part accurate, many scientists felt they overstated the importance of the early years and of early brain development. This point is made by John Bruer (1999), for example.

For a balanced presentation of the evidence on early experiences and early brain development, the best source is *Neurons to Neighborhoods*, the report of the National Academy of Sciences Committee on the Science of Early Childhood Development (Shonkoff and Phillips 2000).

4. Shonkoff and Phillips 2000, 162.

5. These primate studies by Stephen Suomi are summarized in Ridley 2003, 255. See also a more extensive discussion in Hrdy 1999.

6. Shonkoff and Phillips 2000, 127.

7. There are several famous examples of such children—the Wild Boy of Aveyron, who evidently lived in the wild until he was twelve, Kaspar Hauser, who was kept in isolation until the age of sixteen, and Genie, a modern-day wild child from Los Angeles who was kept in isolation until she was thirteen. For a more extended discussion, see Ridley 2003, 168–170.

8. Children who learn a language in adolescence or later have particular trouble with morphology (understanding the building blocks of words), rather than syntax (understanding the order of works in sentences). For a more detailed discussion of timing and language development, see Shonkoff and Phillips 2000, 133–136.

9. See Hart and Risley 1995; and Hutternlocher et al. 1991. There is a good deal of variation in how much language children hear as toddlers. Hart and Risley (1995) recorded the number of utterances addressed to children age eleven to eighteen months and found that some children heard nearly 800 utterances per hour, while others heard fewer than 100 (the overall average was 325).

10. See, for instance, Snow 1972; Snow and Ferguson 1977; Katz and Snow in press.

11. Cognitive theory has long recognized the importance of interactions with caregivers during the first years of life for children's cognitive development (Nelson 1973; Bruner 1975).

12. For a more detailed discussion, see Hrdy 1999.

13. Quote from John Bowlby, *Maternal Care and Mental Health*, published in 1951, quoted in Ann Hulbert 2003, 205.

14. Shonkoff and Phillips 2000, 166. See also the NICHD Early Child Care Research Network (1997b), who found that 72 percent of infants received some nonparental care in the first year of life, entering care on average when they were three months old.

15. Shonkoff and Phillips 2000 165–169.

16. Rubin, Mills, and Rose-Krasnor 1989.

17. Shonkoff and Phillips 2000, 169.

18. Thompson 2001, 28.

19. See, for instance, Brazelton 1986 and Leach 1997. For an overview of childrearing guides over the past century, see Hulbert 2003.

20. For reviews of the research on maternal employment, see Gottfried, Gottfried, and Bathurst 1995; Hoffman et al. 1999; Shonkoff and Phillips 2000; Smolensky and Gootman 2003. For reviews of the research on child care, see Lamb 1998; Love, Schochet, and Meckstroth 1996; Scarr and Eisenberg 1993; Shonkoff and Phillips 2000.

21. For details, see Ruhm 2000. See also work by Winegarden and Bracy (1995), who cover a smaller number of countries and years but also find that longer periods of maternity leave are associated with lower infant mortality.

22. For details, see Tanaka 2005.

23. The American Academy of Pediatrics recommends exclusive breastfeeding for the first six months and continued breastfeeding (alongside solid foods, which may be gradually introduced in the second six months) through the first year of life, citing its advantages for infants' health, growth, and development as well as benefits for women's health (see American Academy of Pediatrics, Work Group on Breastfeeding 1997). However, actual breastfeeding practices in the United States do not meet these goals (Philipp, Merewood, and O'Brien 2001). As of 2001, about two-thirds of infants and toddlers had ever been breast-fed, but smaller shares were still being breast-fed at six and twelve months postbirth (27 percent and 12 percent respectively) (Li et al. 2003).

24. The American Academy of Pediatrics recommends that infants be placed on their back or sides to sleep, because of the elevated risk of SIDS for infants sleeping in a prone position (American Academy of Pediatrics, Task Force on Infant Positioning and SIDS 1992). A "Back to Sleep" campaign was launched in 1994 to increase parents' knowledge about the links between infants' sleeping position and the risk of SIDS (Willinger, Hoffman, and Hartford 1994). However, this campaign may not have been as effective in reaching child care centers, where an estimated 20 percent of SIDS deaths occur; for instance, a survey of child care centers in 1996 found that 43 percent were not aware of the campaign and 49 percent were still putting children to sleep on their stomachs at least some of the time (Moon and Biliter 2000). Subsequent surveys have found increased awareness of the Back to Sleep campaign but have still found 20 to 28 percent still putting infants to sleep on their stomachs at least some of the time (Moon and Biliter 2000; Moon, Weese-Mayer, and Silvestri 2003). Measures proposed to raise the adoption of Back to Sleep practices among child care providers include tightening state regulations (Moon, Biliter, and Croskell 2001) and providing health education training (Moon and Oden 2003).

25. This study used data from the National Longitudinal Survey of Youth, for women giving birth between 1988 and 1996. See Berger, Hill, and Waldfogel (2003) for details.

26. Instrumental variables models first predict a particular behavior, such as parental employment, based on individual and family characteristics as well as an instrument that is external to the individual, and then estimate the effect of that predicted behavior on the outcome in question, as a way to correct for potential bias associated with the individual's choosing that behavior. For an overview, see Angrist, Imbens, and Krueger 1996; and Angrist and Krueger 1999.

27. Propensity score matching models estimate effects of a treatment of interest (such as having an employed parent) by comparing outcomes for individuals who received the treatment compared to those who did not receive the treatment but were most similar, as a way of correcting for bias associated with selection into treatment. For an overview, see Rosenbaum and Rubin 1983 and 1985.

28. Analyses of fathers' leave taking in the Millennium Cohort Study are from Tanaka and Waldfogel 2004.

29. For a more extensive discussion of the health effects of day care, see Meyers et al. 2004.

30. Shonkoff and Phillips 2000, 138. See also McCartney 1984 and NICHD Early Child Care Research Network 2000a.

31. Although the evidence is not conclusive, many studies have found that breastfeeding is associated with better cognitive development (see, for example, Hor-

wood and Fergusson 1998; Mortensen et al. 2002). For a critical review, see Jain, Concato, and Leventhal (2002), who conclude that although most studies suggest that breast-feeding promotes intelligence, the more rigorous studies tend to find weaker results.

32. For evidence that parental working conditions and satisfaction with work matter, see Parcel and Menaghan 1990 and 1994.

33. Galinsky (1999) cites evidence that parents' attitudes toward working influence how their children are affected by their employment. See also NICHD Early Child Care Research Network 1998b.

34. See, for example, Desai, Chase-Lansdale, and Michael 1989; Baydar and Brooks-Gunn 1991; Blau and Grossberg 1992; Smith 1994; Han, Waldfogel, and Brooks-Gunn 2001.

35. Studies that have found that effects of early maternal employment vary by child care include Howes 1988 and 1990; Baydar and Brooks-Gunn 1991; and Field 1991. Studies that have found effects vary by family socioeconomic status include Desai, Chase-Lansdale, and Michael 1989; Vandell and Ramanan 1992; and Caughy, DiPietro, and Strobino 1994. There is also a large amount of research on the effects of early nonmaternal child care on cognitive development (see reviews in Shonkoff and Phillips 2000; Vandell and Wolfe 2000; Smolensky and Gootman 2003). Most recently, the NICHD Early Child Care Research Network (1999b, 2000a, 2002a, 2002b, 2003b) has found that the quality of care affects children's cognitive and linguistic development. Quantity and type of care matter as well (Shonkoff and Phillips 2000; Vandell and Wolfe 2000; Smolensky and Gootman 2003).

36. For details, see Han, Waldfogel, and Brooks-Gunn 2001 and Waldfogel, Han, and Brooks-Gunn 2002. See also Ruhm (2003), who finds effects persisting to age ten and eleven, but see also Harvey (1999) who assessed children as late as age twelve and did not find persistent effects (however, her methodology was sufficiently different that the results are not readily comparable). There has also been an active debate on the effects of early maternal employment in Britain, and two sets of longitudinal studies have recently been carried out there. Studying young adults who were born in the 1970s and were included in the British Household Panel Study in the early-to-mid-1990s, Ermisch and Francesconi (2000) found that children whose mothers worked more extensively during their preschool years had somewhat lower educational attainment as young adults and that these effects held up (in fact, become even stronger) when they controlled for unobserved heterogeneity among mothers by estimating family fixed effects models. A second set of studies analyzed data from two large national birth cohort studies (the National Child Development Study of children born in 1958 and the British Cohort Study of children born in 1970). Joshi and Verropoulou (2000) first examined outcomes for children born in the 1970s and 1980s to mothers from the 1958 birth cohort and found that these children born in the 1970s and 1980s tended to have slightly poorer outcomes when assessed at ages five to seventeen in 1991 if their mothers worked in the first year of life, although only the effect on children's reading performance was statistically significant. They next examined children born in 1970 (from the British Cohort Study) and found, consistent with the results of Ermisch and Francesconi (2000), that children whose mothers worked more extensively during the preschool years had somewhat lower educational attainment as young adults. There is also one recent longitudinal study of maternal employment effects in New Zealand (Horwood and Fergusson 1999); however, because this study did not separate out the effects of early maternal employment

and because few of its sample members worked before the child's third birthday, its results are not readily comparable to the U.S. studies. There is also some literature from other countries on the effects of early child care. Studies in Sweden have found that children who had been in day care before the age of two had better socioemotional and cognitive outcomes at ages eight and thirteen than children who had not attended out-of-home care, with the best outcomes for children who began day care before age one (Andersson 1989 and 1992; see also Broberg et al. 1989 and Cochran and Gunnarson 1985). In France as well, several studies indicate that the effects on cognitive achievement of center care begun as early as age two are generally positive (see Boocock 1995 and Rayna and Plaisance 1998 for reviews).

37. For further discussion of the selection problem, see Currie 2003; see also Neidell 2000; Ruhm 2004.

38. For details, see Ruhm 2004.

39. For details, see Baum 2003. See also a later study by the same author, Baum in press.

40. For details, see Waldfogel, Han, and Brooks-Gunn 2002. See also James-Burdumy 2005.

41. For details of this study, see Hill et al. in press. For an introduction to propensity score methods, see Rosenbaum and Rubin 1983 and 1985.

42. For details of this study, see Brooks-Gunn, Han, and Waldfogel 2002. The findings for the effect of long hours of employment in the first year on maternal sensitivity are consistent with the NICHD Early Child Care Research Network (1999a), who found that children who were in more hours of child care in the first year of life were rated as having less sensitive mothers.

43. Both maternal sensitivity and quality of care have been found to be important influences on child outcomes in other work with the NICHD Study of Early Child Care. And there is evidence that high-quality child care can improve parenting, at least in high-risk families. For instance, the NICHD Early Child Care Research Network (1997d) found that mothers who were in or near poverty engaged more positively with their six-month-olds when they were in high-quality child care, when compared to similar mothers whose children were in lower-quality child care or were at home full time.

44. Evidence on experimental studies of high-quality interventions is reviewed in Barnett, W. S. 1995; Currie 2001; Haskins 2004; Karoly et al. 1998; and Waldfogel 2002. Evidence on observational studies of center-based care programs is reviewed in Clarke-Stewart and Allhusen 2005; and Smolensky and Gootman 2003.

45. When child care teachers provide more verbal stimulation, children show greater language and cognitive gains (McCartney 1984; NICHD Early Child Care Research Network 2000a). As discussed later in this chapter, center-based care teachers are much more highly educated on average than other types of child care providers.

46. For details, see Han 2005.

47. For details of this study, see Han, Brooks-Gunn, and Waldfogel 2004. For other analyses showing the effect of income on child development in the NICHD-SECC, see Dearing, McCartney, and Taylor 2001.

48. The NLSY-CS studies have tended to find neutral or positive effects of maternal employment in the second and third year of life. However, recent work by Ruhm (2004) finds some negative effects of mothers' working full-time in the second and third year of life.

49. Ruhm 2004.

50. Han, Waldfogel, and Brooks-Gunn 2001.

51. Classic works on attachment include Ainsworth 1973; Ainsworth et al. 1978; Belsky and Cassidy 1994; Bowlby 1969; Cassidy 1999; and Sroufe 1996. See also the discussion in Shonkoff and Phillips 2000, 229–238.

52. These opposing viewpoints are summarized in Belsky (1988), who argues that early child care is problematic for the development of secure attachment, and Clarke-Stewart (1988), who argues that it is not. As the effects of nonmaternal child care on infant-mother attachment were debated, less attention was paid to the question of attachment relationships between children and their child care providers. Studies that have examined these relationships have found that the security of the infant-mother relationship is most important for how a child functions in other social situations, but children who have established secure relationships with both their mothers and their child care providers are the most socially skilled (see, for instance, Howes et al. 1995), and in general children who have secure attachments with their child care providers are more socially competent in their encounters with other children and adults (see, for example, Howes and Hamilton 1993; Howes et al. 1988; Howes, Matheson, and Hamilton 1994; and Howes 2000). However, it is also true that because of high turnover and frequent changes in child care arrangements, children are often not securely attached to their child care providers. See, for instance, Galinsky et al. 1994; Howes 1999; Seltenheim et al. 1997; and Whitebrook, Howes, and Phillips 1990, as well as discussion in Shonkoff and Phillips 2000, 234–235.

53. There has been a very active debate on these topics in Britain as well (McGurk, Hennessy, and Moss 1993; Morgan 1996). Studies in Britain have produced mixed results: for instance, Osborn and Milbank (1987), using data on children born in 1970, found negative effects of preschool child care on socioemotional development, but Melhuish and Moss (1991), using data on children born in 1983, did not.

54. Baydar and Brooks-Gunn (1991) analyzed 572 non-Hispanic white children aged three and four in 1986 and found significant effects of first-year maternal employment on the children's BPI scores at age three or four. Belsky and Eggebeen (1991) studied 565 white and black children aged four to six in 1986 and found that children whose mothers were employed full-time in the first or second year of life scored worse on a composite measure of behavioral adjustment than did children whose mothers were not employed during their first three years. Parcel and Menaghan (1994) studied 526 children aged four to six in 1986 and found no effect on children's behavioral problems. Greenstein (1995) analyzed 2,040 children aged four to six in 1986, 1988, or 1990.

55. For details, see Han, Waldfogel, and Brooks-Gunn 2002.

56. For details, see Berger, Hill, and Waldfogel 2003.

57. See Han, Waldfogel, and Brooks-Gunn (2002), who find that the effects that are present for non-Hispanic white children at age four are generally attenuated and no longer significant after that age. See also Ruhm (2003), who followed children from the NLSY-CS to age ten and eleven and found no significant effects of first-year employment (or second- and third-year employment) on children's behavior problems at those ages.

58. For further information, see the NICHD-SECC website, secc.rti.org [accessed 10/12/05].

59. NICHD Early Child Care Research Network 1997a.

60. For details, see NICHD Early Child Care Research Network 2003a.

61. Watamura et al. 2003.

62. Shonkoff and Phillips 2000.

63. Han, Brooks-Gunn, and Waldfogel 2004.

64. This study measured child temperament along two dimensions, emotionality and effortful control. See Li-Grining et al. 2004.

65. See Crockenberg 2003; Ahnert and Lamb 2003; and Fabes, Hanish, and Martin 2003. Further evidence on the importance of quality comes from studies that have examined the effects of child care quality on children's later social competence. These studies, reviewed in Shonkoff and Phillips (2000, 169) have tended to find that when the quality of care is higher, children go on to have more competent relationships with peers. See also reviews by Lamb 1998; Hayes, Palmer, and Zaslow 1990; and Scarr and Eisenberg 1993.

66. For further information on IHDP, see Karoly et al. 1998; Waldfogel 2002.

67. Karoly et al. 1998; Yoshikawa 1995.

68. For details, see Han, Waldfogel, and Brooks-Gunn 2002.

69. NICHD Early Child Care Research Network 1997b.

70. Flanagan and West 2004.

71. NICHD Early Child Care Research Network 1997c.

72. Martin Malin (1994 and 1998) makes the case that fathers would like to take more leave and would take more if offered. But we lack hard data on these points.

73. For details, see Waldfogel 2001c, 21. For further information on the two surveys that have been conducted since the FMLA was enacted, see Commisson on Family and Medical Leave 1996 and Cantor et al. 2001.

74. For details, see Berger and Waldfogel 2004.

75. For details, see Gregg, Gutierrez-Domenech, and Waldfogel 2003.

76. For details, see Burgess et al. 2002.

77. For details, see Tanaka 2005.

78. Tanaka 2005.

79. The theory on this point is provided by Summers 1989; see also Gruber and Krueger (1991) and Gruber (1992 and 1994) for useful discussions and applications to workmen's compensation and health insurance coverage for maternity respectively.

80. Whether employers are able to pass on these costs to employees depends on how the market is working. If the market is working well, there is no reason to believe that employers would be able to pass on the costs to employees. But if there is some type of market failure that prevents the optimal level of benefits being offered, employers should be able to pass on the costs to employees. In the case of family leave, several types of market failure are possible, including, for example, incomplete information (if workers do not have full information as to the value of family leave), externalities (if some of the benefits to leave accrue to other individuals), or adverse selection (if firms are deterred from providing otherwise optimal levels of leave for fear of attracting workers who will take long leaves). See discussion in Waldfogel 2001b; see also Mitchell 1990; Ruhm 1997a.

81. For details on the California program, see Smolensky and Gootman 2003.

82. Another consideration is that any time the government sets up a social program funded by payroll taxes, there will be some amount of deadweight loss associated with that tax. Deadweight loss refers to the loss to the economy associated with money being taken from individuals and spent by the government. However,

given that the overall size of the program would be fairly small, the size of that deadweight loss is likely to be small as well.

83. Another option would be to fund such programs through general revenues, as New Zealand has done, in order to avoid imposing costs on employers (Levin-Epstein 2004).

84. For details on the European Union directive on part-time work, see Gornick and Meyers 2003.

85. Blank 1990; Ferber and Waldfogel 1998; Tilly 1996.

86. Galinsky, Bond, and Hill 2004.

87. Information on the United Kingdom's part-time and flexible hours policy is from Camp 2004; Maternity Alliance 2004; and Work Foundation 2004.

88. Statistics on the share of women not working prebirth and the share of these nonworking women returning post birth are from Berger and Waldfogel (2004), estimated for women in the NLSY-CS who gave birth from 1988 to 1996.

89. For further details on policies for exempting women with young children from welfare-related work requirements, see Brady-Smith et al. 2001.

90. Haider, Jacknowitz, and Schoeni 2003.

91. For further details on at-home infant child care programs, see Smolensky and Gootman 2003.

92. For more information on Finland and Norway's early childhood benefits programs, see Waldfogel 2001c.

93. For some recent evidence on the income mothers forgo when they have children, see Sigle-Rushton and Waldfogel 2004.

94. See Waldfogel 1998b.

95. Harriet Presser has written extensively on split-shift working and parenting. For a recent overview, see Presser 2004.

96. Han 2005.

97. Galinsky et al. 1994. This study included 226 providers (60 relative providers, 112 regulated family day care providers, and 54 nonregulated providers), caring for children up to the age of sixty-five months, with about two-thirds of the children under age thirty months.

98. Figure for 1977 is from the U.S. Bureau of the Census 1982.

99. See, for instance, NICHD Early Child Care Research Network, 1996 and 2000b. For evidence on the importance of child-to-staff ratios and provider education for child outcomes, see review in Shonkoff and Phillips 2000, 315–317; and see also Blau 2000.

100. Data on centers in 1990 from the Profile of Child Care Settings, conducted by Mathematica Policy Research, as summarized in Smolensky and Gootman 2003.

101. Data on child care quality is summarized in Smolensky and Gootman 2003.

102. These tabulations on child care quality in the NICHD-SECC were produced for the Committee on Work and Family Policies of the National Academy of Sciences and are presented in its report (Smolensky and Gootman 2003). The NICHD Early Child Care Research Network (1996) also reported especially poor quality of child care for infants, as measured by the sensitivity of the caregivers, with only one in four rated as moderately or highly stimulating of cognitive development, while another one in four were rated as moderately insensitive and one in five were rated as moderately or highly detached.

103. The evidence on high-quality center-based interventions has been reviewed by Karoly et al. (1998). See also reviews by Barnett, W. S. 1995; Currie 2001; Has-

kins 2004; Waldfogel 2002; Yoshikawa 1995; and recent evidence in Hill, Waldfogel, and Brooks-Gunn 2003. For evidence on the effects of high-quality care in more-typical child care settings, see Burchinal et al. 1995 and 1996; Field 1991; Galinsky et al. 1994; Howes and Rubenstein 1985; McCartney 1984; NICHD Early Child Care Research Network 1999c and 2000a; Peisner-Feinberg and Burchinal 1997; and Peisner-Feinberg et al. 1999. Another approach to defining quality is to set out standards for teaching and instruction, based on developmental research about how children learn in these years. For an example of this approach, see National Research Council 2000.

104. Galinsky et al. 1994, Table 18, p. 47. This study included children up to the age of sixty-five months, but two-thirds were under age thirty months.

105. These statistics on quality are summarized in Smolensky and Gootman 2003.

106. See, for instance, the findings of two recent National Academy of Sciences panels, as reported in Shonkoff and Phillips 2000 and Smolensky and Gootman 2003.

107. See Blau 2001. In a survey carried out in the 1990s, 27 percent of low-income families who used child care for their preschoolers said they would like to change their arrangements; of these, two-thirds said they would prefer center-based care and over two-thirds said the reason they wanted to change was to gain higher-quality care (see Brayfield, Deich, and Hofferth 1995).

108. Information on Mississippi's regulations from Mississippi State Department of Health 2003, "Regulations Governing Licensure of Child Care Facilities." Available at www.msdh.state.ms.us (accessed 12/10/03).

109. NICHD Early Child Care Research Network 1999b.

110. Information on the Early Head Start program is available from U.S. Department of Health and Human Services, Administration for Children and Families 2002a. Information on the evaluation is available from U.S. Department of Health and Human Services, Administration for Children and Families 2002b; Early Head Start Research Consortium 2001; and Love et al. 2002. Figure on the share of eligible children served by Early Head Start is calculated by dividing the number of children age zero to two served in 2002 (64,000) by the number of poor children in that age range (2 million), which yields 3 percent.

3. Preschool-Age Children

1. Shonkoff and Phillips (2000) provide a comprehensive overview of preschoolers' developmental needs and the role of parents and others in meeting those needs.

2. For evidence on the importance of parents' language, see Hart and Risley 1995; Huttenlocher et al. 1991. For evidence on the importance of child care providers' verbal skills for children's language and cognitive development, see McCartney 1984 and NICHD Early Child Care Research Network 2000.

3. Technically, there are three distinct types of self-regulation—attention, emotion, and behavior (see Shonkoff and Phillips 2000, 121).

4. See, for instance, Stipek 2001.

5. This is probably an understatement of all the tasks that parents have to do in these years. Parents are also working to build children's character, introducing concepts of morality and manners. Parents may also be introducing children to religion or to other aspects of their culture. There is also tremendous variation among children and over time in how challenging parenting can be in these years. Some chil-

dren are more "difficult" than others, but it is also true that even the "easiest" children can encounter rough spots during the preschool years.

6. In 2000, about 40 percent of three-year-olds and 60 percent of four-year-olds who did not have working mothers were enrolled in some form of preschool (Meyers, et al. 2004). At the same time, 15 to 20 percent of three- or four-year-olds who did have working mothers were not in any form of nonparental child care (because they were cared for by their fathers or, more rarely, because their mothers cared for them while they were working); Table 3.1 in this chapter.

7. As we shall see, with the exception of a study by Ruhm (2004), which examined the effects of maternal and paternal employment in the first three years of life, most studies have examined the effects of maternal employment but not paternal employment. In part, this is due to data limitations: because paternal employment is so common, and because men who do not work may be different from those who do, it is difficult to estimate the effects of having a father who does not work. But it is also true that few researchers have tried to include fathers in their analyses.

8. A useful discussion of parental employment and child health is found in Leibowitz 2005. See also Huston (2002), who emphasizes the importance of income. For recent evidence on the links between income and child health, see Case, Lubotsky, and Paxson 2002 and Deaton 2002.

9. Morris et al. 2001. Health effects for children aged three to five at the time of random assignment are summarized in Figure 3.3, p. 49.

10. See discussion in Shonkoff and Phillips 2000, 71–75.

11. Anderson, Butcher, and Levine 2003; Ruhm 2003.

12. According to Roberts et al. (1999), the average child aged two to four spends over four hours per day watching television, and more than one in four have a TV in their bedroom.

13. Morris et al. 2001. Effects of programs on the school achievement of children aged three to five at the time of random assignment are summarized in Figure 3.1, p. 45.

14. Han, Brooks-Gunn, and Waldfogel 2004.

15. Ruhm 2004.

16. Ruhm 2004.

17. Morris et al. 2001. The effects of welfare-to-work programs on behavior problems for children who were aged three to five at the time of random assignment are summarized in Figure 3.2, p. 47. Results for the time-limited welfare program, which reduced positive behavior among children who were aged one to eight at the time of random assignment, are summarized in Figure 4.1, p. 54. A common limitation of these studies is that children's behavior is reported by parents, and thus differences in behavior may be clouded by differences in parents rather than in the children. Other MDRC studies have used more-objective reports of children's behavior, but in these particular studies, only parent reports were available.

18. Han, Waldfogel, and Brooks-Gunn 2001 and 2002.

19. Han, Brooks-Gunn, and Waldfogel 2004.

20. Ruhm 2003. As discussed in chapter 4, Ruhm also found no link between maternal employment when children were aged three to eight and children's involvement in substance use at age eleven.

21. See reviews of the literature on child care and child health in Meyers et al. 2004; and Leibowitz 2005.

22. Currie and Neidell 2003.

23. U.S. Department of Health and Human Services, Administration for Children and Families 2005.

24. For further information on the Child and Adult Care Food Program, see U.S. Department of Agriculture 2002.

25. Currie and Hotz 2004, 2.

26. Currie and Hotz (2004, 4) cite an estimate that the rate of injuries requiring medical attention is 14.3 per 100 children in day care centers compared to 35 per 100 children in the community at large.

27. See U.S. Consumer Product Safety Commission 1999 and Office of the Inspector General 1994.

28. Currie and Hotz 2004.

29. For background on the rise of sexual abuse allegations in the 1980s, see Waldfogel 1998a.

30. Statistics from U.S. Department of Health and Human Services, Administration on Children, Youth, and Families 2003. This report refers to children found to be abused or neglected as "victims." Percent of victims for whom a child day care provider was the perpetrator was 0.8 percent (Figure 4-2, p. 44). Total number of victims was 903,000 (Table 3-7, p. 46).

31. Statistics on rates of abuse from U.S. Department of Health and Human Services, Administration on Children, Youth, and Families 2003. Overall victimization rate in 2001 (twelve per one thousand children) is from Figure 3-2, p. 22. Number of children in some form of day care is estimated using data from Smolensky and Gootman 2003, 42–48.

32. Magnuson and Waldfogel in press; U.S. Department of Health and Human Services, Administration for Children and Families 2005.

33. Figure on number of reports made by child care providers from U.S. Department of Health and Human Services, Administration on Children, Youth, and Families 2003, Table 2-3, p. 14. For a discussion of ways in which child care may reduce parental discipline, see Magnuson and Waldfogel in press.

34. For reviews of the evidence on early childhood interventions including IHDP, see Barnett, W. S. 1995; Currie 2001; Haskins 1989 and 2004; Karoly et al. 1998; and Waldfogel 2002.

35. Recent studies of Head Start's effectiveness include Currie and Thomas 1995, 1999, 2000, and 2001; see also Magnuson, Meyers, et al. 2004. For reviews of the research on Head Start, see Haskins 2004; Magnuson and Waldfogel 2005; Waldfogel 2002. Cost figures for Head Start and other programs are from Currie and Neidell 2003, 15. Results from the random assignment evaluation are reported in U.S. Department of Health and Human Services, Administration for Children and Families 2005.

36. Observational studies that have found positive effects of center-based care on preschoolers' cognitive outcomes include Clarke-Stewart et al. 1994 and NICHD Early Child Care Research Network 2000a and 2003b. In contrast, more time in family day care has been found to be associated with poorer cognitive outcomes; see Yoshikawa 1999. For a review, see Shonkoff and Phillips 2000, 121.

37. NICHD Early Child Care Research Network and Duncan 2003.

38. Magnuson, Meyers, et al. 2004.

39. There is also a multistate study underway at the National Center for Early Development and Learning, at the University of North Carolina-Chapel Hill. See www.ncedl.org for more information [accessed 2/1/05].

40. See, for instance, the report of the National Academy of Sciences Committee on Early Childhood Pedagogy (Bowman, Donovan, and Burns 2000), as well as the report of the National Academy of Sciences Panel of the Science of Early Childhood Development (Shonkoff and Phillips 2000).

41. Ruopp et al. 1979; see also discussion in Blau 2001.

42. Howes 1997.

43. This literature is reviewed in Blau 2001; Shonkoff and Phillips 2000; and Vandell and Wolfe 2000.

44. For an overview, see Meyers, et al. 2004; and Shonkoff and Phillips 2000. For evidence on differentials in enrollment in center-based care by family income, see Bainbridge et al. 2005. For evidence on differentials in quality by family income, see Shonkoff and Phillips 2000, Table A5–4, pp. 172–177.

45. These studies are reviewed in Shonkoff and Phillips (2000, 111–115) and summarized in their Tables A5–2 and Table A5–3 (pp. 150–171). See also reviews by Blau 2001; and Vandell and Wolfe 2000. On the effects of current versus past quality, see NICHD Early Child Care Research Network 2000b. On effects persisting into elementary school, see, for example, Peisner-Feinberg et al. 1999.

46. Ruopp et al. 1979.

47. Further details on the Perry Preschool and other programs can be found in Haskins 2004; Karoly et al. 1998; and Waldfogel 2002. Evidence on outcomes to age forty is reported in Schweinhart et al. in press. See also discussion in Carneiro and Heckman 2003.

48. For further information on the Chicago Child-Parent Centers, see Haskins 2004; Karoly et al. 1998; and Waldfogel 2002.

49. NICHD Early Child Care Research Network 2003a. See especially their conclusions on pp. 999–1000.

50. For further details on the ECLS-K results, see Magnuson, Meyers, et al. 2004.

51. For an excellent summary of perspectives on why effects of child care on child social and emotional development might not be uniform, see Langlois and Liben 2003.

52. Smolensky and Gootman 2003.

53. In the spring of 1999, about 40 percent of three- and four-year-olds with working mothers attended some center-based care, according to the U.S. Bureau of the Census 2004, Table 1B (Child care arrangements for preschoolers by family characteristics and employment status of mothers: Spring 1999).

54. Meyers et al. 2004, Figures 6.2, 6.3, and 6.4.

55. For details on the Profile of Child Care Settings Study, see Kisker et al. 1991.

56. U.S. Department of Health and Human Services, Adminstration for Children and Families, 2005.

57. According to Smith et al. (2003), 82 percent of prekindergarten teachers earn public school teacher salaries.

58. See also Galinsky et al. (1994), who found in the Families and Work Institute Study of Children in Family Child Care and Relative Care that only 31 percent of relatives were rated good or adequate, while 69 percent were rated inadequate. The results of this study are discussed further in chapter 2, since the majority of the children in this study were under the age of thirty months.

59. Among families with children aged zero to five, parental care is the primary form of care in a third of families where mothers work a nonday shift; see Table 3–1, p. 44, in Smolensky and Gootman 2003.

60. Smolensky and Gootman 2003, Table 3–4, p. 58. For further details on the Profile of Child Care Settings Study, see Kisker et al. 1991. Galinsky et al. (1994) also provide evidence on family day care providers, but as noted above, this study mainly focused on younger children and is therefore discussed in chapter 2.

61. See, for instance, Galinsky et al. 1994.

62. Bainbridge et al. 2005, Figures 1 and 2, p. 731. For other evidence on income-differentials in enrollment, see Meyers et al. 2004.

63. Figures from Smolensky and Gootman 2000, Table A5–4 (Distribution of child care quality by type of care and family income), pp. 172–177. For a review of other evidence on how quality of care varies by family income, see Meyers et al. 2004.

64. Meyers et al. 2004.

65. Bainbridge et al. 2005, Figure 3, p. 732.

66. For further discussion of the market system in the United States, see Kamerman and Waldfogel 2005.

67. Blau (2001) argues for quality-related vouchers but is skeptical about the effectiveness of regulations. Gormley (1995), in contrast, argues that tighter regulations could play an important role in boosting quality. Helburn and Bergmann (2002) argue for pursuing both, as do Smolensky and Gootman (2003).

68. National Association for the Education of Young Children 2003. Tiered rating systems are diffusing rapidly. For instance, in January 2005, Wisconsin's governor proposed establishing a star-rating system in that state (Early Childhood Focus 2005).

69. Information on North Carolina's child care improvement initiative, Smart Start, and other aspects of North Carolina's approach to child care and education is available from the North Carolina Division of Child Development Web site at http://ncchildcare.dhhs.stats.nc.us and from the Smart Start Web site at www.smart start-nc.org.

70. For evidence on the effect of the reforms, see North Carolina Partnership for Children 2003; see also various reports available from the Web site of the Frank Porter Graham Child Development Institute at the University of North Carolina-Chapel Hill at www. fpg.unc.edu/ [accessed 2/1/05].

71. For more details on Australia's quality improvement initiative, see Organization for Economic Cooperation and Development 2001, Box 3.4, p. 69.

72. Details are in the United Kingdom background study prepared for the Organization for Economic Cooperation and Development 2001.

73. Figures on Head Start are from Currie and Neidell 2003. Figures on preschools and prekindergarten are from Magnuson et al. 2004. Average elementary school teacher's salary is from National Education Association 2001.

74. Data on programs' curriculums was gathered as part of the Head Start FACES study. See U.S. Deparment of Health and Human Services, Administration for Children and Families, 2000.

75. For details, see Currie and Neidell 2003.

76. For details, see Currie and Neidell 2003.

77. The report is *Starting Strong: Early Childhood Education and Care*, by the Organization for Economic Cooperation and Development 2001. For further details on countries not included in the OECD report, see the Clearinghouse on International Developments in Child, Youth, and Family Policies at Columbia University 2002; Meyers and Gornick 2001; and Waldfogel 2004a and in press.

78. Following the work of Gosta Esping-Anderson (1990), comparative scholars

typically divide social welfare regimes into three distinct groups: the continental European countries; Nordic countries; and English-speaking countries. I follow that convention here.

79. Information on France and other countries not included in the OECD report comes from the Clearinghouse on International Development in Child, Youth, and Family Policy at Columbia University 2002; Meyers and Gornick 2001; and Waldfogel 2004a and in press.

80. Meltzer 1994, Table 4.1, p. 15.

81. This is the child-to-staff ratio recommended by the European Commission's Childcare Network; see Organization for Economic Cooperation and Development 2001 for details.

82. The U.K. permits a higher child-to-staff ratio, up to thirty to one, for five-year-olds if they are enrolled in a reception class in school (the equivalent of a U.S. kindergarten class). Details on child-to-staff ratios are from Organization for Economic Cooperation and Development 2001, Table 3.3., p. 67. Information on the European Commission (EC) Childcare Network recommended child-to-staff ratio is from OECD 2001, p. 66.

83. Details on training and qualification of staff in the various countries are from the country summaries in Organization for Economic Cooperation and Development 2001, appendix 1, pp. 150–184.

84. Some of the most effective programs were Early Excellence Centres, model child care and education programs that integrate services to children and families with high-quality preschool programming. There are now over one hundred of these programs nationwide, and they have been found to provide exceptionally high-quality care, boosting children's school readiness on cognitive and social and emotional dimensions. Findings from the EPPE project are reported in Sammons et al. 2002 and 2003.

85. For details of the ten-year child care strategy, see HM Treasury 2004. For a review of the research that informed the strategy, see Waldfogel 2004a.

86. Bainbridge et al. 2005.

87. Evidence on summer learning loss is reviewed in Bracey 2002. Evidence on the effects of kindergarten is reviewed in Magnuson, Meyers et al. 2004. The recent push to more academic instruction is discussed in Strauss 2004.

88. My tabulations are from the Early Childhood Longitudinal Survey, Kindergarten Cohort.

89. For more details on the effects of out-of-school care on kindergartners' outcomes, see Magnuson, Meyers et al. 2004; and Magnuson, Ruhm, and Waldfogel in press.

90. Cost figures are from National Institute for Early Education Research 2002.

91. See Magnuson, Meyers et al. 2004; Magnuson, Ruhm, and Waldfogel in press.

92. Grissmer et al. 2000.

93. Duncan, Claesens, and Engel 2004.

94. Further evidence on prekindergarten will come from a study being carried out by the National Center for Early Development and Learning (2003) of programs in six states. For early results from this study, see Clifford et al. in press; Pianta et al. in press.

95. Details on the Georgia prekindergarten program and its effects are available in a series of papers, including Henry and Gordon 2004; Henry, Henderson, and Ponder 2004; Henry et al. 2003; Henry et al. 2004.

96. Quote from Gormley and Phillips 2003, 20. For further information on the Oklahoma program and the results of the Tulsa evaluation, see also Gormley and Gayer 2003. As noted earlier, there is also a multistate study of prekindergarten programs underway; for more information, see National Center for Early Development and Learning at www.fpg.unc.edu/-ncedl [accessed 2/1/05].

4. School-Age Children

1. Maccoby and Martin, cited in Maccoby (1984), found more than three times as many studies of children under age six as of school-age children. If anything, the imbalance has only increased subsequently, given the explosion of interest in early childhood development.

2. Erikson 1968. For an authoritative overview of middle childhood, see Collins 1984. For a more recent and excellent overview, see the introduction in Huston and Ripke, in press. See also Eccles (1999), which offers a very useful overview of development in middle childhood as it relates to out-of-school time for children.

3. Collins 1984, 1. See also Sameroff and Haith 1996.

4. Statistic on the share of children having sexual intercourse before the age of thirteen is from Centers for Disease Control and Prevention (2004) Table 42, p. 71.

5. For an excellent overview of health in middle childhood, see Shonkoff 1984.

6. Collins 1984, 18. The Panel Study of Time Use in American Households reported in 1981 that children six to eight years old were watching thirteen hours of TV a week; this rose to seventeen hours a week among children nine to ten years old, and nineteen hours a week among children eleven to twelve years old (Collins 1984, Table 1.14, p. 18).

7. The Panel Study of Time Use in American Households found that children eleven to twelve years old were watching nineteen hours of television per week in 1981 (Collins 1984, Table 1.14, p. 18). This compares to fifteen hours per week reported by twelve-year-olds in 1997 (Hofferth 1998). And by 1999, school-age children were watching less than three hours of TV a day, on average, compared to three to four hours a day in 1983 (Kaiser Family Foundation 1999).

8. Figures on obesity rates for school-age children in 2000 and thirty years earlier are from National Center for Health Statistics 2003.

9. Centers for Disease Control and Prevention 2004, Table 36, p. 65.

10. Huston and Ripke in press.

11. See, for instance, Chase-Lansdale and Pittman 2002.

12. Huston in press.

13. Bianchi 2000.

14. Morris et al. 2001.

15. Anderson, Butcher, and Levine 2003.

16. Ruhm 2003.

17. Heymann 2000, chap. 3.

18. Waldfogel 2005.

19. Recent reviews on the role of parents in children's school achievement include Barton 2003; Fan and Chen 2001; Henderson and Mapp 2002; Levin and Belfield 2002; Nord, Brimhall, and West 1997; Weiss et al. 2003.

20. Morris, Duncan, and Clark-Kauffman 2003.

21. This extensive literature has been reviewed by Hoffman 1979, 1984, 1989;

Hoffman et al. 1999; Kamerman and Hayes 1982; Smolensky and Gootman 2003 (chap. 4); and Zaslow and Emig 1997.

22. Ruhm 2003.

23. Heymann (2000, appendix C, Table C1 and C2, pp. 229–230) reports that children whose parents work during the evening score more poorly in math, and children whose parents work at night are at higher risk of being suspended from school.

24. Smolensky and Gootman 2003, chap. 4. See also Hoffman et al. 1999, chaps. 1 and 7.

25. Ruhm 2003.

26. See Barnett and Baruch (1987), Crouter and Crowley (1990), Crouter et al. (1987), and Hoffman et al. (1999) for evidence that maternal employment may affect father involvement in two-parent families.

27. For instance, in an in-depth study of 485 third- and fourth-graders, Hoffman et al. (1999) concluded that the higher aggressiveness of children with employed mothers was due to the effects of mothers working in the first year of life.

28. Ruhm 2003.

29. Hoffman et al. 1999, chap. 10.

30. Smolensky and Gootman 2003, chap. 4.

31. This literature is reviewed in Repetti in press; and Zaslow, Jekielek, and Gallagher in press.

32. Repetti 1994.

33. See Cooksey, Meneghan, and Jekielek 1997; Galinsky 1999, chap. 8; Hoffman et al. 1999; Menaghan, Kowaleski-Jones, and Mott 1997; Smolensky and Gootman 2003, chap. 4; Zaslow, Jekielek, and Gallagher in press.

34. Yankelovich, Clark, and Martin 1977.

35. Galinsky 1999. Galinsky and colleagues at the Families and Work Institute surveyed a nationally representative sample of children in third through twelfth grade (age eight to eighteen). They also surveyed parents. Statistics on satisfaction with time with fathers are from Galinsky 1999, 69.

36. Galinsky 1999, 65–66.

37. Galinsky 1999, 93–94.

38. Galinsky 1999, 93–94.

39. Galinsky 1999, 68.

40. Galinksy 1999, 29–30 and 49–50.

41. See for example Conger et al. 1992, 1993, 1994; Elder 1974; Elder, Van Nguyen, and Caspi 1985.

42. Galinsky 1999, 38.

43. Galinsky 1999, 85.

44. Galinsky 1999, 215.

45. Jacobs and Gerson 2004, 30.

46. Jacobs and Gerson 2004, 65.

47. See discussion in Galinsky 1999, chap. 6; and Jacobs and Gerson 2004, chap. 4.

48. Bianchi 2000; Smolensky and Gootman 2003.

49. Smolensky and Gootman 2003, Table 3–2, p. 48. Both these results hold up in multivariate analyses for children aged five to seven, eight to ten, and eleven to thirteen: controlling for other characteristics, children are more likely to be in self-care rather than parental care if they live with two parents who work full-time or

with a single parent who works full-time or if they do not live with married parents; see Casper and Smith 2004.

50. Blau and Currie in press, Table 4.

51. Smolensky and Gootman 2003, chap. 5.

52. Smolensky and Gootman 2003. For a broader discussion of families' decisions about using self-care, see Smolensky and Gootman 2003, chap. 5; and also Belle 1997; Capizzano, Tout, and Adams 2000; Galambos and Maggs 1991b; Vandell and Su 1999; Vandivere et al. 2003.

53. Kerrebrock and Lewit 1999.

54. Vandell and Su 1999.

55. Kraizer et al. 1990.

56. Fox and Newman 1998; Snyder and Sickmund 1997.

57. See, for instance, Carnegie Council on Adolescent Development 1992; Dryfoos 1998; Burt, Resnick, and Novick 1998; and Resnick et al. 1997.

58. Chin and Newman 2002; Halpern 1999; Heymann and Earle 2000; Quinn 1999; Weiss et al. 2003.

59. Recent studies of the effects of self-care, reviewed in Blau and Currie (in press), include Aizer 2004; Belle 1997; Galambos and Maggs 1989; Marshall et al. 1997; McHale, Crouter, and Tucker 2001; Pettit et al. 1997, 1999; Richardson et al. 1999; Rodman, Pratto, and Nelson 1985; Steinberg 1986; Vandell and Corasiniti 1988; Vandell and Posner 1999; Vandell and Ramanan 1991.

60. Aizer 2004.

61. See, for example, Pettit et al. 1997 and Vandell and Posner 1999.

62. Pettit et al. 1999.

63. McHale, Crouter, and Tucker 2001.

64. Smolensky and Gootman 2003, Table 3.2, p. 48.

65. Smolensky and Gootman 2003, Table 3.2, p. 48.

66. More detailed data from the SIPP (see Smolensky and Gootman 2003, Table 3.2, p. 48) indicate that as children get older, they are less likely to be in something called a child care center and more likely to be in something called an organized activity. Although the differences between these two categories of out-of-school program are not clear cut, one distinction is that centers are more likely to be everyday programs, whereas organized activities may be offered on more of a part-week basis.

67. Blau and Currie in press, Table 2.

68. Blau and Currie in press, Table 2.

69. Blau and Currie in press, Table 2; Halpern 1999.

70. See, for example, Hofferth 1995.

71. Seppanen et al. 1993.

72. Hofferth et al. 1991; Pettit et al. 1997; Vandell and Shumow 1999.

73. Data are from 2001 National Household Survey, as reported in National Center for Education Statistics 2004, Table 34-1, pp. 176–177.

74. Halpern 1999; Vandell and Shumow 1999. See also Duffett et al. 2004.

75. Lareau 2003.

76. Seppanen et al. 1993, p. 56.

77. These studies on after-school programs are reviewed in Vandell and Shumow 1999.

78. Morris and Kalil in press.

79. Alter 1998; California Center for Health Improvement 1998; Charles Stewart Mott Foundation 1998.

80. Blau and Currie in press, 55; Vandell and Shumow 1999.

81. Dryfoos 1999.

82. Sylvester and Reich 2000.

83. Figures for 1988 and 1994 are from Dryfoos 1999; figures for 2000 from National Center for Education Statistics 2002.

84. Dryfoos 1999, 125.

85. Dryfoos 1999, 123.

86. Huang et al. 2000.

87. Kane 2004.

88. The results of the 21st CCLC evaluation were released in January 2003 (Dynarski et al. 2003). This evaluation was criticized by members of its scientific advisory board (Bissell et al. 2003) and other experts (see, for instance, Mahoney and Zigler 2003; see also discussion in Jacobson 2003). Granger and Kane (2004) and Kane (2004), provide a balanced overview of the 21st CCLC evaluation, as well as evaluations of three other major after-school programs (New York City's The After-School Corporation [TASC], the Extended-Service Schools Initiative [ESS] which operated in six cities, and San Francisco Beacons Initiative [SFBI]).

89. Afterschool Alliance 2003, 1, 3.

90. The National Governors Association also publishes a newsletter on extra learning opportunities. This newsletter and other information are available at www.nga.org [accessed 2/1/05].

91. For further information on The National School-Age Child Care Alliance, see their Web site at naaweb.org [accessed 2/1/05].

92. See, for instance, the Harvard Family Research Project at www.gse.web.harvard.edu [accessed 2/1/05] and the National Institute on Out-of-School Time at www.niost.org [accessed 2/1/05].

93. Only about a third of child care subsidy funds go to cover the costs of care for school-age children; see Meyers et al. 2004.

94. Halpern 1999.

95. See, for instance, evidence from the New Hope study, carried out by MDRC, summarized in Bos et al. 1999.

96. For further information on the Child Care Development Fund and the Child and Dependent Care Tax Credit, see Smolensky and Gootman 2003, chap. 8.

97. Information on school schedules in other countries is from Gornick and Meyers 2003, Table 7.9, pp. 230–231.

98. Bracey 2002.

99. Information on San Diego's program is available from the City of San Diego at www.sannet/gov/6to6/ [accessed 2/1/05]. Quotation is from City of San Diego 2004, p. 1.

100. Information on scheduling and school calendar reforms is available from the Education Commission of the States, at www.ecs.org [accessed 2/1/05].

5. *Adolescents*

1. See discussion in Eccles and Gootman 2002, chap. 2. See also Adams, Montemayor, and Gullotta 1989; Brooks-Gunn and Reiter 1990; Brooks-Gunn, Graber, and Paikoff 1994; Buchanan, Eccles, and Becker 1992; Caspi, Moffitt, and Silva 1993; National Research Council 1999.

2. Erikson 1968.

3. See, for instance, Arnett 1999; Carnegie Council on Adolescent Development 1989; Cicchetti and Toth 1996; Eccles and Gootman 2002; Eccles et al. 1993; Eccles, Lord, and Roeser 1996; Giddens 1990; Jessor, Donovan, and Costa 1991; Moffitt 1993; Rutter and Smith 1995; Sampson and Laub 1995; Steinberg and Morris 2001.

4. Centers for Disease Control and Prevention 2004, Table 48, p. 77.

5. Centers for Disease Control and Prevention 2004, Table 50, p. 79. Over the same period, enrollment in physical education at school falls from 71 percent to 57 percent; see Table 54, p. 83.

6. Centers for Disease Control and Prevention 2004, Table 58, p. 87.

7. Centers for Disease Control and Prevention 2004, Table 20, p. 49.

8. Centers for Disease Control and Prevention 2004, Table 26, p. 55.

9. Centers for Disease Control and Prevention 2004, Table 28, p. 57.

10. National Center on Addiction and Substance Abuse 1994 and 2003a.

11. Centers for Disease Control and Prevention 2004, Table 4, p. 33.

12. Centers for Disease Control and Prevention 2004, Table 42, p. 71.

13. Data on condom and birth control use are from Centers for Disease Control and Prevention 2004, Table 42, p. 71. Data on multiple partners are from the same source, Table 28, p. 57.

14. Centers for Disease Control and Prevention 2004, Table 6, p. 35. For an overview of the rise in criminal involvement during adolescence, see McCord, Widom, and Crowell 2001; and Smolensky and Gootman 2003, chap. 6.

15. Centers for Disease Control and Prevention 2004, Table 16, p. 45.

16. For an overview of brain development during adolescence, see McCord, Widom and Crowell 2001.

17. National Academy of Sciences 1998; Mortimer et al. 1996; Steinberg and Dornbusch 1991.

18. See review in Smolensky and Gootman 2003, chap. 6. See also Eccles and Gootman 2002, chap. 2; Laursen, Coy, and Collins 1998.

19. See discussion in Roth and Brooks-Gunn 2000; see also Council of Economic Advisors 2000; and Resnick et al. 1997.

20. See discussion in Council of Economic Advisors 2000; Larson et al. 1996; Roth and Brooks-Gunn 2000. Analyses from the National Longitudinal Survey of Adolescent Health are reported in Council of Economic Advisors 2000. See also analyses of the same data set reported by Resnick et al. 1997, and related evidence in Moore et al. 1999; Tepper 1999.

21. Baker and Stevenson 1986; Chilcoat and Anthony 1996; Dishion and McMahon 1998; Patterson, Bank, and Stoolmiller 1990. See also overview in McCord, Widom, and Crowell 2001.

22. See, for instance, Rhodes 1994.

23. See discussion in Roth and Brooks-Gunn 1999.

24. See, for instance, Mayer 1997; McLanahan and Sandefur 1994; E. Thompson, Hanson, and McLanahan 1994.

25. For an overview of the literature on the effects of low income on the home environment and parenting practices, see Duncan and Brooks-Gunn 1997; McLeod and Shanahan 1993; McLoyd 1990 and 1998. For evidence on adolescent financial strain, see Moore, Coley, and Chase-Lansdale 2004, and also McLoyd et al. 1994; Wadsworth and Compas 2002.

26. See, for instance, Armistead, Wierson, and Forehand 1990; Hillman and Sawilosky 1991; Orthner 1991; Wright, Peterson, and Barners 1990.

27. Parallel analyses of children aged twelve to fifteen at the time of the intervention found negative but not statistically significant effects on school achievement; see Morris, Duncan, and Clark-Kauffman 2003, Table 3. However, when programs were analyzed individually, significant negative effects for this age group did emerge in two of the programs (no significant effects were found in the other four); see Morris, Duncan, and Clark-Kauffman 2003, appendix, Table 2. See also Brooks, Hair, and Zaslow (2001), who find a pattern of negative effects for adolescents in two studies.

28. These analyses are reported in Gennetian et al. 2002.

29. For a further elaboration of the idea of a developmental "mismatch" associated with parental employment, see Zaslow, Jekielek, and Gallagher in press.

30. A few studies have found that boys in middle-class families have poorer grades if their mothers work full-time but no effects for girls; see Bogenschneider and Steinberg 1994; Bronfenbrenner and Crouter 1982; and Montemayor 1984. Galinsky (1999) reports that employed mothers with adolescents spend more time with daughters than they do with sons.

31. See Gennetian et al. 2002.

32. Armistead, Wierson, and Forehand 1990; Orthner 1991; Ross Phillips 2002.

33. For an overview, see Smolensky and Gootman 2003, chap. 6. See also Conger et al. 1992, 1993, 1994; R. D. Conger, K. J. Conger, and Elder 1997; Elder 1974, Elder, Van Nguyen, and Caspi 1985, Elder et al. 1995; Gutman and Eccles 1999; Lempers, Clark-Lempers, and Simons 1989; McLoyd 1990 and 1998; McLoyd et al. 1994; McLoyd and Wilson 1990; Moore, Coley, and Chase-Lansdale 2004; Skinner, Elder, and Conger 1992; Whitbeck et al. 1991 and 1997.

34. The results of this survey are reported in Galinsky 1999.

35. Galinsky 1999, chap. 2.

36. Galinsky 1999, 75. The survey also found that if you ask parents, they report eating together more often than their children do (there are similar gaps when it comes to other activities). It may be that parents tend to overstate the time they spend with their children because it is socially desirable, or that children tend to overstate time not spent with parents because they notice it more.

37. Galinsky 1999, p. 80.

38. Galinksy 1999, chap. 5.

39. Galinsky 1999, pp. 270–271.

40. National Institute on Out-of-School Time 2001.

41. Zill, Moore, et al. 1995. See also Marshall et al. 1997; Richardson et al. 1999.

42. See discussion in Smolensky and Gootman 2003, chap. 6; see also Coolson, Seligson, and Garbarino 1985; Galambos and Maggs 1991a and 1991b; Rodman, Pratto, and Smith Nelson 1985; Steinberg 1986; Stewart 2001; Zill, Moore et al. 1995.

43. Smolensky and Gootman 2003, chap. 6.

44. Smolensky and Gootman 2003, chap. 6. See also Aizer 2001; Dishion, McCord, and Poulin 1999; Galambos and Maggs 1991a and 1991b; Mahoney, Stattin, and Magnusson 2001; McCord 1978; Osgood et al. 1996; Steinberg 1986.

45. See, for example, Dishion and McMahon 1998; Dishion et al. 1995; Furstenberg et al. 1999; Pettit et al. 1999; Reid and Patterson 1989.

46. Roth and Brooks-Gunn 2000.

47. Quinn 1999.

48. See discussion in Lauver 2004. See also Eccles and Gootman 2002; Hollister 2003; Kirby 2001; Kane and Sawhill 2003.

49. See review in Eccles and Gootman 2002, chap. 1. See also National Center for Education Statistics (2004, Table 34-1, p. 177), which finds 42 percent of children in grades six to eight (roughly, ages eleven to fourteen) participating in after-school activities on a weekly basis. The National Survey of America's Families finds a higher share of youths—60 percent—participating in some kind of activity after school or on weekends; see National Survey of America's Families 1997.

50. National Survey of America's Families 1997; Newman et al. 2000.

51. Centers for Disease Control and Prevention 2004, Table 56, p. 85.

52. For an in-depth discussion of different types of programs, with a particular focus on youth development, see Eccles and Gootman 2002; Roth and Brooks-Gunn 2003a and 2003b.

53. This literature is reviewed in Chaput 2004; Eccles and Gootman 2002, Roth and Brooks-Gunn 2000. See in particular Barber, Eccles, and Stone in press; Cairns and Cairns 1994; Clark 1988; Eccles and Barber 1999; Elder et al. 2000; Larson 2000; Marsh and Kleitman 2002; Vandell and Posner 1999; Zill, Nord, and Loomis 1995.

54. See in particular Dishion and Andrews 1995; Dishion, McCord, and Poulin 1999. See also an overview of this literature in McCord, Widom, and Crowell 2001.

55. For an overview, see Eccles and Gootman 2002, chap. 9.

56. For an overview of these and other programs, see Blau and Currie in press; Eccles and Gootman 2002; Heckman and Lochner 2000; Roth et al. 1998.

57. Details of the evaluation are available in Tierney, Grossman, and Resch 1995.

58. Details of the evaluation are available in Hahn, Leavitt, and Aaron 1994.

59. Details of the evaluation are available in Kahne and Bailey 1999.

60. Details of the evaluation are available in Allen et al. 1996.

61. Csikszentmihalyi, Rathunde, and Whalen 1993; Mahoney 2000; Mahoney and Magnusson 2001; Tierney, Grossman, and Resch 1995.

62. Bureau of Labor Statistics 2004, Table 1, p. 5

63. Bureau of Labor Statistics 2004, Table 4, p. 9

64. See, for example, Lerman 2000.

65. For a useful overview, see Donahoe and Tienda 2000. A separate body of literature has considered the health risks related to hazards on the job; see review in Roth and Brooks-Gunn 2000.

66. Tyler 2003.

67. See Donahoe and Tienda 2000.

68. For evidence on the labor market returns to adolescents' working, see Ruhm 1997b and 1997c.

69. See Hoffman (1974 and 1979) on the influence of mothers' work and Galambos and Sears (1998) and Ryu and Mortimer (1996) on the influence of fathers' work.

70. See, for instance, research reported by the Sleep Foundation 2004.

71. Larson and Verma 1999; Zill, Nord, and Loomis 1995.

72. Centers for Disease Control and Prevention 2004, Table 56, p. 85.

73. Lemke et al. 2004, Table 2, p. 14; Table 3, p. 29; and p. 34.

74. National Center for Education Statistics 2002, 60–62 and 150–152.
75. See discussion in Donahoe and Tienda 2000.

6. *Where Do We Go from Here?*

1. Galinsky, Bond, and Hill 2004, p. 21. See also Christensen 2005; Stark et al. 2005; Waldfogel 2005.
2. Ku and Broaddus 2000; Lambrew 2001; Dubay and Kenney 2001.
3. This figure is based on estimates in Duncan and Magnuson (2003), who propose something like an early childhood benefit. They propose a child allowance payable to all families with children under age five with incomes under $60,000 per year. The benefit would be $300 per month for infants and $200 per month for children up to age five. The benefit would be taxable, and the costs would also be offset by reducing other benefits. The net cost of this proposal is about $10 billion per year (Table 2–1, p. 28), but Duncan and Magnuson argue that the net developmental benefits are many times greater. The cost of an early childhood benefit limited to low- and moderate-income families with a child under one would be considerably less. According to Duncan and Magnuson, there are fewer than 3 million children under the age of one living in families with incomes below $60,000 per year. Thus, the cost of a $300 per month benefit would be about $900 million per year. However, if we take into account savings in other programs (which would amount to a projected $675 million), the net cost would be roughly $225 million per year.
4. Figure for children of employed mothers in the 1999 Survey of Income and Program Participation is from Blau and Currie in press, Table 1, p. 84.
5. In 2001, the maximum reimbursement rate for care for a preschool-age child ranged from a low of $2,600 per year in Missouri to a high of $14,935 in California; see Blau and Currie in press, Table 10.
6. Head Start figure is in 1999 dollars and is from Magnuson and Waldfogel in press b.
7. See estimates in Magnuson, Meyers, et al. (2004), who argue that a year of prekindergarten (at a cost of $8,800 in 2002 dollars) will increase lifetime earnings by $7,600 and will yield other benefits in reduced grade retention and possibly increased school attainment, reduced teen pregnancy, or reduced criminal justice involvement.
8. Early intervention cost is in 1999 dollars and is from Magnuson, Meyers, et al. 2004.
9. See, for instance, Heckman and Lochner 2000; Carneiro and Heckman 2003.
10. See Magnuson and Waldfogel 2005.
11. HM Treasury 2004.
12. Meyers et al. 2004, Table 6.6, p. 255.
13. Gornick and Meyers 2003, Table 7.4, p. 214.
14. Mitchell and Stoney 2004.
15. Labor Project for Working Families 2003.
16. Levin-Epstein 2004.
17. See, for instance, the report of the Committee for Economic Development 2002.
18. Afterschool Alliance 2003.
19. Afterschool Alliance 2003.

20. Farkas et al. 2000.
21. Public Agenda 1999, 6.
22. Ad Council 2004, 6.
23. Evidence on this generational change is provided in Galinsky and Bond 2004.
24. For an extended discussion of what parents can do, see Bookman 2004.
25. Friedman and Galinsky (2000 and 2001) provide useful overviews. See also Friedman and Greenhaus 2000.
26. In a 1998 survey of large firms, the Families and Work Institute found that over a third said they did not make a real and ongoing effort to inform employees of available assistance with work-family needs, while over half said they did provide training to supervisors in responding to work-family needs (Galinsky and Bond 1998, Tables H and I, pp. 8–9).
27. Galinsky and Bond 1998, Table L, p. 11.
28. Friedman and Galinsky 2001.
29. Ad Council 2004, 7.
30. National Partnership for Women and Families 2004.
31. The Trust for Early Education 2004.
32. National Center for Education Statistics 2002.
33. Labor Project for Working Families 2003.
34. Beatty 2004; Kirp 2004.

References

Adams, G. R., R. Montemayor, and T. P. Gullotta. 1989. *Biology of Adolescent Behavior and Development*. Newbury Park, Calif.: Sage Publications.

Ad Council. 2004. *Turning Point: Engaging the Public on Behalf of Children*. New York: Ad Council. Available at www.adcouncil.org (accessed 1/12/05).

Afterschool Alliance. 2003. *Afterschool Alert: Poll Report, No. 6*. December, 2003. Available at www.afterschoolalliance.org (accessed 8/1/04).

Ahnert, L. and Michael Lamb. 2003. "Shared Care: Establishing a Balance between Home and Child Care Settings." *Child Development* 74 (4): 1044–1049.

Ainsworth, Mary D. S. 1973. "The Development of Infant-Mother Attachment." In *Review of Child Development Research*, ed. B. M. Caldwell and H. N. Ricciutti, vol. 3, 1–94. Chicago, Ill.: University of Chicago Press.

Ainsworth, Mary D. S., M. C. Blehar, E. Waters, and S. Wall. 1978. *Patterns of Attachment*. Hillsdale, N.J.: Lawrence Erlbaum Associates.

Aizer, Anna. 2001. "Home Alone: Maternal Employment, Child Care, and Adolescent Behavior." Working Paper 807, University of California at Los Angeles.

Aizer, Anna. 2004. "Home Alone: Supervision After School and Child Behavior." *Journal of Public Economics*. 88(9–10): 1835–1848.

Allen, J. P., S. Philliber, S. Herrling, and Gabriel P. Kuperminc. 1996. "Preventing Teen Pregnancy and Academic Failure." *Child Development* 64: 729–742.

Alter, J. 1998. "Do You Know Where Your Kids Are?" *Newsweek* April 27: 28–33.

American Academy of Pediatrics, Task Force on Infant Positioning and SIDS. 1992. "Positioning and SIDS." *Pediatrics* 89 (June): 1120–1126.

American Academy of Pediatrics, Work Group on Breastfeeding. 1997. "Breastfeeding and the Use of Human Milk." *Pediatrics* 100(6): 1035–1039.

Anderson, Patricia, Kristin Butcher, and Philip Levine. 2003. "Maternal Employment and Overweight Children." *Journal of Health Economics* 22(3): 477–504.

Andersson, Bengt-Eric. 1989. "Effects of Public Day Care: A Longitudinal Study." *Child Development* 60: 857–867.

Andersson, Bengt-Eric. 1992. "Effects of Day-Care on Cognitive and Socioemotional Competence of Thirteen-Year-Old Swedish Schoolchildren." *Child Development* 63: 20–36.

Angrist, Joshua D., Guido Imbens, and Alan Krueger. 1996. "Identification of Causal Effects Using Instrumental Variables." *Journal of the American Statistical Association* 91: 444–472.

Angrist, Joshua D. and Alan Krueger. 1999. "Empirical Strategies in Labor Economics." In *Handbook of Labor Economics*, ed. Orley Ashenfelter and David Card, vol. 3A. Amsterdam: North-Holland.

Armistead, L., M. Wierson, and R. Forehand. 1990. "Adolescents and Maternal Employment: Is It Harmful for a Young Adolescent to Have an Employed Mother?" *Journal of Early Adolescence* 10(3): 260–278.

Arnett, J. J. 1999. "Adolescent Storm and Stress, Reconsidered." *American Psychologist* 54: 317–326.

Bainbridge, Jay, Marcia Meyers, Sakiko Tanaka, and Jane Waldfogel. 2005. "Who Gets an Early Education? Family Income and the Gaps in Enrollment of 3–5 Year Olds from 1968–2000." *Social Science Quarterly* 86(3): 724–745.

Baker, C. O. and L. D. L. Stevenson. 1986. "Mothers' Strategies for Children's School Achievement: Managing the Transition to High School." *Sociology of Education* 59: 156–166.

Barber, B. L., J. S. Eccles, and M. R. Stone. In press. "Whatever Happened to the Jock, the Brain, and the Princess?" *Journal of Adolescent Research*.

Barnett, R. C. and G. K. Baruch. 1987. "Determinants of Fathers' Participation in Family Work." *Journal of Marriage and the Family* 49: 29–40.

Barnett, Rosalind C. and Caryl Rivers. 1996. *She Works/He Works: How Two Income Families Are Happier, Healthier, and Better-Off.* San Francisco: Harper Collins.

Barnett, W. S. 1995. "Long-Term Effects of Early Childhood Programs on Cognitive and School Outcomes." *Future of Children* 5(3): 25–50.

Barton, P. E. 2003. "Parsing the Achievement Gap: Baselines for Tracking Progress." Princeton, N.J.: Policy Information Center, Educational Testing Service. Available from www.ets.org. (accessed 8/1/04).

Baum, Charles L. 2003. "Does Early Maternal Employment Harm Child Development? An Analysis of the Potential Benefits of Leave-Taking." *Journal of Labor Economics* 21(2): 409–448.

Baum, Charles L. In press. "The Long-Term Effects of Early and Recent Maternal Employment on a Child's Academic Achievement." *Journal of Family Issues*.

Baydar, Nazli and Jeanne Brooks-Gunn. 1991. "Effects of Maternal Employment and Child Care Arrangements in Infancy on Preschoolers' Cognitive and Behavioral Outcomes: Evidence from the Children of the NLSY." *Developmental Psychology* 27: 918–931.

Beatty, Barbara. 2004. "Past, Present, and Future: What Can We Learn from the History of Preschool Education?" *American Prospect* November 1: 1–5.

Belle, Deborah. 1997. "Varieties of Self-Care: A Qualitative Look at Children's Experiences in the After-School Hours." *Merrill-Palmer Quarterly* 43(3): 478–496.

Belle, Deborah. 1999. *The After-School Lives of Children: Alone and With Others.* Mahwah, N.J.: Lawrence Erlbaum Associates.

Belsky, Jay. 1988. "The 'Effects' of Infant Day Care Reconsidered." *Early Childhood Research Quarterly* 3: 235–272.

Belsky, Jay. 2001. "Developmental Risk (Still) Associated with Early Child Care." *Journal of Child Psychology and Psychiatry* 42: 845–860.

Belsky, Jay and J. Cassidy. 1994. "Attachment: Theory and Evidence." In *Development through Life*, ed. Michael Rutter and D. Hay, 373–402. Oxford, U.K.: Blackwell.

Belsky, Jay and David Eggebeen. 1991. "Early and Extensive Maternal Employment/Child Care and 4–6 Year Olds Socioemotional Development: Children of the National Longitudinal Survey of Youth." *Journal of Marriage and the Family* 53: 1083–1099.

Berger, Lawrence, Jennifer Hill, and Jane Waldfogel. 2003. "Parental Leave Policies, Early Maternal Employment, and Child Outcomes." Paper presented at the annual meeting of the European Society for Population Economics, New York.

Berger, Lawrence, Jennifer Hill, and Jane Waldfogel. 2005. "Maternity Leave, Early Maternal Employment, and Child Outcomes in the United States." *Ecomonic Journal* 115: F29–F47.

Berger, Lawrence and Jane Waldfogel. 2004. "Maternity Leave and the Employment of New Mothers in the United States." *Journal of Population Economics* 17: 331–349.

Bianchi, Suzanne. 2000. "Maternal Employment and Time with Children: Dramatic Change or Surprising Continuity?" *Demography* 37(4): 401–414.

Bissell, Joan S., Christopher Cross, Karen Mapp, Elizabeth Reisner, Deborah Lowe Vandell, Constancia Warren, and Richard Weissbourd. 2003. "Statement Released by Members of the Scientific Advisory Board for the 21st Century Community Learning Center Evaluation." May 10.

Blank, R. M. 1990. "Are Part-Time Jobs Bad Jobs?" In *A Future of Lousy Jobs?* ed. Gary Burtless, 123–155. Washington, D.C.: Brookings Institution.

Blank, Rebecca. 1998. "Contingent Work in a Changing Labor Market." In *Generating Jobs*, ed. Richard Freeman and Peter Gottschalk, 258–294. New York: Russell Sage Foundation.

Blau, David. 1999. "The Effect of Income on Child Development." *Review of Economics and Statistics* 34(4): 261–276.

Blau, David. 2000. "The Production of Quality in Child Care Centers: Another Look." *Applied Developmental Science* 4(3): 136–148.

Blau, David. 2001. *The Child Care Problem*. New York: Russell Sage Foundation.

Blau, David and Janet Currie. In press. "Pre-School, Day Care, and After-School Care: Who's Minding the Kids?" *Handbook of the Economics of Education*. New York: North Holland.

Blau, Francine D. and Adam J. Grossberg. 1992. "Maternal Labor Supply and Children's Cognitive Development." *Review of Economics and Statistics* 74(3): 474–481.

Bogenschneider, K. and L. Steinberg. 1994. "Maternal Employment and Adolescent Academic Achievement: A Developmental Analysis." *Sociology of Education* 67: 60–77.

Boocock, S. S. 1995. "Early Childhood Programs in Other Nations: Goals and Outcomes." *Future of Children* 5(3): 94–114.

Bookman, A. 2004. *Starting in Our Own Backyards: How Working Families Can Build Community and Survive the New Economy*. New York: Routledge.

Borkowski, J., Sharon Landesman Ramey, and M. Bristol-Powers. In press. *Parent-*

ing and the Child's World: Influences on Academic, Intellectual, and Socioemotional Development. Hillsdale, N.J.: Lawrence Erlbaum Associates.

Bornstein, M., N. Gist, C. Hahn, O. Haynes, and M. Voigt. 2001. "Long-Term Cumulative Effects of Daycare Experience on Children's Mental and Socioemotional Development." Washington, D.C.: National Institute of Child Health and Human Development.

Bos, Johannes, Thomas Brock, Greg Duncan, Robert Granger, Aletha Huston, and Vonnie McLoyd. 1999. *New Hope for People With Low Incomes: Two-Year Results of a Program to Reduce Poverty and Reform Welfare.* Available at www.mdrc. org (accessed 6/15/03).

Bowlby, John. 1969. *Attachment and Loss,* vol. 1. New York: Basic Books.

Bowman, Barbara, Suzanne Donovan, and Susan Burns. 2000. *Eager to Learn: Educating Our Preschoolers.* Report of the National Academy of Sciences Committee on Early Childhood Pedagogy. Washington, D.C.: National Academy Press.

Bracey, G. 2002. "Summer Loss: The Phenomenon No One Wants to Deal With." *Phi Delta Kappan* 84(1): 12–13.

Brady-Smith, Christy, Jeanne Brooks-Gunn, Jane Waldfogel, and Rebecca Fauth. 2001. "Work or Welfare? Assessing the Impacts of Recent Employment and Policy Changes on Very Young Children." *Evaluation and Program Planning* 24: 409–425.

Brayfield, A. A., S. G. Deich, and S. L. Hofferth. 1995. *Caring for Children in Low-Income Families: A Substudy of the National Child Care Survey, 1990.* Washington, D.C.: Urban Institute Press.

Brazelton, T. Berry. 1986. "Issues for Working Parents." *American Journal of Orthopsychiatry* 56: 14–25.

Brazelton, T. Berry and Stanley I. Greenspan. 2000. *The Irreducible Needs of Children: What Every Child Must Have to Grow, Learn, and Flourish.* Cambridge, Mass.: Perseus Books.

Broberg, A. G., C. P. Hwang, M. E. Lamb, and R. D. Ketterlinus. 1989. "Child Care Effects on Socioemotional and Intellectual Competence in Swedish Preschoolers." In *Caring for Children: Challenge for America,* ed. J. S. Lande, S. Scarr, and N. Gunzenhauser, Hillsdale, N.J.: Lawrence Erlbaum Associates.

Broberg, A. G., C. P. Hwang, H. Wessels, and M. E. Lamb. 1997. "Effects of Day Care on the Development of Cognitive Abilities in 8-Year Olds: A Longitudinal Study." *Developmental Psychology* 33(1): 62–69.

Bronfenbrenner, Urie and Nan Crouter. 1982. "Work and Family through Time and Space." In *Families that Work: Children in a Changing World,* ed. Sheila Kamerman and Cheryl Hayes, Washington, D.C.: National Academy Press.

Brooks, J. L., E. C. Hair, and M. J. Zaslow. 2001. *Welfare Reform's Impacts on Adolescents: Early Warning Signs.* Washington, D.C.: Child Trends.

Brooks-Gunn, Jeanne, Wen-Jui Han, and Jane Waldfogel. 2002. "Maternal Employment and Child Cognitive Outcomes in the First Three Years of Life: The NICHD Study of Early Child Care." *Child Development* 73(4): 1052–1072.

Brooks-Gunn, Jeanne and E. O. Reiter. 1990. "The Role of Pubertal Processes." In *At the Threshold: The Development Adolescent,* ed. S. S. Feldman and G. R. Elliott, 16–53. Cambridge, Mass.: Harvard University Press.

Brooks-Gunn, Jeanne, J. A. Graber, and R. L. Paikoff. 1994. "Studying the Links between Hormones and Negative Affect: Models and Measures." *Journal of Research on Adolescence* 4: 469–486.

Bruer, John T. 1999. *The Myth of the First Three Years.* New York: The Free Press.

Bruner, J. 1975. "The Ontogenesis of Speech Activities." *Journal of Child Language* 2: 1–19.

Buchanan, C. M., J. S. Eccles, and J. B. Becker. 1992. "Are Adolescents the Victims of Raging Hormones: Evidence for Activational Effects of Hormones on Moods and Behaviors in Adolescence." *Psychological Bulletin* 111: 62–107.

Burchinal, M. R., Sharon Ramey, M. K. Reid, and J. Jaccard. 1995. "Early Child Care Experiences and Their Association with Family and Child Characteristics during Middle Childhood." *Early Childhood Research Quarterly* 10: 33–41.

Burchinal, M. R., J. E. Roberts, L. A. Nabors, and D. M. Bryant. 1996. "Quality of Center Child Care and Infant Cognitive and Language Development." *Child Development* 67: 606–620.

Bureau of Labor Statistics. 2004. "Employment of Teenagers during the School Year and Summer." Washington, D.C.: Goverment Printing Office.

Burgess, Simon, Paul Gregg, Carol Propper, Elizabeth Washbrook, and the ALSPAC Study Team. 2002. "Maternity Rights and Mothers' Return to Work." CMPO Working Paper no. 02/055, University of Bristol, England.

Burt, Martha G., Gary Resnick, and Emily Novick. 1998. *Building Supportive Communities for At-Risk Adolescents: It Takes More Than Services.* Washington, D.C.: American Psychological Association.

Cairns, R. B. and B. D. Cairns. 1994. *Lifelines and Risks: Pathways of Youth in Our Time.* New York: Cambridge University Press.

California Center for Health Improvement. 1998. *Growing Up Well: Focus on Prevention. Californians Favor Investing In After-School, Mentoring, Education Programs.* Sacramento: California Center for Health Improvement.

Camp, Christine. 2004. *Right to Request Flexible Working: Review of Impact in First Year of Legislation.* Report for the Department of Trade and Industry. Available at www.dti.gov.uk (accessed 10/12/05).

Cantor, David, Jane Waldfogel, Jeff Kerwin, Mareena McKinley Wright, Kerry Levin, John Rauch, Tracey Hagerty, and Martha Stapleton Kudela. 2001. *Balancing the Needs of Families and Employers: Family and Medical Leave Surveys, 2000 Update.* Rockville, Md.: Westat.

Capizzano, J., K. Tout, and G. Adams. 2000. *Child Care Patterns of School-Age Children with Employed Mothers.* Washington, D.C.: Urban Institute.

Capizzano, J., S. Adelman, and M. Stagner. 2002. *What Happens When the School Year Is Over? The Use and Costs of Child Care for School-Age Children during the Summer Months.* Washington, D.C.: Urban Institute.

Carnegie Council on Adolescent Development. 1989. *Turning Points: Preparing American Youth for the 21st Century.* New York: Carnegie Corporation.

Carnegie Council on Adolescent Development. 1992. *A Matter of Time: Risk and Opportunity in the Nonschool Hours.* New York: Carnegie Corporation.

Carnegie Task Force on Meeting the Needs of Young Children. 1994. *Starting Points: Meeting the Needs of Our Youngest Children.* New York: Carnegie Corporation.

Carneiro, Pedro and James J. Heckman. 2003. "Human Capital Policy." In *Inequality in America: What Role for Human Capital Policies?* ed. Benjamin W. Friedman, Cambridge, Mass.: MIT Press.

Case, Anne, Darren Lubotsky, and Christina Paxson. 2002. "Economic Status and Health in Childhood: The Origin of the Gradient." *American Economic Review* 92(5): 1308–1334.

Case, Anne and Christina Paxson. 2001. "Mothers and Others: Who Invests in Children's Health?" *Journal of Health Economics* 20: 301–328.

Casper, Lynne M. and Kristin E. Smith. 2004. "Self-Care: Why Do Parents Leave Their Children Unsupervised?" *Demography* 41(2): 285–301.

Caspi, A., D. Lynam, T. E. Moffitt, and P. A. Silva. 1993. "Unraveling Girls' Delinquency: Biological, Dispositional, and Contextual Contributions to Adolescent Misbehavior." *Developmental Psychology* 29: 19–30.

Caspi, A., J. McClay, T. Moffitt, J. Mill, J. Martin, I. W. Craig, A. Taylor, and R. Poulton. 2002. "Role of Genotype in the Cycle of Violence in Maltreated Children." *Science* 297: 851–854.

Cassidy, J. 1999. "The Nature of the Child's Ties." In *Handbook of Attachment: Theory, Research, and Clinical Applications,* ed. J. Cassidy and P. R. Shaver, 3–20. New York: Guilford Press.

Caughy, M. O., J. DiPietro, and D. Strobino. 1994. "Day-Care Participation as a Protective Factor in the Cognitive Development of Low-Income Children." *Child Development* 65, 457–471.

Centers for Disease Control and Prevention. 2004. "Youth Risk Behavior Surveillance—United States, 2003." *Morbidity and Mortality Weekly Report* 53 (SS-2, May 21): 1–96.

Chaput, Sandra Simpkins. 2004. "Characterizing and Measuring Participation in Out-of-School Time Programs." *Harvard Family Research Project Evaluation Exchange* 10(1): 2–3, 29.

Charles Stewart Mott Foundation. 1998. "Poll Finds Overwhelming Support for Afterschool Enrichment Programs to Keep Kids Safe and Smart." Flint, Mich.: Charles Stewart Mott Foundation. Available at www.mott.org (accessed 8/1/04).

Chase-Lansdale, P. L. and L. D. Pittman. 2002. "Welfare Reform and Parenting: Reasonable Expectations." *Future of Children* 12(1): 167–185.

Chatterji, Pinka and Sara Markowitz. 2004. "Does the Length of Maternity Leave Affect Maternal Health?" NBER Working Paper no. 10206, National Bureau for Economic Research, Cambridge, Mass.

Chilcoat, H. D. and J. C. Anthony. 1996. "Impact of Parental Monitoring on Initiation of Drug Use Through Late Childhood." *Journal of American Academy of Child and Adolescent Psychiatry* 35: 91–100.

Chin, M. M. and K. S. Newman. 2002. *High Stakes: Time Poverty, Testing, and the Children of the Working Poor.* New York: Foundation for Child Development.

Chira, Susan. 1994. "Still Guilty After All These Years." *New York Times Book Review.* May 8, 1994, p. 11.

Christensen, Kathleen. 2005. "Achieving Work-Life Balance: Strategies for Dual Earner Families." In *Being Together, Working Apart,* ed. Barbara Schneider and Linda Waite. Cambridge, UK: Cambridge University Press.

Cicchetti, Dante and S. L. Toth, eds. 1996. *Adolescence: Opportunities and Challenges—Rochester Symposium on Developmental Psychopathology,* vol. 8. Rochester, N.Y.: University of Rochester Press.

City of San Diego. 2004. "'6 to 6' Extended School Day Program." Available from the City of San Diego at www.sannet.gov (accessed 8/1/04).

Clark, R. M. 1988. *Critical Factors in Why Disadvantaged Students Succeed or Fail in School.* New York: Academy for Educational Development.

Clarke-Stewart, K. A. 1988. " 'The "Effects" of Infant Day Care Reconsidered' Reconsidered: Risks for Parents, Children, and Researchers." *Early Childhood Research Quarterly* 3, 293–318.

Clarke-Stewart, Alison and Virginia D. Allhusen. 2005. *What We Know about Childcare.* Cambridge, Mass.: Harvard University Press.

Clarke-Stewart, K. A., C. P. Gruber, and L. M. Fitzgerald. 1994. *Children at Home and in Day Care.* Hillsdale, N.J.: Lawrence Erlbaum Associates.

Clearinghouse on International Developments in Child, Youth, and Family Policies at Columbia University. 2002. "Early Childhood Education and Care." Available at www.childpolicyintl.org (accessed 1/6/04).

Clifford, R. M., O. Barbarin, F. Chang, D. Early, D. Bryant, C. Howes, M. Burchinal, and R. Pianta. In press. "What is Pre-Kindergarten? Characteristics of Public Pre-Kindergarten Programs." *Applied Developmental Science.*

Cochran, M. S. and L. Gunnarson. 1985. "A Follow-Up Study of Group Day Care and Family-Based Childrearing Patterns." *Journal of Marriage and the Family* 47: 297–309.

Coletrane, Scott. 1996. *Family Man: Fatherhood, Housework, and Gender Equity.* New York: Oxford University Press.

Collins, W. Andrew. 1984. *Development during Middle Childhood: The Years from Six to Twelve.* Washington, D.C.: National Academy Press.

Commission on Family and Medical Leave. 1996. *A Workable Balance: Report to the Congress on Family and Medical Leave Policies.* Washington, D.C.: Women's Bureau, U.S. Department of Labor.

Committee for Economic Development. 2002. *Preschool for All: Investing in a Productive and Just Society.* New York: Committee for Economic Development. Available at www.ced.org (accessed 7/26/04).

Conger, R. D., K. J. Conger, and Glen E. Elder. 1997. "Family Economic Hardship and Adolescent Adjustment: Mediating and Moderating Processes." In *Consequences of Growing Up Poor,* ed. Greg Duncan and Jeanne Brooks-Gunn, chap. 10. New York: Russell Sage Foundation.

Conger, Rand, K. Conger, G. Elder, F. Lorenz, R. Simons, and L. Whitbeck. 1992. "A Family Process Model of Economic Hardship and Adjustment of Early Adolescent Boys." *Child Development* 63: 526–541.

Conger, Rand, K. Conger, G. Elder, F. Lorenz, R. Simons, and L. Whitbeck. 1993. "Family Economic Stress and Adjustment of Early Adolescent Girls." *Developmental Psychology* 29: 206–219.

Conger, Rand, X. Ge, G. Elder, F. Lorenz, and R. Simons. 1994. "Economic Stress, Coercive Family Process, and Developmental Problems of Adolescents." *Child Development* 65: 541–561.

Cooksey, E. C., E. G. Menaghan, and S. M. Jekielek. 1997. "Life Course Effect of Work and Family Circumstances on Children." *Social Forces* 76: 637–667.

Coolson, P., M. Seligson, and J. Garbarino. 1985. *When School's Out and Nobody's Home.* Chicago, Ill.: National Committee for the Prevention of Child Abuse.

Council of Economic Advisors. 2000. *Teens and Their Parents in the 21st Century: An Examination of Trends in Teen Behavior and the Role of Parent Involvement.* Washington, D.C.: Council of Economic Advisors.

Crittenden, Ann. 2001. *The Price of Motherhood: Why the Most Important Job in the World is Still the Least Valued.* New York: Metropolitan Books.

Crittenden, Ann. 2004. "The Price of Motherhood—Author Meets the Critics." Presentation to annual meeting of the Population Association of America, Boston.

Crockenberg, S. C. 2003. "Rescuing the Baby from the Bathwater: How Gender and Temperament (May) Influence How Child Care Affects Child Development." *Child Development* 74(4): 1034–1038.

Crouter, A. C. and M. S. Crowley. 1990. "School-Age Children's Time Alone with Fathers in Single- and Dual-Earner Families." *Journal of Early Adolescence* 10: 296–312.

Crouter, A. C., H. Helms-Erikson, K. Updegraff, and S. M. McHale. 1999. "Conditions Underlying Parents' Knowledge about Children's Daily Lives: Between- and Within-Family Comparisons." *Child Development* 70: 246–259.

Crouter, A. C., M. Perry-Jenkins, T. L. Huston, and S. M. McHale. 1987. "Processes Underlying Father Involvement in Dual-Earner and Single-Earner Families." *Developmental Psychology* 23: 431–440.

Csikszentmihalyi, M., K. Rathunde, and W. Whalen. 1993. *Talented Teenagers: The Roots of Success and Failure.* Cambridge, U.K.: Cambridge University Press.

Cunningham, Allan S., Derrick B. Jelliffe, and E. F. Patrice Jelliffe. 1991. "Breastfeeding and Health in the 1980s: A Global Epidemiological Review." *The Journal of Pediatrics* 118(5): 659–666.

Currie, Janet. 2001. "Early Childhood Intervention Programs: What Do We Know?" *Journal of Economic Perspectives* 15: 213–238.

Currie, Janet. 2003. "When Do We Really Know What We Think We Know?" Paper presented at the NICHD Conference on Work, Family, Health, and Well-Being, Washington, D.C.

Currie, Janet and V. Joseph Hotz. 2004. "Accidents Will Happen? Unintentional Injury, Maternal Employment, and Child Care Policy." *Journal of Health Economics.* 23(1): 25–59.

Currie, Janet and Matthew Neidell. 2003. "Getting Inside the 'Black Box' of Head Start Quality: What Matters and What Doesn't?" NBER Working Paper 10091. Available at www.nber.org (accessed 7/1/04).

Currie, J. and D. Thomas. 1995. "Does Head Start Make a Difference?" *American Economic Review* 85(3): 341–364.

Currie, J. and D. Thomas. 1999. "Does Head Start Help Hispanic Children?" *Journal of Public Economics* 74(2): 235–262.

Currie, J. and D. Thomas. 2000. "School Quality and the Longer-Term Effects of Head Start." *Journal of Human Resources* 35(4): 755–774.

Currie, Janet and Duncan Thomas. 2001. "Early Test Scores, Socioeconomic Status, School Quality, and Future Outcomes." *Research in Labor Economics* 20: 103–132.

Damon, William, ed. 1988. *The Moral Child: Nurturing Children's Natural Moral Growth.* New York: Free Press.

Damon, William, ed. 1998. *Handbook of Child Psychology.* 5th ed. New York: John Wiley and Sons.

Dearing, E., K. McCartney, and B. A. Taylor. 2001. "Change in Family Income-to-Needs Matters More for Children with Less." *Child Development* 72(6): 1779–1793.

Deaton, Angus. 2002. "Health, Inequality, and Economic Development." *Journal of Economic Literature* 41: 113–158.

Desai, Sonalde, Lindsay Chase-Lansdale, and Robert Michael. 1989. "Mother or Market? Effects of Maternal Employment on Cognitive Development of Four-Year-Old Children." *Demography* 26: 545–561.

Deutsch, Francine M. 1999. *Halving It All: How Equally Shared Parenting Works.* Cambridge, Mass.: Harvard University Press.

Dishion, T. J. 1990. "The Family Ecology of Boys' Peer Relations in Middle Childhood." *Child Development* 61: 874–892.

Dishion, T. J. and D. W. Andrews. 1995. "Preventing Escalation in Problem Behaviors with High-Risk Young Adolescents: Immediate and 1-Year Outcomes." *Journal of Consulting and Clinical Psychology* 63(4): 538–548.

Dishion, T. J., D. Capaldi, K. M. Spacklen, and F. Li. 1995. "Peer Ecology of Male Adolescent Drug Use: Developmental Processes in Peer Relations and Psychopathology." *Developmental and Psychopathology* 7: 803–824.

Dishion, T. J., J. McCord, and F. Poulin. 1999. "When Interventions Harm: Peer Groups and Problem Behavior." *American Psychologist* 55: 755–764.

Dishion, T. J. and R. J. McMahon. 1998. "Parental Monitoring and the Prevention of Child and Adolescent Problem Behavior: A Conceptual and Empirical Formulation." *Family Psychology Review* 1: 61–75.

Donahoe, Debra and Marta Tienda. 2000. "The Transition from School to Work: Is there a Crisis? What Can Be Done?" In *Securing the Future: Investing in Children from Birth to College,* ed. Sheldon Danziger and Jane Waldfogel, 231–264. New York: Russell Sage Foundation.

Douglas, Susan J. and Meredith W. Michaels. 2004. *The Mommy Myth: The Idealization of Motherhood and How It Has Undermined Women.* New York: Free Press.

Dryfoos, Joy G. 1998. *Safe Passage: Making It through Adolescence in a Risky Society.* New York: Oxford University Press.

Dryfoos, Joy G. 1999. "The Role of the School in Children's Out-of-School Time." *Future of Children* 9(2): 117–134.

Dubay, K. and G. Kenney. 2001. "Covering Parents through Medicaid and SCHIP: Potential Benefits to Low-Income Parents and Children." Washington, D.C.: Urban Institute.

Duffett, A. and J. Johnson, with S. Farkas, S. Kung, and A. Ott. 2004. *All Work and No Play? Listening to What Kids and Parents Really Want from Out-of-School Time.* New York: Public Agenda. Available at www.publicagenda.org (accessed 1/12/05).

Duncan, Greg and Jeanne Brooks-Gunn, eds. 1997. *Consequences of Growing Up Poor.* New York: Russell Sage Foundation.

Duncan, Greg, Amy Claessens, and Mimi Engel. 2004. "The Contributions of Hard Skills and Socioemotional Behavior to School Readiness." Evanston, Ill.: Northwestern University.

Duncan, Greg and Katherine Magnuson. 2003. "Promoting the Healthy Development of Young Children." In *One Percent for the Kids: New Policies, Brighter Futures for America's Children,* ed. Isabel Sawhill, 16–39. Washington, D.C.: Brookings Institution.

Duyme, M., A. C. Dumaret, and S. Tomkiewicz. 1999. "How Can We Boost the IQs of 'Dull Children'? A Late Adoption Study." *Proceedings of the National Academy of Sciences* 96(15): 8790–8794.

Early Childhood Focus. 2005. "Wisconsin Governor Proposes Child Care Rating System." Available at www.earlychildhoodfocus.org (accessed 1/13/05).

Early Head Start Research Consortium. 2001. *Building Their Futures: How Early Head Start Programs Are Enhancing the Lives of Infants and Toddlers in Low-Income Families: Summary Report.* Washington, D.C.: U.S. Department of Health and Human Services, Administration for Children and Families.

Eccles, Jacquelynne S. 1999. "The Development of Children Ages 6 to 14." *Future of Children* 9(2): 30–44.

Eccles, Jacquelynne S. and Bonnie L. Barber. 1999. "Student Council, Volunteering, Basketball, or Marching Band: What Kind of Extracurricular Involvement Matters?" *Journal of Adolescent Research* 14: 10–43.

Eccles, Jacquelynne and Jennifer Appleton Gootman. 2002. *Community Programs to Promote Youth Development.* Washington, D.C.: National Academy Press.

Eccles, J. S., S. Lord, and R. Roeser. 1996. "Round Holes, Square Pegs, Rocky Roads, and Sore Feet: The Impact of Stage/Environment Fit on Young Adolescents' Experiences in Schools and Families." In *Adolescence: Challenges and Opportunities—Rochester Symposium on Developmental Psychopathology,* vol. 8, ed. D. Cicchetti and S. L. Toth, 47–93. Rochester, N.Y.: University of Rochester Press.

Eccles, J. S., C. Midgley, A. Wigfield, C. M. Buchanon, D. Reuman, C. Flanagan, and D. MacIver. 1993. "Development during Adolescence." *American Psychologist* 48: 90–101.

Education Commission of the States. 2004. "Scheduling/School Calendar." Available at www.ecs.org. (accessed 6/15/04).

Elder, Glen. 1974. *Children of the Great Depression: Social Change in Life Experience.* Chicago, Ill.: University of Chicago.

Elder, G. H., J. S. Eccles, M. Ardelt, and S. Lord. 1995. "Inner-City Parents under Economic Pressure: Perspectives on the Strategies of Parenting." *Journal of Marriage and the Family* 57(3): 771–784.

Elder, G., D. Leaver-Dunn, M. Q. Wang, S. Nagy, and L. Green. 2000. "Organized Group Activity as a Protective Factor against Adolescent Substance Abuse." *American Journal of Health Behavior* 24: 108–113.

Elder, G., T. Van Nguyen, and A. Caspi. 1985. "Linking Family Hardship to Children's Lives." *Child Development* 56: 361–375.

Ellwood, David T. 1988. *Poor Support: Poverty in the American Family.* New York: Basic Books.

Erikson, Eric H. 1968. *Identity: Youth and Crisis.* New York: W. W. Norton.

Ermisch, J. and M. Francesconi. 2000. "The Effects of Parents' Working on Children's Outcomes." Paper presented at the British Society for Population Studies, London.

Esping-Anderson, Gosta. 1990. *Three Worlds of Welfare Capitalism.* Princeton, N.J.: Princeton University Press.

European Foundation for the Improvement of Living and Working Conditions. N.d. *European Industrial Relations Observatory Online.* Available at www.eiro. eurofound.ie. (accessed 2/11/04).

Fabes, R. A., L. D. Hanish, and C. L. Martin. 2003. "Children at Play: The Role of Peers in Understanding the Effects of Child Care." *Child Development* 74(4): 1039–1043.

Fan, X. and M. Chen. 2001. "Parental Involvement and Students' Academic Achievement: A Meta-Analysis." *Educational Psychology Review* 13(1): 1–22.

Farkas, S., A. Duffett, and J. Johnson, with T. Foleno and P. Foley. 2000. *Necessary Compromises: How Parents, Employers, and Children's Advocates View Child Care Today.* New York: Public Agenda. Available at www.publicagenda.org (accessed 1/12/05).

Farkas, S., J. Johnson, and A. Duffett, with L. Wilson and J. Vine. 2002. *A Lot Easier Said Than Done: Parents Talking about Raising Children in Today's America.* New York: Public Agenda. Available at www.publicagenda.org (accessed 1/12/05).

Ferber, Marianne and Jane Waldfogel. 1998. "The Long-Term Consequences of Nontraditional Employment." *Monthly Labor Review* (May): 3–12.

Field, Tiffany. 1991. "Quality Infant Day Care and Grade School Behavior and Performance." *Child Development* 62: 863–870.

Flanagan, K. and J. West. 2004. *Children Born in 2001: First Results from the Base Year of the Early Childhood Longitudinal Study, Birth Cohort (ECLS-B).* U.S. Department of Education, Washington, D.C.: National Center for Education Statistics.

Fox, J. A. and S. A. Newman. 1998. *After-School Crime or After-School Programs: Tuning into the Prime Time for Violent Juvenile Crime and Implications for National Policy.* Washington, D.C.: Fight Crime and Invest in Kids.

Friedman, S. D. and E. Galinsky. 2000. "Private Sector Initiatives in Caring for the Young Children of Working Parents." Paper presented at the Wharton School Impact Conference, Caring for Young Children of Working Parents. Philadelphia.

Friedman, S. D. and E. Galinsky. 2001. "Corporate Help Is at Hand for Working Parents." *Financial Times,* November 5.

Friedman, S. D. and J. Greenhaus. 2000. *Work and Family: Allies or Enemies?* New York: Oxford University Press.

Furstenberg, Frank. 1995. "Fathering in the Inner City: Paternal Participation and Public Policy." In *Fatherhood: Contemporary Theory, Research, and Social Policy,* ed. William Marsiglio, 119–147. Thousand Oaks, Calif.: Sage Publications.

Furstenberg, Frank, Tom Cook, Jacquelynne Eccles, Glen Elder, and Arnold Sameroff. 1999. *Managing to Make It: Urban Families and Adolescent Success.* Chicago, Ill.: University of Chicago Press.

Galambos, N. L. and J. L. Maggs. 1991a. "Out-of-School Care of Young Adolescents and Self-Reported Behavior." *Developmental Psychology* 27(4): 644–655.

Galambos, N. L. and J. L. Maggs. 1991b. "Children in Self-Care: Figures, Facts, and Fiction." In *Employed Mothers and Their Children,* ed. Jacqueline Lerner and Nancy Galambos, 131–157. New York: Garland Press.

Galambos, N. L. and H. A. Sears. 1998. "Adolescents' Perceptions of Parents' Work and Adolescents' Work Values in Two-Earner Families." *Journal of Early Adolescence* 18(4): 397–420.

Galinsky, Ellen. 1999. *Ask the Children: What America's Children Really Think About Working Parents.* New York: William Morrow and Company.

Galinsky, Ellen and James T. Bond. 1998. *The 1998 Business Work-Life Study: A Sourcebook.* Executive Summary available at http://familiesandwork.org (accessed 1/11/05).

Galinsky, Ellen and James T. Bond. 2004. *Generation and Gender in the Workplace.*

New York: Families and Work Institute. Available at http://familiesandwork. org (accessed 1/11/05).

Galinsky, Ellen, James T. Bond, and E. Jeffrey Hill. 2004. *When Work Works: A Status Report on Workplace Flexibility.* New York: Families and Work Institute. Available at http://familiesandwork.org (accessed 1/11/05).

Galinsky, Ellen, Carollee Howes, Susan Kontos, and Marybeth Shinn. 1994. *The Study of Children in Family Child Care and Relative Care.* New York: Families and Work Institute.

Gennetian, Lisa A., Greg J. Duncan, Virginia W. Knox, Wanda G. Vargas, Elizabeth Clark-Kauffman, and Andrew S. London. 2002. *How Welfare and Work Policies for Parents Affect Adolescents: A Synthesis of Research.* New York: Manpower Demonstration Research Corporation.

Gerson, Kathleen. 1993. *No Man's Land: Men's Changing Commitments to Family and Work.* New York: Basic Books.

Giddens, Anthony. 1990. *The Consequences of Modernity.* Stanford, Calif.: Stanford University Press.

Gormley, William T. 1995. *Everybody's Children: Child Care as a Public Problem.* Washington, D.C.: Brookings Institution.

Gormley, William T. and Ted Gayer. 2003. "Promoting School Readiness in Oklahoma: An Evaluation of Tulsa's Pre-K Program." Working Paper no. 1, Center for Research on Children in the United States, Georgetown University.

Gormley, William T. and Deborah Phillips. 2003. "The Effects of Universal Pre-K in Oklahoma: Research Highlights and Policy Implications." Working Paper no. 2, Center for Research on Children in the United States, Georgetown University.

Gornick, Janet C. and Marcia K. Meyers. 2003. *Families That Work: Policies for Reconciling Parenthood and Employment.* New York: Russell Sage Foundation.

Gottfried, A. E., A. W. Gottfried, and K. Bathurst. 1995. "Maternal and Dual-Earner Employment Status and Parenting." In *Handbook of Parenting*, vol. 2, ed. Marc Bornstein, 139–160. Mahwah, N.J.: Lawrence Erlbaum Associates.

Granger, Robert C. and Thomas J. Kane. 2004. "Improving the Quality of After-School Programs." Available from the William T. Grant Foundation at www.wtgrantfoundation.org (accessed 7/1/04).

Greenstein, Theodore N. 1995. "Are the 'Most Advantaged' Children Truly Disadvantaged by Early Maternal Employment? Effects on Child Cognitive Outcomes." *Journal of Family Issues* 16(2): 149–169.

Gregg, Paul, Maria Gutierrez-Domenech, and Jane Waldfogel. 2003. "The Employment of Married Mothers in Great Britain: 1974–2000." CEP Discussion Paper no. 596. London: Centre for Economic Performance, London School of Economics.

Grissmer, David W., Ann Flanagan, Jennifer Kawata, and Stephanie Williamson. 2000. *Improving Student Achievement: What State NAEP Test Scores Tell Us.* Santa Monica, Calif.: RAND.

Gruber, Jonathan. 1992. "The Efficiency of a Group-Specific Mandated Benefit: Evidence from Health Insurance Benefits for Maternity." Working Paper 4157, National Bureau of Economic Research, Cambridge, Mass.

Gruber, Jonathan. 1994. "The Incidence of Mandated Maternity Benefits." *American Economic Review* (June): 622–641.

Gruber, Jonathan and Alan Krueger. 1991. "The Incidence of Mandated Employer-Provided Insurance: Lessons from Workers' Compensation Insurance." In *Tax Policy and the Economy*, ed. David Bradford. Cambridge, Mass.: MIT Press.

Gutman, L. M. and Jacquelynne Eccles. 1999. "Financial Strain, Parenting Behaviors, and Adolescents' Achievement: Testing Model Equivalence between African American and European American Single and Two Parent Families." *Child Development* 70(6): 1464–1474.

Haas, Linda and Philip Hwang. 1999. "Parental Leave in Sweden." In *Parental Leave: Progress or Pitfall? Research and Policy Issues in Europe*, ed. Peter Moss and Fred Deven, 45–68. Brussels: CBGS Publications.

Hahn, A., T. Leavitt, and P. Aaron. 1994. "Evaluation of the Quantum Opportunities Program: Did the Program Work?" Waltham, Mass.: Brandeis University, Heller Graduate School, Center for Human Resources.

Haider, Steven J., Alison Jacknowitz, and Robert F. Schoeni. 2003. "Welfare Work Requirements and Child Well-Being: Evidence from the Effects on Breast-Feeding." *Demography* 40(3): 479–497.

Halpern, Robert. 1999. "After-School Programs for Low-Income Children: Promise and Challenges." *Future of Children* 9(2): 81–95.

Han, Wen-Jui. 2005. "Maternal Nonstandard Work Schedules and Child Cognitive Outcomes." *Child Development* 76(1): 137–154.

Han, Wen-Jui, Jeanne Brooks-Gunn, and Jane Waldfogel. 2004. "Are There Persistent Effects of Early Maternal Employment on Child Cognitive Outcomes? The NICHD Study of Early Child Care." Paper presented at the annual meeting of the Population Association of America, Boston.

Han, Wen-Jui and Jane Waldfogel. 2003. "Parental Leave: The Impact of Recent Legislation on Parents' Leave-Taking." *Demography* 40(1): 191–200.

Han, Wen-Jui, Jane Waldfogel, and Jeanne Brooks-Gunn. 2001. "The Effects of Early Maternal Employment on Later Cognitive and Behavioral Outcomes." *Journal of Marriage and the Family* 63: 336–354.

Han, Wen-Jui, Jane Waldfogel, and Jeanne Brooks-Gunn. 2002. "Maternal Employment in the First Year and Preschoolers' Behavior Outcomes: Evidence from the NLSY and NICHD Study of Early Child Care." Mimeo, Columbia University.

Harris, Judith R. 1995. "Where is the Child's Environment? A Group Socialization Theory of Development." *Psychological Review* 102(3): 458–489.

Harris, Judith R. 1998. *The Nature Assumption: Why Children Turn Out the Way They Do*. New York: Free Press.

Hart, B. and T. R. Risley. 1995. *Meaningful Differences in the Everyday Experiences of Young American Children*. Baltimore, Md.: Paul H. Brookes.

Harvey, Elizabeth. 1999. "Short-Term and Long-Term Effects of Early Parental Employment on Children of the National Longitudinal Survey of Youth." *Developmental Psychology* 35(2): 445–459.

Haskins, Ron. 1989. "Beyond Metaphor: The Efficacy of Early Childhood Education." *American Psychologist* 44: 274–282.

Haskins, Ron. 2004. "Preschool Programs and the Achievement Gap: The Little Train that Could." Washington, D.C.: Brookings Institution.

Hayes, C. D., J. L. Palmer, and M. J. Zaslow, eds. 1990. *Who Cares for America's*

Children? Child Care Policy for the 1990s. Committee on Child Development Research and Public Policy. Washington, D.C.: National Academy Press.

Hays, Sharon. 1996. *The Cultural Contradictions of Motherhood.* New Haven, Conn.: Yale University Press.

Heckman, James J. and Lance Lochner. 2000. "Rethinking Education and Training Policy: Understanding the Sources of Skill Formation in a Modern Economy." In *Securing the Future: Investing in Children from Birth to College,* ed. Sheldon Danziger and Jane Waldfogel, 47–86. New York: Russell Sage Foundation.

Helburn, Suzanne and Barbara Bergmann. 2002. *America's Child Care Problem: The Way Out.* New York: Palgrave for St. Martin's Press.

Henderson, A. T. and K. L. Mapp. 2002. *A New Wave of Evidence: The Impact of Family, School, Community Connections on Student Achievement.* Austin, Tex.: Southwest Educational Development Laboratory.

Henry, Gary T. and Craig S. Gordon. 2004. "Competition in the Sandbox: A Test of the Effects of Preschool Competition on Educational Outcomes." Atlanta, Ga.: Andrew Young School of Policy Studies, Georgia State University.

Henry, Gary T., Laura W. Henderson, and Bentley D. Ponder. 2004. "Ready or Not: A Snapshot of Children Entering Kindergarten in Georgia." Atlanta, Ga.: Andrew Young School of Policy Studies, Georgia State University.

Henry, Gary T., Laura W. Henderson, Bentley D. Ponder, Craig S. Gordon, Andrew J. Mashburn, and Dana K. Rickman. 2003. "Report of the Findings from the Early Childhood Study: 2001–02." Atlanta, Ga.: Andrew Young School of Policy Studies, Georgia State University.

Henry, Gary T., Andrew J. Mashburn, Bentley D. Ponder, Laura W. Henderson, Craig S. Gordon, and Dana K. Rickman. 2004. "Impacts of Georgia's Pre-K Program: 2002–03 Report of the Findings from the Early Childhood Study." Atlanta, Ga.: Andrew Young School of Policy Studies, Georgia State University.

Hertz, Rosanna. 1986. *More Equal than Others: Women and Men in Dual-Career Marriages.* Berkeley: University of California Press.

Heymann, Jody. 2000. *The Widening Gap: Why America's Working Families Are in Jeopardy and What Can Be Done About It.* New York: Basic Books.

Heymann, Jody and Alison Earle. 2000. "Low-Income Parents: How Do Working Conditions Affect Their Opportunity to Help School-Age Children At Risk?" *American Educational Research Journal* 37: 833–848.

Hill, Jennifer, Jane Waldfogel, and Jeanne Brooks-Gunn. 2003. "Sustained Effects of High Participation in an Early Intervention for Low-Birth-Weight Premature Infants." *Developmental Psychology* 39(4): 730–744.

Hill, Jennifer, Jane Waldfogel, Jeanne Brooks-Gunn, and Wen-Jui Han. In Press. "Towards a Better Estimate of Causal Links in Child Policy: The Case of Maternal Employment and Child Outcomes." Forthcoming in *Developmental Psychology.*

Hillman, S. B. and S. Sawilowsky. 1991. "Maternal Employment and Early Adolescent Substance Abuse." *Adolescence* 26: 829–837.

HM Treasury. 2004. *Choice for Parents, the Best Start for Children: A Ten Year Strategy for Childcare.* London: The Stationery Office.

Hochschild, Arlie R. 1989. *The Second Shift.* New York: Avon Books.

Hofferth, Sandra L. 1995. "Out-of-School Time: Risk and Opportunity." In *America's Working Poor,* ed. T. Swartz and K. M. Weigert, 123–153. Notre Dame, Ind.: University of Notre Dame.

Hofferth, S. L. 1998. *Healthy Environments, Healthy Children: Children in Families: A Report on the 1997 Panel Study of Income Dynamics Child Development Supplement.* Ann Arbor, Mich.: University of Michigan.

Hofferth, S. L., A. Brayfield, S. Deich, and P. Holcomb. 1991. *National Child Care Survey, 1990.* Washington, D.C.: Urban Institute.

Hoffman, L. 1974. "Effects of Maternal Employment on the Child: A Review of the Research." *Developmental Psychology* 10: 204–228.

Hoffman, L. 1979. "Maternal Employment." *American Psychologist* 34: 859–865.

Hoffman, L. 1984. "Maternal Employment and the Young Child." In *Minnesota Symposium on Child Psychology,* ed. M. Perlmutter, 101–128. Hillsdale, N.J.: Lawrence Erlbaum Associates.

Hoffman, L. 1989. "Effects of Maternal Employment in the Two-Parent Family." *American Psychologist* 44: 283–292.

Hoffman, L., and L. M. Youngblade, with R. L. Coley, A. S. Fuligni, and D. D. Kovacs. 1999. *Mothers at Work: Effects on Children's Well Being.* New York: Cambridge University Press.

Hollister, R. 2003. *The Growth in After-School Programs and Their Impact.* Washington, D.C.: Brookings Institution.

Horwood, L. John and David M. Ferguson. 1998. "Breastfeeding and Later Cognitive and Academic Outcomes." *Pediatrics* 101(1): 9–16.

Horwood, L. John and David M. Ferguson. 1999. "A Longitudinal Study of Maternal Labour Force Participation and Child Academic Achievement." *Journal of Child Psychology and Psychiatry* 40(7): 1013–1024.

Howes, C. 1988. "Relations between Early Child Care and Schooling." *Developmental Psychology* 24(1): 53–57.

Howes, C. 1990. "Can the Age of Entry into Child Care and the Quality of Child Care Predict Adjustment in Kindergarten?" *Developmental Psychology* 26(2): 292–303.

Howes, C. 1997. "Children's Experiences in Center-Based Care as a Function of Teacher Background and Adult:Child Ratio." *Merrill-Palmer Quarterly* 43: 404–425.

Howes, Carolee. 1999. "Attachment Relationships in the Context of Multiple Caregivers." In *Handbook of Attachment: Theory, Research, and Clinical Applications,* ed. J. Cassidy and P. R. Shaver, 671–687. New York: Guilford Press.

Howes, Carolee. 2000. "Social-Emotional Classroom Climate in Child Care, Child-Teacher Relationships, and Children's Second Grade Peer Relations." *Social Development* 9(2): 191–205.

Howes, Carolee and C. E. Hamilton. 1993. "The Changing Experience of Child Care: Changes in Teachers and in Teacher-Child Relationships and Children's Social Competence with Peers." *Early Childhood Research Quarterly* 8: 15–32.

Howes, Carolee, C. C. Matheson, and C. E. Hamilton. 1994. "Maternal, Teacher, and Child Correlates of Children's Relationships with Peers." *Child Development* 65: 253–263.

Howes, Carolee, C. Rodning, D. Galluzzo, and I. Myers. 1988. "Attachment and Childcare: Relationships with Mother and Caregiver." *Early Childhood Research Quarterly* 3:403–416.

Howes, Carolee and J. L. Rubinstein. 1985. "Determinants of Toddlers' Experiences in Day Care: Age of Entry and Quality of Setting." *Child Care Quarterly* 14: 140–153.

Howes, Carolee, L. Sakai, Marybeth Shinn, Deborah A. Phillips, Ellen Galinsky, and Marcy Whitebook. 1995. "Race, Social Class, and Maternal Working Conditions as Influences on Children's Development." *Journal of Applied Development Psychology* 16: 107–124.

Hrdy, Sarah Blaffer. 1999. *Mother Nature: A History of Mothers, Infants, and Natural Selection*. New York: Pantheon Books.

Huang, Denise, Barry Gribbons, Kyung Sung Kim, Charlotte Lee, and Eva L. Baker. 2000. *A Decade of Results: The Impact of LA's BEST After-School Enrichment Program on Subsequent Student Achievement and Performance*. Available from UCLA Center for the Study of Evaluation at www.cse.ucla.edu (accessed 7/1/05).

Hubel, D. H., T. N. Wiesel, and S. LeVay. 1977. "Plasticity of Ocular Dominance Columns in Monkey Striate Cortex." *Philosophical Transactions of the Royal Society of London* 278: 307–409.

Hulbert, Ann. 2003. *Raising America: Experts, Parents, and a Century of Advice About Children*. New York: Alfred A. Knopf.

Huston, Aletha. 2002. "Reforms and Child Development." *Future of Children* 12(1): 59–77.

Huston, Aletha. In press. "Middle Childhood: Developmental Tasks and Challenges." Aletha C. Huston and Marika N. Ripke, eds. *Development Contexts in Middle Childhood*.

Huston, Aletha C. and Marika N. Ripke. In press. *Development Contexts in Middle Childhood*. Cambridge, Mass.: Cambridge University Press.

Huttenlocher, J., W. Haight, A. Bryk, M. Seltzer, and T. Lyons. 1991. "Early Vocabulary Growth: Relation to Language Input and Gender." *Developmental Psychology* 27(2): 236–248.

Ilmakunnas, Seija. 1997. *Female Labour Supply and Work Incentives*. Helsinki: Labor Institute for Economic Research.

Jacobs, Jerry A. and Kathleen Gerson. 2004. *The Time Divide: Work, Family, and Gender Inequality*. Cambridge, Mass.: Harvard University Press.

Jacobson, Linda. 2003. "After-School Report Called Into Question." *Education Week* 22(37): 1, 15.

Jain, Anjali, John Concato, and John Leventhal. 2002. "How Good Is the Evidence Linking Breastfeeding and Intelligence?" *Pediatrics* 109(6): 1044–1053.

James-Burdumy, Suzanne. 2005. "The Effect of Maternal Labor Force Participation on Child Development." *Journal of Labor Economics* 25(1): 177–211.

Jessor, R., J. E. Donovan, and F. M. Costa. 1991. *Beyond Adolescence: Problem Behavior and Young Adult Development*. New York: Cambridge University Press.

Joshi, H. and G. Verropoulou. 2000. *Maternal Employment and Child Outcomes: Analysis of Two Birth Cohort Studies*. London: Smith Institute.

Kahne, Joseph and Kim Bailey. 1999. "The Role of Social Capital in Youth Development: The Case of 'I Have a Dream Programs.'" *Educational Evaluation and Policy Analysis* 21(3): 321–343.

Kaiser Family Foundation. 1999. *Kids and Media at the New Millennium*. Available from the Kaiser Family Foundation at www.kff.org (accessed 10/12/05).

Kamerman, Sheila B. 1994. "Family Policy and the Under-3s: Money, Services, and Time in a Policy Package." *International Social Security Review* 47(3–4): 31–43.

Kamerman, Sheila B. 2000a. "Early Childhood Education and Care: An Overview of Developments in the OECD Countries." *International Journal of Educational Research* 33: 7–29.

Kamerman, Sheila B. 2000b. "Parental Leave Policies: An Essential Ingredient in Early Childhood Education and Care Policies." *Social Policy Report* 14(2): 3–15.

Kamerman, Sheila B. 2000c. "From Maternity to Parenting Policies: Women's Health, Employment, and Child and Family Well-Being." *Journal of the American Women's Medical Association.* 55(2): 96–99.

Kamerman, Sheila B. and Cheryl D Hayes. 1982. *Families That Work: Children in a Changing World.* Washington, D.C.: National Academy Press.

Kamerman, Sheila B. and Alfred J. Kahn, eds. 1991. *Child Care, Parental Leave, and the Under 3s: Policy Innovation in Europe.* New York: Auburn House.

Kamerman, Sheila B. and Alfred J. Kahn. 1995. *Starting Right: How America Neglects Its Youngest Children and What We Can Do About It.* New York: Oxford University Press.

Kamerman, Sheila B. and Jane Waldfogel. 2005. "Market and Non-Market Institutions in Early Childhood Education and Care." In *Market and Non-Market Institutions,* ed. Richard Nelson. New York: Russell Sage Foundation.

Kane, Andrea and Isabel V. Sawhill. 2003. "Preventing Early Childbearing." In *One Percent for the Kids: New Policies, Brighter Futures for America's Children,* ed. Isabel V. Sawhill, 56–75. Washington, D.C.: Brookings Institution.

Kane, Thomas J. 2004. "The Impact of After-School Programs: Interpreting the Results of Four Recent Evaluations." Available from the William T. Grant Foundation at www.wtgrantfoundation.org (accessed 7/1/04).

Karoly, Lynn, Peter Greenwood, Susan Everingham, Jill Hoube, Rebecca Kilburn, Peter Rydell, Matthew Sanders, and James Chiesa. 1998. *Investing in Our Children: What We Know and Don't Know about the Costs and Benefits of Early Childhood Interventions.* Santa Monica, Calif.: RAND.

Katz, J. and C. E. Snow. In press. "Language Development in Early Childhood: The Role of Social Interaction in Different Care Environments." In *Infants and Toddlers in Out-of-Home Care,* ed. D. Bailey. Baltimore, Md.: Paul H. Brookes.

Kerrebrock, Nancy and Eugene M. Lewit. 1999. "Children in Self-Care." *Future of Children* 9(2): 151–160.

Kirby, D. 2001. *Emerging Answers: Research Findings on Programs to Reduce Teen Pregnancy.* Washington, D.C.: National Campaign to Prevent Teen Pregnancy.

Kirp, David. 2004. "You're Doing Fine, Oklahoma! The Universal Pre-K Movement Takes Off in Unlikely Places." *American Prospect,* November 1: 1–5.

Kisker, E., S. L. Hofferth, D. A. Phillips, and E. Farquhar. 1991. *A Profile of Child Care Settings: Early Education and Care in 1990.* Princeton, N.J.: Mathematica Policy Research.

Klerman, Jacob Alex and Arleen Leibowitz. 1998. "FMLA and the Labor Supply of New Mothers: Evidence from the June CPS." Paper presented at the Population Association of America Annual Meeting, Chicago.

Kmec, Julie A. 1999. "Multiple Aspects of Work-Family Conflict." *Sociological Forces* 32(3): 265–285.

Kraizer, S., S. Witte, G. Fryer, and T. Miyoshi. 1990. "Children in Self-Care: A New Perspective." *Child Welfare* 69 (November/December): 571–580.

Ku, L. and M. Broaddus. 2000. "The Importance of Family-based Health Insurance Expansions: New Research Findings about State Health Reforms." Washington, D.C.: Center on Budget and Policy Priorities.

Labor Project for Working Families. 2003. *Putting Families First: How California Won the Right for Paid Family Leave.* Berkeley, Calif.: Labor Project for Working Families. Available at http://laborproject.berkeley.edu (accessed 1/13/05).

Lamb, Michael E., ed. 1996. *The Role of the Father in Child Development.* New York: John Wiley and Sons.

Lamb, Michael E. 1998. "Nonparental Child Care: Context, Quality, Correlates." In *Handbook of Child Psychology*, ed. William Damon, vol. 4, pp. 73–134, 5th ed. New York: John Wiley and Sons.

Lambrew, J. M. 2001. "Health Insurance: A Family Affair." New York: Commonwealth Fund.

Langlois, Judith H. and Lynn S. Liben. 2003. "Child Care Research: An Editorial Perspective." *Child Development* 74 (4): 969–975.

Lareau, Annette. 2003. *Unequal Childhoods: Class, Race, and Family Life.* Berkeley: University of California Press.

Larson, R. W. 2000. "Toward a Psychology of Positive Youth Development." *American Psychologist* 55: 170–183.

Larson, R., M. H. Richards, G. Moneta, G. Holmbeck, and E. Duckett. 1996. "Changes in Adolescents' Daily Interactions with Their Families from Ages 10 to 18: Disengagement and Transformation." *Developmental Psychology* 32: 744–754.

Larson, R. W. and S. Verma. 1999. "How Children and Adolescents Spend Time Across the World: Work, Play, and Developmental Opportunities." *Psychological Bulletin* 125(6): 701–736.

Laursen, B., K. C. Coy, and W. A. Collins. 1998. "Reconsidering Changes in Parent-Child Conflict Across Adolescence: A Meta-Analysis." *Child Development* 69: 817–832.

Lauver, Sherri. 2004. "Attracting and Sustaining Youth Participation in After-School Programs." *Harvard Family Research Project Evaluation Exchange* 10(1): 4–5, 31.

Leach, Penelope. 1994. *Children First: What Society Must Do—and is Not Doing—for Children Today.* New York: Alfred A. Knopf.

Leach, Penelope. 1997. *Your Baby and Child.* New York: Alfred A. Knopf.

Leibowitz, Arleen. 2005. "An Economic Perspective on Work, Family, and Well-Being." In *Work, Family, Health, and Well-Being*, ed. Suzanne Bianchi and Lynne Casper, Mahwah, N.J.: Lawrence Erlbaum Associates.

Leira, Arnlaug. 1999. "Cash-for-Child Care and Daddy Leave." In *Parental Leave: Progress or Pitfall? Research and Policy Issues in Europe*, ed. Peter Moss and Fred Deven. Brussels: CBGS Publications.

Lemke, M., A. Sen, E. Pahlke, L. Partelow, D. Miller, T. Williams, D. Kastberg, and L. Jocelyn. 2004. *International Outcomes of Learning in Mathematics Literacy and Problem-Solving: PISA 2003: Results from the U.S. Perspective.* Washington, D.C.: National Center for Education Statistics, U.S. Department of Education.

Lempers, J., D. Clark-Lempers, and R. Simons. 1989. "Economic Hardship, Parenting, and Distress in Adolescence." *Child Development* 60:25–39.

Lerman, Robert. 2000. *Are Teens in Low-Income and Welfare Families Working Too Much?* Report B-25. Washington, D.C.: Urban Institute.

LeVay, S., T. N. Wiesel, and D. H. Hubel. 1980. "The Development of Ocular

Dominance Columns in Normal and Visually Deprived Monkeys." *Journal of Comparative Neurology* 19: 11–51.

Levin, Henry M. and Clive R. Belfield. 2002. "Families as Contractual Partners in Education." *UCLA Law Review* 49(6): 1799–1824.

Levine, J. A. and T. L. Pittinsky. 1997. *Working Fathers: New Strategies for Balancing Work and Family.* New York: Harcourt Brace.

Levin-Epstein, J. 2004. "Taking the Next Step: What Can the U.S. Learn About Parental Leave from New Zealand?" Washington, D.C.: Center for Law and Social Policy.

Li, Ruowei, Zhen Zhao, Ali Mokdad, Lawrence Barket, and Laurence Grummer-Strawn. 2003. "Prevalence of Breastfeeding in the United States: The 2001 National Immunization Survey." *Pediatrics* 111(5): 1198–1201.

Li-Grining, Christine P., Elizabeth Votruba-Drzal, Heather Bachman, and P. Lindsay Chase-Lansdale. 2004. "Welfare Reform and Preschoolers: Are Certain Children at Risk?" Paper presented at the annual meeting of the Population Association of America, Boston.

Lindberg, Laura. 1996. "Women's Decisions about Breast-Feeding and Maternal Employment." *Journal of Marriage and the Family* 58(1): 239–251.

Love, John M., P. Z. Schochet, and A. L. Meckstroth. 1996. *Are They in Any Real Danger? What Research Does—and Doesn't—Tell Us About Child Care Quality and Children's Well-Being.* Princeton, N.J.: Mathematica Policy Research.

Love, John M., Ellen Eliason-Kisker, Christine M. Ross, P. Z. Schochet, Jeanne Brooks-Gunn, and D. Paulsell. 2002. *Making a Difference in the Lives of Infants and Toddlers and Their Families: The Impacts of Early Head Start.* Washington, D.C.: Administration for Children and Families, U.S. Department of Health and Human Services.

Maccoby, Eleanor E. 1984. "Middle Childhood in the Context of the Family." In *Development during Middle Childhood: The Years from Six to Twelve,* ed. Andrew W. Collins, chap. 5, 184–239. Washington, D.C.: National Academy Press.

Maccoby, Eleanor E. and J. A. Martin. 1983. "Socialization in the Context of the Family: Parent-Child Interaction." In *Manual of Child Psychology,* ed. E. M. Hetherington, vol. 4, 4th edition. New York: John Wiley and Sons.

Magnuson, Katherine and Jane Waldfogel. In press. "Preschool Enrollment and Parents' Use of Physical Discipline." *Infant and Child Development.*

Magnuson, Katherine and Jane Waldfogel. 2005. "Early Childhood Care and Education and Racial and Ethnic Test Score Gaps at School Entry." *Future of Children.* 15(1): 169–196.

Magnuson, Katherine, Marcia Meyers, Christopher Ruhm, and Jane Waldfogel. 2004. "Inequality in Preschool Education and School Readiness." *American Educational Research Journal.* 41(1): 115–157.

Magnuson, Katherine, Christopher Ruhm, and Jane Waldfogel. In press. "Does Prekindergarten Improve School Preparation and Performance?" *Economics of Education Review.*

Mahoney, Joseph L. 2000. "Participation in School Extracurricular Activities as Moderator in the Development of Antisocial Patterns." *Child Development* 71: 502–516.

Mahoney, Joseph L. and D. Magnusson. 2001. "Parent Community Engagement and the Persistence of Criminality." *Development and Psychopathology* 13(1): 125–141.

Mahoney, Joseph L., H. Stattin, and D. Magnusson. 2001. "Youth Recreation Centre Participation and Criminal Offending: A 20-Year Longitudinal Study of Swedish Boys." *International Journal of Behavioral Development* 25(6): 509–530.

Mahoney, Joseph L. and Edward F. Zigler. 2003. "The National Evaluation of the 21st Century Community Learning Centers: A Critical Analysis of First-Year Findings." Working Paper, Department of Psychology, Yale University.

Malin, Martin. 1994. "Fathers and Parental Leave." *Texas Law Review* 72: 1047–1095.

Malin, Martin. 1998. "Fathers and Parental Leave Revisited." *Northern University Law Review* 19: 25–56.

Marsh, H. W. and S. Kleitman. 2002. "Extracurricular School Activities: The Good, the Bad, and the Nonlinear." *Educational Review* 72: 464–514.

Marshall, N. L., C. Garcia-Coll, F. Marx, K. McCartney, N. Keefe, and J. Ruh. 1997. "After-School Time and Children's Behavioral Adjustment." *Merrill-Palmer Quarterly* 43(3): 497–514.

Maternity Alliance. 2004. *Happy Anniversary? The Right to Request Flexible Work One Year On.* London: Maternity Alliance.

Mayer, Susan. 1997. *What Money Can't Buy: The Effect of Parental Income on Children's Outcomes.* Cambridge, Mass.: Harvard University Press.

McCartney, Kathleen. 1984. "The Effect of Quality of Day Care Environment upon Children's Language Development." *Developmental Psychology* 20: 244–260.

McCord, J. 1978. "A 30-Year Follow-Up of Treatment Effects." *American Psychologist* 33: 284–289.

McCord, Joan, Cathy Spatz Widom, and Nancy A. Crowell, eds. 2001. *Juvenile Crime, Juvenile Justice.* Washington, D.C.: National Academy Press.

McGurk, H. M., E. Hennessy Kaplan, and P. Moss. 1993. "Controversy, Theory, and Social Context in Contemporary Day Care Research." *Journal of Child Psychology and Psychiatry* 34: 3–23.

McHale, S. M., A. C. Crouter, and C. J. Tucker. 2001. "Free-Time Activities in Middle Childhood: Links with Adjustment in Early Adolescence." *Child Development* 72(6): 1764–1778.

McLanahan, Sara and Gary Sandefur. 1994. *Growing Up with a Single Parent: What Helps, and What Hurts.* Cambridge, Mass.: Harvard University Press.

McLeod, J. and M. Shanahan. 1993. "Poverty, Parenting, and Children's Mental Health." *American Sociological Review* 58: 351–366.

McLoyd, V. 1990. "The Impact of Economic Hardship on Black Families and Children: Psychological Distress, Parenting, and Socioemotional Development." *Child Development* 61: 311–346.

McLoyd, V. 1998. "Socioeconomic Disadvantage and Child Development." *American Psychologist* 53: 185–204.

McLoyd, V. C., T. B. Jayaratne, R. Ceballo, and J. Borquez. 1994. "Unemployment and Work Interruptions among African American Single Mothers: Effects on Parenting and Adolescent Socioemotional Functioning." *Child Development* 65(2): 562–584.

Mednick, S. A., W. F. Gabrielli, and B. Hutchings. 1984. "Genetic Influences in Criminal Convictions: Evidence from an Adoption Cohort." *Science* 224: 50–79.

Melhuish, E. C. and P. Moss. 1991. *Day Care for Young Children: International Perspectives.* London: Tavistock/Routledge.

Meltzer, H. 1994. *Day Care Services for Children: A Survey Carried Out on Behalf of the Department of Public Health in 1990.* London: HMSO (Her Majesty's Stationery Office).

Menaghan, E. G., L. Kowaleski-Jones, and F. L. Mott. 1997. "The Intergenerational Costs of Parental Social Stressors: Academic and Social Difficulties in Early Adolescence for Children of Young Mothers." *Journal of Health and Social Behavior* 38: 72–86.

Meyers, Marcia and Janet Gornick. 2001. "Cross-National Variation in ECEC Service Organization and Financing." In *Early Childhood Education and Care: International Perspectives,* ed. Sheila B. Kamerman, 141–176. New York: Institute for Child and Family Policy, Columbia University.

Meyers, Marcia, Dan Rosenbaum, Christopher Ruhm, and Jane Waldfogel. 2004. "Inequality in Early Childhood Care and Education: What Do We Know?" In *Social Inequality,* ed. Kathryn Neckerman, 223–269. New York: Russell Sage Foundation.

Mississippi State Department of Health. 2003. "Regulations Governing Licensure of Child Care Facilities." Available at www.msdh.state.ms.us (accessed on 12/10/03).

Mitchell, Anne and Louise Stoney. 2004. "Public Engagement: How Do We Make Paid Family Leave a Part of the Early Care and Education System?" Available from Smart Start National Technical Assistance Center at www.ncsmart start.org (accessed 7/24/04).

Mitchell, Olivia. 1990. "The Effects of Mandating Benefits Packages." *Research in Labor Economics* 11:297–320.

Moffitt, T. E. 1993. "Adolescence-Limited and Life-Course-Persistent Antisocial Behavior: A Developmental Taxonomy." *Psychology Review* 100: 674–701.

Montemayor, R. 1984. "Maternal Employment and Adolescents' Relations with Parents, Siblings, and Peers." *Journal of Youth and Adolescence* 13: 543–557.

Moon, Rachel Y. and Wendy M. Biliter. 2000. "Infant Sleep Position Policies in Licensed Child Care Centers After Back to Sleep Campaign." *Pediatrics* 106(3): 576–580.

Moon, Rachel Y., Wendy M. Biliter, and Sarah E. Croskell. 2001. "Examination of State Regulations Regarding Infants and Sleep in Licensed Child Care Centers and Family Child Care Settings." *Pediatrics* 107(5): 1029–1036.

Moon, Rachel Y. and Rosalind P. Oden. 2003. "Back to Sleep: Can We Influence Child Care Providers?" *Pediatrics* 112(4): 878–882.

Moon, Rachel Y., Debra E. Weese-Mayer, and Jean M. Silvestri. 2003. "Nighttime Child Care: Inadequate Sudden Infant Death Syndrome Risk Factors, Knowledge, Practice, and Policies." *Pediatrics* 111(4): 795–799.

Moore, Kristin A. 1999. "Family Process and Adolescent Outcome Measures." Washington, D.C.: Child Trends.

Moore, Mignon R., Rebekah Levine Coley, and P. Lindsay Chase-Lansdale. 2004. "Perceived Financial Strain and Psychological Adjustment among Disadvantaged Adolescents." Mimeo. Columbia University.

Morgan, Patricia. 1996. *Who Needs Parents?* London: Institute for Economic Affairs.

Morris, Pamela A., Greg J. Duncan, and Elizabeth Clark-Kauffman. 2003. Child

Well-Being in an Era of Welfare Reform: The Sensitivity of Transitions in Development to Policy Change." Mimeo, Manpower Demonstration Research Corporation.

Morris, Pamela A., Aletha C. Huston, Greg J. Duncan, Danielle A. Crosby, and Johannes M. Bos. 2001. *How Welfare and Work Policies Affect Children: A Synthesis of Research.* New York: Manpower Demonstration Research Corporation.

Morris, Pamela A. and Ariel Kalil. In press. "Out-of-School Time Use during Middle Childhood in a Low-Income Sample: Do Combinations of Activities Affect Achievement and Behavior?" In *Middle Childhood: Development Contexts in Middle Childhood*, ed. Aletha C. Huston and Marika N. Ripke.

Mortensen, Erik Lykke, Kim Fleisher Michaelsen, Stephanie A. Sanders, and June Machover Reinisch. 2002. "The Association Between Duration of Breast-Feeding and Adult Intelligence." *Journal of the American Medical Association* 287(18): 2365–2371.

Mortimer, J. T., M. D. Finch, S. Ryu, M. J. Shanahan, and K. T. Call. 1996. "The Effects of Work Intensity on Adolescent Mental Health, Achievement, and Behavioral Adjustment: New Evidence from a Prospective Study." *Child Development* 67(June): 1243–1261.

Moss, Peter and Fred Deven, eds. 1999. *Parental Leave: Progress or Pitfall? Research and Policy Issues in Europe.* Brussels: CBGS Publications.

Muller, C. 1995. "Maternal Employment, Parent Involvement, and Mathematics Achievement Among Adolescents." *Journal of Marriage and the Family* 57(1): 85–100.

Murnane, Richard J. and Frank Levy. 1996. *Teaching the New Basic Skills: Principles for Educating Children to Thrive in a Changing Economy.* New York: Free Press.

National Academy of Sciences. 1998. *Protecting Youth at Work: Health, Safety, and Development of Working Children and Adolescents in the United States.* Washington, D.C.: National Academy Press.

National Association for the Education of Young Children. 2003. "State Policies on Accreditation and Tiered Reimbursement." Available at www.naeyc.org (accessed 1/12/05).

National Center for Early Development and Learning. 2003. *Multi-State Study of Pre-Kindergarten.* Chapel Hill: Frank Porter Graham Child Development Institute, University of North Carolina. Available at www.ncedl.com (accessed 2/1/05).

National Center for Education Statistics. 2002. *The Condition of Education 2002.* Washington, D.C.: U.S. Department of Education.

National Center for Education Statistics. 2004. *The Condition of Education 2004.* Washington, D.C.: U.S. Department of Education.

National Center for Health Statistics. 2003. *Health, United States, 2003.* Washington, D.C.: U.S. Department of Health and Human Services.

National Center on Addiction and Substance Abuse at Columbia University. 1994. *Cigarettes, Alcohol, Marijuana: Gateways to Illicit Drug Use.* New York: National Center on Addiction and Substance Abuse.

National Center on Addiction and Substance Abuse at Columbia University. 2003a. *The Formative Years: Pathways to Substance Abuse Among Girls and Young Women, Ages 8–22.* New York: National Center on Addiction and Substance Abuse at Columbia University.

National Center on Addiction and Substance Abuse at Columbia University. 2003b. *The Importance of Family Dinners.* New York: National Center on Addiction and Substance Abuse at Columbia University.

National Education Association. 2001. *Status of the American Public School Teacher, 2000–2001.* Washington, D.C.: National Education Association. Available at www.nea.org (accessed 7/23/04).

National Institute for Early Education Research. 2002. "Fast Facts." New Brunswick, N.J.: National Institute for Early Education Research. Available at www.nieer.org (accessed 7/24/04).

National Institute on Out-of-School Time. 2001. "Fact Sheet on School-Age Children's Out-of-School Time." Wellesley, Mass.: National Institute on Out-of-School Time.

National Partnership for Women and Families. 2004. "State Legislative Round-Up." Washington, D.C.: National Partnership for Women and Families. Available at www.nationalpartnership.org (accessed 1/13/05).

National Research Council. 1999. *Adolescent Development and the Biology of Puberty: Summary of a Workshop on New Research.* Washington, D.C.: National Academy Press.

National Survey of America's Families. 1997. *1997 NSAF Benchmarking Measures of Child and Family Well-Being,* Report 6. Washington, D.C.: Urban Institute.

Neidell, Matthew. 2000. "Early Parental Time Investments in Children's Human Capital Development: Effects of Time in the First Year on Cognitive and Non-Cognitive Outcomes." Mimeo, University of California at Los Angeles.

Nelson, K. 1973. "Structure and Strategy in Learning to Talk." *Monographs of the Society for Research in Child Development:* 38(149).

Newsweek. 2000. "What Mattters Most." Special issue, fall/winter.

Newman, S., J. A. Fox, E. Flynn, and W. Christensen. 2000. *America's After-School Choices: The Prime Time for Juvenile Crime, Or Youth Enrichment and Achievement.* Washington, D.C.: Fight Crime: Invest in Kids.

NICHD Early Child Care Research Network. 1996. "Characteristics of Infant Child Care: Factors Contributing to Positive Caregiving." *Early Childhood Research Quarterly* 11(3): 269–306.

NICHD Early Child Care Research Network. 1997a. "The Effects of Infant Child Care on Infant-Mother Attachment Security: Results of the NICHD Study of Early Child Care." *Child Development* 68(5): 860–879.

NICHD Early Child Care Research Network. 1997b. "Child Care in the First Year of Life." *Merrill-Palmer Quarterly* 43(3): 340–360.

NICHD Early Child Care Research Network. 1997c. "Poverty and Patterns of Child Care." In *Consequences of Growing Up Poor,* ed. Jeanne Brooks-Gunn and Greg J. Duncan, 100–131. New York: Russell Sage.

NICHD Early Child Care Research Network. 1997d. "Child Care in the First Year of Life." *Merrill-Palmer Quarterly* 11: 340–360.

NICHD Early Child Care Research Network. 1998a. "Early Child Care and Self-Control, Compliance, and Problem Behavior at Twenty-Four and Thirty-Six Months." *Child Development* 69(3): 1145–1170.

NICHD Early Child Care Research Network. 1998b. "Relations between Family Predictors and Child Outcomes: Are They Weaker for Children in Child Care?" *Developmental Psychology* 34: 1119–1128.

NICHD Early Child Care Research Network. 1999a. "Child Care and Mother-Child Interaction in the First Three Years of Life." *Developmental Psychology* 35(6): 1399–1413.

NICHD Early Child Care Research Network. 1999b. "Child Outcomes When Child Care Center Classes Meet Recommended Standards of Quality." *American Journal of Public Health* 89(7): 1072–1077.

NICHD Early Child Care Research Network. 1999c. "Effect Sizes from the NICHD Study of Early Child Care." Paper presented at the biennial meeting of the Society for Research in Child Development, Albuquerque.

NICHD Early Child Care Research Network. 2000a. "The Relation of Child Care to Cognitive and Language Development." *Child Development* 71(4): 958–978.

NICHD Early Child Care Research Network. 2000b. "Characteristics and Quality of Child Care for Toddlers and Preschoolers." *Applied Developmental Science.* 4: 116–135.

NICHD Early Child Care Research Network. 2002a. "Child Care and Children's Peer Interaction at 24 and 36 Months." *Child Development* 72: 1478–1500.

NICHD Early Child Care Research Network. 2002b. "Early Child Care and Children's Development Prior to School Entry: Results from the NICHD Study of Early Child Care." *American Educational Research Journal* 39: 133–164.

NICHD Early Child Care Research Network. 2003a. "Does Amount of Time Spent in Child Care Predict Socioemotional Adjustment during the Transition to Kindergarten?" *Child Development* 74(4): 976–1005.

NICHD Early Child Care Research Network. 2003b. "Age of Entry to Kindergarten and Children's Academic Achievement and Socioemotional Development." Manuscript under review.

NICHD Early Child Care Research Network and Greg Duncan. 2003. "Modeling the Impacts of Child Care Quality on Children's Preschool Cognitive Development." *Child Development* 74: 1454–1475.

Nord, C., D. Brimhall, and J. West. 1997. *Fathers' Involvement in Their Children's Schools.* Washington, D.C.: National Center for Educational Statistics, U.S. Department of Education.

North Carolina Partnership for Children. 2003. "Why Smart Start?" Available from Smart Start at www.smartstart-nc.org (accessed 7/21/04).

Office of the Inspector General. 1994. *Nationwide Review of Health and Safety Standards at Child Care Facilities.* Washington, D.C.: U.S. Department of Health and Human Services.

Organization for Economic Cooperation and Development. 2001. *Starting Strong: Early Childhood Education and Care.* Paris: Organization for Economic Cooperation and Development.

Orthner, D. K. 1991. "Parental Work and Early Adolescence: Issues for Research and Practice." *Journal of Early Adolescence* 10: 246–259.

Osborn, A. F. and J. E. Milbank. 1987. *The Effects of Early Education: A Report from the Child Health and Education Study.* Oxford, U.K.: Clarendon Press.

Osgood, D. W., J. K. Wilson, P. M. O'Malley, J. G. Bachman, and L. D. Johnson. 1996. "Routine Activities and Individual Deviant Behavior." *American Sociological Review* 61: 635–655.

Parcel, T. L. and E. G. Menaghan. 1990. "Maternal Working Conditions and Child Verbal Facility: Studying the Intergenerational Transmission of Inequality from Mothers to Young Children." *Social Psychology Quarterly* 53: 132–147.

Parcel, T. L. and E. G. Menaghan. 1994. "Early Parental Work, Family Social Capital, and Early Childhood Outcomes." *American Journal of Sociology*, 99(4): 972–1009.

Parke, Ross D. 1996. *Fathers.* Cambridge, Mass.: Harvard University Press.

Patterson, G. R., L. Bank, and M. Stoolmiller. 1990. "The Preadolescent's Contributions to Disrupted Family Process." In *From Childhood to Adolescence: A Transitional Period*, ed. R. Montemayor, G. R. Adams, and T. P. Gullotta, 107–155. Newbury Park, Calif.: Sage Publications.

Peisner-Feinberg, E. S. and M. R. Burchinal. 1997. "Relationships between Preschool Children's Child-Care Experiences and Concurrent Development: The Cost, Quality, and Outcome Study." *Merrill-Palmer Quarterly* 43(3): 451–477.

Peisner-Feinberg, E. S., M. R. Burchinal, R. M. Clifford, M. L. Culkin, C. Howes, S. L. Kagan, N. Yazejian, P. Byler, J. Rustici, and J. Zelazo. 1999. *The Children of the Cost, Quality, and Outcomes Study Go to School: Technical Report.* Chapel Hill: Frank Porter Graham Child Development Center, University of North Carolina at Chapel Hill.

Pettit, G. S., J. E. Bates, K. A. Dodge, and D. W. Meese. 1999. "The Impact of After-School Peer Contact Is Moderated by Parental Monitoring, Perceived Neighborhood Safety, and Prior Adjustment." *Child Development* 72(5): 1534–1553.

Pettit, G. S., R. D. Laird, J. E. Bates, and K. A. Dodge. 1997. "Patterns of After-School Care in Middle-Childhood: Risk Factors and Developmental Outcomes." *Merrill-Palmer Quarterly* 43: 515–538.

Philipp, Barbara, Anne Merewood, and Susan O'Brien. 2001. "Physicians and Breastfeeding Promotion in the United States: A Call for Action." *Pediatrics* 107(3): 584–587.

Phillips, Deborah and Kathleen McCartney. In press. "Child Care and Early Childhood Education." In *Handbook of Early Childhood Development*, ed. Kathleen McCartney and Deborah Phillips. Oxford: Blackwell.

Phillips, Deborah and Debra Mekos. 1993. "The Myth of Child Care Regulation: Rates of Compliance in Center-Based Child Care Settings." Paper presented at the annual research conference of the Association for Public Policy Analysis and Management, Washington, D.C.

Phillips, Deborah, Miriam Voran, Ellen Kisker, Carollee Howes, and Marcy Whitebrook. 1994. "Child Care for Children in Poverty: Opportunity or Inequity?" *Child Development* 65: 772–792.

Pianta, R., C. Howes, M. Burchinal, D. Bryant, R. Clifford, D. Early, and O. Barbarin. In press. "Features of Pre-Kindergarten Programs, Classrooms, and Teachers: Do They Predict Observed Classroom Quality and Child-Teacher Interactions?" *Applied Developmental Science.*

Plomin, R., J. C. DeFries, G. E. McClearn, and M. Rutter. 1997. *Behavioral Genetics.* 3rd ed. New York: W. H. Freeman and Company.

Presser, Harriet. 2004. *Working in a 24/7 Economy: Challenges for American Families.* New York: Russell Sage Foundation.

Public Agenda. 1999. *Kids These Days '99: What Americans Really Think about the Next Generation.* New York: Public Agenda. Available at www.adcouncil.org (accessed 1/12/05).

Quinn, Jane. 1999. "Where Need Meets Opportunity: Youth Development Programs for Early Teens." *Future of Children* 9(2): 96–116.

Ramey, Craig T. and Sharon Landesman Ramey. 1999. *Right from Birth: Building Your Child's Foundation for Life from Birth to 18 Months.* New York: Goddard Press.

Rayna, S. and E. Plaisance. 1998. "Early Childhood Education Research in France." In *Research Early Childhood Education: European Perspectives,* ed. T. David. London: Paul Chapman.

Reid, J. B. and G. R. Patterson. 1989. "The Development of Antisocial Behavior Patterns in Childhood and Adolescence: Personality and Aggression." *European Journal of Personality* 3: 107–119.

Repetti, Rena. 1994. "Short-Term and Long-Term Processes Linking Job Stressors to Father-Child Interaction." *Social Development* 3: 1–15.

Repetti, Rena. In press. "A Psychological Perspective on the Health and Well-Being Consequences of Employment Experiences for Children and Families." In *Work, Family, Health, and Well-Being,* ed. Suzanne Bianchi, Lynne Capser, and Rosalind King. Mahwah, N.J.: Lawrence Erlbaum Associates.

Resnick, M. D., P. S. Bearman, R. Blum, K. E. Bauman, K. M. Harris, J. Jones, J. Tabor, T. Beuhring, R. E. Sieving, M. Shew, M. Ireland, L. H. Bearinger, and J. R. Udry. 1997. "Protecting Adolescents from Harm: Findings from the National Longitudinal Study on Adolescent Health." *Journal of the American Medical Association* 278(10): 823–832.

Rhodes, J. E. 1994. "Older and Wiser: Mentoring Relationships in Childhood and Adolescence." *Journal of Primary Prevention* 14: 187–196.

Richardson, Jean, Kathleen Dwyer, Kimberley McGugan, William B. Hansen, Clyde Dent, C. Anderson Johnson, Steven Sussman, Bonnie Brannon, and Brian Flay. 1999. "Substance Abuse among Eighth-Grade Students Who Take Care of Themselves after School." *Pediatrics* 84(3): 556–566.

Ridley, Matt. 2003. *Nature Via Nurture: Genes, Experience, and What Makes Us Human.* New York: HarperCollins.

Roberts, D. F., U. G. Foehr, V. J. Rideout, and M. Brodie. 1999. *Kids and Media in the New Millenium.* Menlo Park, Calif.: Kaiser Family Foundation.

Rodman, Hyman, David J. Pratto, and Rosemary Smith Nelson. 1985. "Child Care Arrangements and Children's Functioning: A Comparison of Self-Care and Adult-Care Children." *Developmental Psychology* 48: 413–418.

Roe, Brian, Leslie Whittington, S. Fein, and M. Teisl. 1996. "The Conflict between Breast-Feeding and Maternal Employment." Paper presented at the Population Association of American Annual Meeting, New Orleans.

Ronsen, Marit. 1999. "Assessing the Impact of Parental Leave: Effects on Fertility and Employment." In *Parental Leave: Progress or Pitfall? Research and Policy Issues in Europe,* ed. Peter Moss and Fred Deven, 193–226. Brussels: CBGS Publications.

Rosenbaum, Paul and Donald Rubin. 1983. "The Central Role of the Propensity Score in Observational Studies for Causal Effects." *Biometrika* 70(1): 41–55.

Rosenbaum, Paul and Donald Rubin. 1985. "Constructing a Control Group Using Multivariate Matched Sampling Methods that Incorporate the Propensity Score." *American Statistician* 39: 33–38.

Ross, Katherin. 1998. "Labor Pains: The Effects of the Family and Medical Leave Act on Recent Mothers' Returns to Work After Childbirth." Paper presented at the Population Association of America Annual Meeting, Chicago.

Ross Phillips, Katherin. 2002. *Parent Work and Child Well-Being in Low-Income Families,* Occasional Paper 56. Washington, D.C.: Urban Institute.

Ross Phillips, Katherin. 2004. "Getting Time Off: Access to Leave Among Working Parents." Washington D.C.: Urban Institute.

Roth, Jodie and Jeanne Brooks-Gunn. 1999. "Implications of Individual Difference Theories for Enhancing Adolescent Development." In *Designing Developmentally Appropriate Middle Schools.* Washington, D.C.: National Association of Secondary School Principals, 54–75.

Roth, Jodie and Jeanne Brooks-Gunn. 2000. "What Do Adolescents Need for Healthy Development? Implications for Youth Policy." *Social Policy Report* 14(1): 3–19.

Roth, Jodie and Jeanne Brooks-Gunn. 2003a. "What Exactly is a Youth Development Program? Answers from Research and Practice." *Applied Developmental Science* 7(2): 94–111.

Roth, Jodie and Jeanne Brooks-Gunn. 2003b. "Youth Development Programs: Risk, Prevention, and Policy." *Journal of Adolescent Health* 32: 170–182.

Roth, Jodie, Jeanne Brooks-Gunn, Lawrence Murray, and William Foster. 1998. "Promoting Healthy Adolescents: Synthesis of Youth Development Program Evaluations." *Journal of Research on Adolescence* 8(4): 423–459.

Rowe, D. C. 1994. *The Limits of Family Influence: Genes, Experience, and Behavior.* New York: Guilford.

Rubin, K. H., W. Bukowski, and J. G. Parker. 1998. "Peer Interactions, Relationships, and Groups." In vol. 3, Social, Emotional, and Personality Development, *Handbook of Child Psychology*, 5th ed., ed. William Damon, 619–700. New York: John Wiley and Sons.

Rubin, K. H., R. S. L. Mills, and I. Rose-Krasnor. 1989. "Maternal Beliefs and Children's Social Competence." In *Social Competence in Developmental Perspective*, ed. B. Schneidier, G. Attili, J. Nadel, and R. Weissberg. Boston, Mass.: Kluwer Academic.

Ruhm, Christopher. 1997a. "Policy Watch: The Family and Medical Leave Act." *Journal of Economic Perspectives* 11(3): 175–186.

Ruhm, Christopher. 1997b. "The Effects of High School Work Experience on Future Economic Attainment." Washington, D.C.: Employment Policies Institute.

Ruhm, Christopher. 1997c. "Is High School Employment Consumption or Investment?" *Journal of Labor Economics* 15(4): 735–776.

Ruhm, Christopher. 1998. "The Economic Consequences of Parental Leave Mandates: Lessons from Europe." *Quarterly Journal of Economics* 113(1): 285–318.

Ruhm, Christopher. 2000. "Parental Leave and Child Health." *Journal of Health Economics* 19(6): 931–960.

Ruhm, Christopher. 2003. "Maternal Employment and Adolescent Development." Mimeo, University of North Carolina at Greensboro.

Ruhm, Christopher. 2004. "Parental Employment and Child Cognitive Development." *Journal of Human Resources* 39(1): 155–192

Ruopp, R., J. Travers, F. Glantz, and C. Coelen. 1979. *Children at the Center: Summary Findings and Their Implications.* Cambridge, Mass.: Abt Books.

Rutter, Michael, J. L. Silberg, T. G. O'Connor, and E. Simonoff. 1999. "Genetics and Child Psychiatry: I. Advances in Quantitative and Molecular Genetics." *Journal of Child Psychology and Psychiatry* 40: 3–18.

Rutter, Michael and D. Smith. 1995. "Towards Causal Explanations of Time Trends in Psychological Disorders in Young People." In *Psychological Disorders in Young People: Time Trends and Their Causes*, ed. M. Rutter and D. Smith, 782–808. New York: John Wiley and Sons.

Ryu, S. and J. T. Mortimer. 1996. "The 'Occupational Linkage Hypothesis' Applied to Occupational Value Formation in Adolescence." In *Adolescents, Work, and Family: An Intergenerational Developmental Analysis*, ed. J. T. Mortimer and M. D. Finch, 167–190. Thousand Oaks, Calif.: Sage Publications.

Salmi, Minna and Johanna Lammi-Taskula. 1999. "Parental Leave in Finland." In *Parental Leave: Progress or Pitfall? Research and Policy Issues in Europe*, ed. Peter Moss and Fred Deven, 85–122. Brussels: CBGS Publications.

Sameroff, A. J. and Haith, M. M., eds. 1996. *The Five to Seven Year Shift: The Age of Reason and Responsibility*. Chicago, Ill.: University of Chicago Press.

Sammons, Pam, Kathy Sylva, Edward Melhuish, Iram Siraj-Blatchford, Brenda Taggart, and Karen Elliot. 2002. "Measuring the Impact of Pre-School on Children's Cognitive Progress over the Pre-School Period," Technical Paper 8a. The Effective Provision of Pre-School Education (EPPE) Project. London: Institute of Education, University of London.

Sammons, Pam, Kathy Sylva, Edward Melhuish, Iram Siraj-Blatchford, Brenda Taggart, and Karen Elliot. 2003. "Measuring the Impact of Pre-School on Children's Social/Behavioral Development over the Pre-School Period," Technical Paper 8b. The Effective Provision of Pre-School Education (EPPE) Project. London: Institute of Education, University of London.

Sampson, Robert J. and John H. Laub. 1995. "Understanding Variability in Lives Through Time." *Studies in Crime and Crime Prevention* 4:143–158.

Scarr, S. and M. Eisenberg. 1993. "Child Care Research: Issues, Perspectives, and Results." *Annual Review of Psychology* 44: 613–644.

Schlesinger, Laura. 2000. *Parenthood by Proxy: Don't Have Them If You Won't Raise Them*. New York: Harper Collins.

Schweinhart, L. J., J. Montie, Z. Xiang, W. S. Barnett, C. R. Belfield, and M. Nores. In press. *Lifetime Effects: The High/Scope Perry Preschool Study through Age 40*. Ypsilanti, Mich.: High/Scope Press.

Seltenheim, K., L. Ahnert, H. Rickert, and M. E. Lamb. 1997. "The Formation of Attachments between Infants and Care Providers in German Daycare Centers." Paper presented to the American Psychological Society, Washington, D.C.

Seppanen, P., J. Love, D. deVries, L. Berstein, M. Seligson, F. Marx, and E. Kisker. 1993. *National Study of Before- and After-School Programs: Final Report*. Washington, D.C.: Office of Policy and Planning, U.S. Department of Education.

Shea, John. 2000. "Does Parents' Money Matter?" *Journal of Health Economics* 77(2): 155–184.

Shonkoff, Jack P. 1984. "The Biological Substrate and Physical Health in Middle Childhood." In *Development during Middle Childhood: The Years from Six to Twelve*, ed. Andrew W. Collins, chap. 2, 24–69 (Report of the Panel to Review the Status of Basic Research on School-Age Children). Washington, D.C.: National Academy Press.

Shonkoff, Jack P. and Deborah A. Phillips, eds. 2000. *From Neurons to Neighborhoods: The Science of Early Childhood Development*. Washington, D.C.: National Academy Press.

Shore, Rima. 1997. *Rethinking the Brain: New Insights into Early Development*. New York: Families and Work Institute.

Sigle-Rushton, Wendy and Jane Waldfogel. 2004. "Motherhood and Women's Earnings in Anglo-American, Continental European, and Nordic Countries."

Paper presented at Conference on Cross-National Comparisons of Expenditures on Children, Princeton, N.J.

Skinner, M. L., G. H. Elder, and R. D. Conger. 1992. "Linking Economic Hardship to Adolescent Aggression." *Journal of Youth and Adolescence* 21(3): 259–276.

Sleebos, Joelle. 2003. "Low Fertility Rates in OECD Countries: Facts and Policy Responses." OECD Social, Employment, and Migration Working Paper no. 15, Organization for Economic and Community Development, Paris. Available at www.oecd.org. (accessed on 2/10/04).

Sleep Foundation. 2004. "Sleep and Teens." Available from the Sleep Foundation at www.sleepfoundation.org (accessed 6/15/04).

Smith, Nina and Elina Pylkkanen. 2004. "Career Interruptions due to Parental Leave: A Comparative Study of Denmark and Sweden." Paper presented at the annual meeting of the Population Association of America, Boston.

Smith, T., A. Kleiner, B. Parsad, E. Farris, and B. Green. 2003. *Prekindergarten in U.S. Public Schools*. Washington, D.C.: U.S. Department of Education, National Center for Education Statistics.

Smolensky, Eugene and Jennifer Gootman, eds. 2003. *Working Families and Growing Kids: Caring for Children and Adolescents*. Washington, D.C.: National Academy Press.

Snow, C. E. 1972. "Mothers' Speech to Children Learning Language." *Child Development* 43: 549–565.

Snow, C. E. and C. A. Ferguson, eds. 1977. *Talking to Children: Language Input and Acquisition*. Cambridge, U.K.: Cambridge University Press.

Snyder, H. and M. Sickmund. 1997. *Juvenile Offenders and Victims: 1997 Update on Violence*. Washington, D.C.: Office of Juvenile Justice and Delinquency Prevention Programs, U.S. Department of Justice.

Sroufe, L. A. 1996. *Emotional Development*. New York: Cambridge University Press.

Steinberg, Laurence. 1986. "Latchkey Children and Susceptibility to Peer Pressure: An Ecological Analysis." *Developmental Psychology* 22: 433–439.

Steinberg, Laurence and S. M. Dornbusch. 1991. "Negative Correlates of Part-Time Employment during Adolescence: Replication and Elaboration." *Developmental Psychology* 27(3): 304–313.

Steinberg, Laurence and A. S. Morris. 2001. "Adolescent Development." *Annual Review of Psychology*. 52: 83–110.

Stewart, R. 2001. "Adolescent Self-Care: Reviewing the Risks." *Families in Society* 82: 119–126.

Stipek, Deborah. 2001. "Pathways to Constructive Lives: The Importance of Early School Success." In *Constructive and Destructive Behavior: Implications for Family, School, and Society*, ed. A. Bohart and D. Stipek. Washington, D.C.: American Psychological Association.

Stork, Diana, Fiona Wilson, Andrea Wicks Bowles, Jenny Sproull, and Jennifer Bena. 2005. "The New Workforce Reality: Insights for Today, Implications for Tomorrow." Simmons School of Management and Bright Horizons Family Solutions.

Strauss, V. 2004. "Jumping into the Rigors of Learning." *Washington Post*, October 26, 2004: A10.

Summers, Lawrence. 1989. "Some Simple Economics of Mandated Benefits." *American Economic Review* 79(2): 177–183.

Sylvester, Kathleen and Kathy Reich. 2000. "After-School Programs: Issues and Ideas." Available from Future of Children at www.futureofchildren.org (accessed 7/1/04).

Tamis-LeMonda, Catherine S. and Natasha J. Cabrera, eds. 2002. *Handbook of Father Involvement: Multidisciplinary Perspectives.* Mahwah, N.J.: Lawrence Erlbaum Associates.

Tanaka, Sakiko. 2004. "Effects of Parental Leave on Child Health and Development." Ph.D. dissertation, Columbia University.

Tanaka, Sakiko. 2005. "Parental Leave and Child Health Across OECD Countries." *Economic Journal* 115: F7–F28.

Tanaka, Sakiko and Jane Waldfogel. 2004. "Effects of Parental Leave and Working Hours on Fathers' Involvement with Their Babies: Evidence from the UK Millennium Cohort Study." Working Paper, Columbia University School of Social Work.

Tepper, Robin. 1999. "Parenting Style, Involvement in Structured Activity, and Adolescent Discretionary Time Use Decisions: Findings from NLSY97." Working Paper, Harris School, University of Chicago.

Thompson, E., T. Hanson, and S. McLanahan. 1994. "Family Structure and Child Well-being: Economic Resources vs. Parental Behaviors." *Social Forces* 73(1): 221–242.

Thompson, R. A. 2001. "Development in the First Years of Life." *Future of Children* 11(1): 21–33.

Thompson, R. A. and C. A. Nelson. 2001. "Developmental Science and the Media: Early Brain Development." *American Psychologist* 56(1): 5–15.

Tierney, J. P., Jean Baldwin Grossman, and N. Resch. 1995. "Making a Difference: An Impact Study of Big Brothers/Big Sisters." Philadelphia, Pa.: Public/Private Ventures.

Tilly, Chris. 1996. *Half a Job: Bad and Good Part-Time Jobs in a Changing Labor Market.* Philadelphia, Pa.: Temple University Press.

Trust for Early Education. 2004. *Quality Pre-Kindergarten for All: State Legislative Report.* Washington, D.C.: Trust for Early Education. Available at www.trust forearlyed.org (accessed 1/13/05).

Tyler, John H. 2003. "Using State Child Labor Laws to Identify the Effect of School-Year Work on High School Achievement." *Journal of Labor Economics* 21(2): 381–408.

U.S. Bureau of the Census. 1982. "Trends in the Child Care Arrangements of Working Mothers." *Current Population Reports.* June: P-23–117. Washington, D.C.: U.S. Government Printing Office.

U.S. Bureau of the Census. 2003. *Statistical Abstract of the United States.* Washington, D.C.: U.S. Bureau of the Census. Available at www.census.gov (accessed 10/12/05).

U.S. Bureau of the Census. 2004. "Child Care Arrangements: Who's Minding the Kids?" Spring 1999. Available at www.census.gov (accessed 10/12/05).

U.S. Consumer Product Safety Commission. 1999. *Safety Hazards in Child Care Settings.* Washington, D.C.: U.S. Government Printing Office.

U.S. Department of Agriculture. 2002. "USDA Child and Adult Care Food Program Data." Available at www.fns.usda.gov (accessed 1/5/03).

U.S. Department of Education, Office of the Under Secretary. 2003. "When Schools Stay Open Late: The National Evaluation of the 21st Century Community Learning Centers Program." Washington, D.C.: U.S. Department of Education, Office of the Under Secretary, January.

U.S. Department of Health and Human Services. Administration for Children and Families. 2000. "FACES Findings: New Research on Head Start Program Quality and Outcomes." Available at www.hhs.gov (accessed 10/12/05).

U.S. Department of Health and Human Services. Administration for Children and Families. 2002a. *Head Start: Promoting Early Childhood Development*. Available at www.hhs.gov (accessed 1/18/04).

U.S. Department of Health and Human Services. Administration for Children and Families. 2002b. "Early Head Start Benefits Children and Families." Available at www.hhs.gov (accessed 10/12/05).

U.S. Department of Health and Human Services. Administration for Children and Families. 2003. *Child Maltreatment 2001*. Washington, D.C.: U.S. Government Printing Office.

U.S. Department of Health and Human Services. Administration for Children and Families. 2005. "Head Start Impact Study: First Year Findings." Available at www.hhs.gov (accessed 10/12/05).

Vandell, Deborah L. and M. A. Corasiniti. 1988. "The Relations Between Third Graders' After-School Care and Social, Academic, and Emotional Functioning." *Child Development* 59: 868–875.

Vandell, Deborah L. and J. K. Posner. 1999. "Conceptualization and Measurement of Children's After-School Environments." In *Measuring Environment Across the Life Span: Emerging Methods and Concepts*, ed. S. L. Friedman and T. D. Wachs, 167–169. Washington, D.C.: American Psychological Association.

Vandell, Deborah Lowe and Janaki Ramanan. 1991. "Children of the National Longitudinal Survey of Youth: Choices in After-School Care and Child Development." *Developmental Psychology* 27(4): 637–643.

Vandell, Deborah and J. Ramanan. 1992. "Effects of Early and Recent Maternal Employment on Children from Low-Income Families." *Child Development* 63: 938–949.

Vandell, Deborah L. and L. Shumow. 1999. "After-School Child Care Programs." *Future of Children* 9(2): 64–80.

Vandell, Deborah L. and H-C Su. 1999. "Child Care and School-Aged Children." *Young Children* 54: 62–71.

Vandell, Deborah L. and Barbara Wolfe. 2000. *Child Care Quality: Does It Matter and Does It Need to Be Improved?* Washington, D.C.: Office of the Assistant Secretary for Planning and Evaluation, U.S. Department of Health and Human Services.

Vandivere, Sharon, Kathryn Tout, Martha Zaslow, Julia Calkins, and Jeff Capizzano. 2003. *Unsupervised Time: Family and Child Factors Associated with Self-Care*. Washington, D.C.: Urban Institute.

Wadsworth, M. and B. Compas. 2002. "Coping with Family Conflict and Economic Strain: The Adolescent Perspective." *Journal of Research on Adolescence* 12: 243–274.

Waldfogel, Jane. 1998a. *The Future of Child Protection: Breaking the Cycle of Abuse and Neglect*. Cambridge, Mass.: Harvard University Press.

Waldfogel, Jane. 1998b. "Understanding the 'Family Gap' in Pay for Women with Children." *Journal of Economic Perspectives* 12(1): 137–156.

Waldfogel, Jane. 1999a. "Family Leave Coverage in the 1990s." *Monthly Labor Review* (October): 13–21.

Waldfogel, Jane. 1999b. "The Impact of the Family and Medical Leave Act." *Journal of Policy Analysis and Management* 18(2): 281–302.

Waldfogel, Jane. 2001a. "Family and Medical Leave: Evidence from the 2000 Surveys." *Monthly Labor Review* (September): 17–23.

Waldfogel, Jane. 2001b. "Family-Friendly Policies for Families with Young Children." *Employee Rights and Employment Policy Journal* 5(1): 101–122.

Waldfogel, Jane. 2001c. "International Policies Toward Parental Leave and Child Care." *Future of Children* 11(1): 99–111.

Waldfogel, Jane. 2002. "Child Care, Women's Employment, and Child Outcomes." *Journal of Population Economics* 15: 527–548.

Waldfogel, Jane. 2004a. "A Cross-National Perspective on Policies to Promote Investments in Children." In *Family Investments in Children's Potential: Resources and Parenting Behaviors that Predict Children's Success*, ed. Ariel Kalil and Thomas DeLeire. Mahwah, N.J.: Lawrence Erlbaum Associates, 237–262.

Waldfogel, Jane. 2004b. "Social Mobility, Life Chances, and the Early Years." CASE paper, Centre for Analysis of Social Exclusion, London School of Economics.

Waldfogel, Jane. 2005. "Work-Family Policies." Paper presented at the Conference on Workforce Policy for the Next Decade and Beyond. Washington, D.C., November 11, 2005.

Waldfogel, Jane. In press. "Early Childhood Policy: A Comparative Perspective." In *Handbook of Early Childhood Development*, ed. Kathleen McCartney and Deborah Phillips. Oxford: Blackwell.

Waldfogel, Jane, Wen-Jui Han, and Jeanne Brooks-Gunn. 2002. "The Effects of Early Maternal Employment on Child Development." *Demography* 39(2): 369–392.

Watamura, S. E., B. Donzella, J. Alwin, and M. R. Gunnar. 2003. "Morning-to-Afternoon Increases in Cortisol Concentrations for Infants and Toddlers at Child Care: Age Differences and Behavioral Correlates." *Child Development* 74 (4): 1006–1020.

Weiss, H., H. Mayer, H. Kreider, P. Vaughn, E. Dearing, R. Hencke, et al. 2003. "Making It Work: Low-Income Working Mothers' Involvement in Their Children's Education." *American Educational Research Journal* 40(4): 879–901.

Whitbeck, L., R. Simons, R. Conger, F. Lorenz, S. Huch, and G. Elder. 1991. "Family Economic Hardship, Parental Support, and Adolescent Self-esteem." *Social Psychology Quarterly* 54: 353–363.

Whitbeck, L., R. Simons, R. Conger, K. Wickrama, K. Ackley, and G. Elder. 1997. "The Effects of Parents' Working Conditions and Family Economic Hardship on Parenting Behaviors and Children's Self-efficacy." *Social Psychology Quarterly* 60(4): 291–303.

Whitebrook, Marcy, Carolee Howes, and Deborah A. Phillips. 1990. *Who Cares? Child Care Teachers and the Quality of Care in America*. Final report of the National Child Care Staffing Study, Child Care Employee Project, Oakland, Calif.

Wiesel, Torsten N. and David H. Hubel. 1965. "Extent of Recovery from the Effects of Visual Deprivation in Kittens." *Journal of Neurophysiology* 28(6): 1060–1072.

Williams, Joan. 2000. *Unbending Gender: Why Family and Work Conflict and What to Do About It*. Oxford, U.K.: Oxford University Press.

Willinger, M., H. J. Hoffman, and R. B. Hartford. 1994. "Infant Sleep Position and Risk for Sudden Infant Death Syndrome: Report of meeting held January 13 and 14, 1994, National Institutes of Health, Bethesda, MD." *Pediatrics* 93(5): 814–819.

Wilson, James Q. 1995. *On Character*. Washington, D.C.: American Enterprise Institute.

Wilson, James Q. 2003. *The Moral Sense*. New York: Free Press.

Winegarden, C. R. and Paula Bracy. 1995. "Demographic Consequences of Maternal-Leave Programs in Industrial Countries: Evidence from Fixed Effects Models." *Southern Economic Journal* 61(4): 1020–1035.

Work Foundation. 2004. "Lowest Paid Losing Out in Right to Request Flexible Working." April 5, 2004. Press Release, available at www.theworkfoundation. com (accessed 4/16/04).

Wright, D. W., L. R. Peterson, and H. L. Barners. 1990. "The Relation of Parental Employment and Contextual Variables with Sexual Permissiveness and Gender Role Attitudes of Rural Early Adolescents." *Journal of Early Adolesence* 10: 382–398.

Yankelovich, D., R. Clark, and G. Martin. 1977. *General Mills American Family Report*. Minneapolis, Minn.: General Mills.

Yeung, Jean W. 2001. "Children's Time with Fathers in Intact Families." *Journal of Marriage and the Family* 63: 136–154.

Yoshikawa, Hiro. 1995. "Long-Term Effects of Early Childhood Programs on Social Outcomes and Delinquency." *Future of Children* 5(3): 51–75.

Yoshikawa, Hiro. 1999. "Welfare Dynamics, Support Services, Mother's Earnings, and Child Cognitive Development: Implications for Contemporary Welfare Reform." *Child Development* 70: 779–801.

Zaslow, M. J. and C. Emig. 1997. "When Low-Income Mothers Go To Work: Implications for Children." *Future of Children* 7(1): 110–115.

Zaslow, Martha, Susan Jekielek, and Megan Gallagher. In press. "Mismatch Through a Developmental Lens: Maternal Employment and Children of Different Ages." In *Work, Family, Health, and Well-Being*, ed. Suzanne Bianchi, Lynne Casper, and Rosalind King. Mahwah, N.J.: Lawrence Erlbaum Associates.

Zill, N., K. Moore, E. Smith, T. Stief, and M. Coiro. 1995. "The Life Circumstances and Development of Children in Welfare Families: A Profile Based on National Survey Data." In *Escape from Poverty: What Makes a Difference for Children?* ed. P. Lindsay Chase-Lansdale and Jeanne Brooks-Gunn, 38–59. New York: Cambridge University Press.

Zill, N., C. W. Nord, and L. S. Loomis. 1995. *Adolescent Time Use, Risky Behavior, and Outcomes: An Analysis of National Data*. Rockville, Md.: Westat.

Zuckerman, Barry and Robert Kahn. 2000. "Pathways to Early Child Health and Development." In *Securing the Future: Investing in Children from Birth to College*, ed. Sheldon Danziger and Jane Waldfogel, 87–121. New York: Russell Sage Foundation.

Acknowledgments

I WAS FORTUNATE to be able to write this book during a sabbatical year (2003–2004) at the Centre for Analysis of Social Exclusion (CASE) at the London School of Economics, where I have been a research associate and visitor for many years. As always, CASE proved to be an ideal place to think and write, and I am deeply grateful to John Hills, Jane Dickson, and the many others at CASE who provided help and support. Another benefit of being at CASE was the opportunity to take part in the policy dialogue occurring nearby at Westminster. During my stay, I was asked to give several talks to senior government policymakers, including the Chancellor of the Exchequer, Treasury officials, and the Prime Minister's advisors at 10 Downing Street. Each of these talks, and the many one-on-one conversations I had with officials, sharpened my thinking. I am grateful to all those with whom I spoke and would particularly like to thank Paul Gregg, Lisa Harker, Liz Kendall, and Kathy Sylva for the insights they shared.

This book is based on research about parental employment, child care, and child outcomes that I carried out over the past ten years with generous funding from the William T. Grant Foundation and the National Institute of Child Health and Human Development (NICHD). The William T. Grant Scholar Award gave me five years of support as well as a network of scholars and mentors to draw upon. I am grateful to all of them and in particular to Betty Hamburg, Karen Hein, and

Bob Granger, whose encouragement meant so much. The NICHD award also provided five years of funding and introduced me to a network of researchers studying work-family issues. I would particularly like to thank Christine Bachrach, Lynne Casper, and Jeff Evans, all at NICHD. I would also like to thank the Ford Foundation, for funding a research project on investing in children from birth to college; the John D. and Catherine T. MacArthur Foundation, for supporting research on child care policies; and especially the Russell Sage Foundation, for funding an ongoing project on inequality in early childhood care and education.

My understanding of the issues discussed in this book has benefited enormously from conversations and collaborative work with students, postdocs, and colleagues—in particular, Jay Bainbridge, Lonnie Berger, Jeanne Brooks-Gunn, Sheldon Danziger, Irv Garfinkel, Wen-Jui Han, Jennifer Hill, Elizabeth Johnson, Sheila Kamerman, Katherine Magnuson, Marcia Meyers, Chris Paxson, Dan Rosenbaum, Chris Ruhm, and Sakiko Tanaka. It is impossible to adequately acknowledge the contribution they have made to my understanding of the issues discussed in this book. Many of the best ideas in this book (and hopefully none of the errors) come directly or indirectly from them. I am also indebted to the members of the National Academy of Sciences Committee on Family and Work Policies, with whom I had the pleasure to serve and from whom I learned so much: Suzanne Bianchi, David Blau, Francine Jacobs, Robin Jarrett, Donna Klein, Sandy Korenman, Joan Lombardi, Joseph Mahoney, Harriet Presser, Gary Sandefur, Deborah Vandell, Eugene Smolensky, Hiro Yoshikawa, and Martha Zaslow. In addition, many others kindly helped by sharing their research or pointing me to other research. In particular, I would like to thank Janet Currie, Greg Duncan, Diane Early, Lisa Gennetian, Aletha Huston, Ginger Knox, Holly Kreider, Kathleen McCartney, Mignon Moore, Pamela Morris, and Deborah Phillips. A special note of thanks goes to two experts on children and families—Jeanne Brooks-Gunn and Ron Haskins—who kindly read portions of the book in draft. Their comments strengthened the book and saved me from making some errors.

I was fortunate to have in Elizabeth Knoll an editor who was deeply committed to this book from the start. Her substantive comments were always helpful, and she and the able staff at Harvard University Press made getting this book published a delight, from start to finish. I am also grateful to two anonymous reviewers who read the manuscript and made many helpful suggestions.

My largest debt is to my family. Katie took a keen interest in this project and provided constant support and encouragement, as well as many useful insights into how children feel. David as always proved to be an astute editor and analyst, making just the right comments and asking just the right questions. Most importantly, they provided a constant reminder of how important families are and proof that it is possible to combine love for family and work.

Index